✳ ✳ ✳ ✳ ✳ ✳ ✳ ✳ ✳ ✳ ✳
Homegrown Terror

A DRIFTLESS CONNECTICUT SERIES BOOK

This book is a 2014 selection in the Driftless Connecticut Series,

for an outstanding book in any field on a Connecticut topic or

written by a Connecticut author.

✳✳✳✳✳✳✳✳✳✳✳✳✳
Homegrown Terror

Benedict Arnold
and the Burning *of*
New London

✳✳✳✳✳✳✳✳✳✳✳✳

ERIC D. LEHMAN

WESLEYAN UNIVERSITY PRESS

Middletown, Connecticut

WESLEYAN UNIVERSITY PRESS
Middletown CT 06459
www.wesleyan.edu/wespress
© 2014 Eric D. Lehman
All rights reserved
Manufactured in the United States of America
Designed by Richard Hendel
Typeset in Garamond Premier Pro by
Tseng Information Systems, Inc.

The Driftless Connecticut Series is funded by the
Beatrice Fox Auerbach Foundation Fund
at the Hartford Foundation for Public Giving.

Wesleyan University Press is a member
of the Green Press Initiative. The paper used in
this book meets their minimum requirement
for recycled paper.

Cloth ISBN: 978-0-8195-7329-2
Ebook ISBN: 978-0-8195-7330-8
Library of Congress Cataloging-in-Publication Data
available upon request

5 4 3 2 1

Contents

Preface	ix
Acknowledgments	xxiii
On the Edge of Spring	1
Flashpoint	14
Resist Even Unto Blood	28
The Shadow War	46
Invasion	62
Villainous Perfidy	79
The Scandal of the Age	97
A Parricide in Old Virginia	113
William Ledyard's Last Summer	127
The Sixth of September	140
The Battle of Groton Heights	151
Remember New London	162
The Fall of Silas Deane	178
Epilogue	197
A Note on Sources	205
Notes	207
Index	255

✳ ✳ ✳

Preface

Just after midnight, a fleet of twenty-four ships slid east on the calm black water of the Devil's Belt. It was late summer in 1781, and the fleet had waited until complete darkness to weigh anchor and move up from the west, with a fair wind behind them. Now they stood near Plum Island, outside Gardiner's Bay, at the very tip of Long Island, ten miles southwest as the crow flies from the entrance to New London harbor. The ships would have to go farther to avoid the reefs on the western side, as they sailed past the jaws of The Race in a few short hours.

On the deck of one of the warships stood a stout, muscular man with dark hair, gray eyes, and a sharp nose. He walked with a limp, his leg shot, then crushed underneath a horse — injuries that might have destroyed a weaker man. He must have tried to see the northern shore, searching for the sleeping town across the wide expanse of the Devil's Belt, sometimes called Long Island Sound. The town was New London, Connecticut, a town he had visited many times to conduct business, to visit friends, or to retrieve his drunken father and bring him home. But he had not returned for years, or returned upriver to Norwich, to the house he had been born in and to the graves of his parents.

It was not a clear night. If it had been clear, without cloud or fog, then someone would have seen the sails, even at this distance, by starlight or moonlight, and cannon would have been fired to warn the militia. One might fire soon enough, as they rowed in for the landing, but by then it would be too late. Besides, the man on the deck knew that the Americans fired two shots to signal for enemy, and he had ordered that another cannon be fired once from the ship. That way the men in their warm beds, far in the wooded backcountry of eastern Connecticut, would not be alarmed and maybe would turn over and go to sleep.

Long Island was held by the British, and though there were Patriot spies there, the man had planned so swiftly that none of the spies could have sent word to Connecticut in time. There would be no welcoming party marched in from Hartford or Providence. Even if the scattered militia rallied, the force on these ships was overwhelming, and only a large city like Boston or Philadelphia could repulse a force under his command without a standing army. New London was not a large town; though it was only two dozen miles from the center of the American Revolution's northern supply lines at Lebanon, he could be reasonably assured that his mission would be successful.

The gray-eyed man on the deck of the flagship of the British fleet was not the only one who had ties to the land. Although the ships held hundreds of German mercenaries and English redcoats sleeping or playing cards or cleaning their muskets in anticipation of the attack, more than half of the 1,732 men were from America. The Third Battalion of the New Jersey volunteers, the Loyalist Refugee Corps, the Loyal Americans, and the so-called American Legion were all waiting below decks. Most wanted to return home, to be part of the mighty British Empire again, to retake their land from what some called "anarchy."

The motive of their leader on the deck was more obscure. Unlike the Loyalists below, he had as recently as a year earlier been fighting for those rebels, and fighting well. His physical courage and quick thinking had won critical battles and had in fact helped turn the tide of the entire war. Now he must have been hoping to turn it the other way. If that happened, perhaps his name would be restored, and he would once again have money, security, fame — enough for his many ambitions.

What he could not know was that those hopes were in vain, and his name would be damned through the ages for his initial treason — a plot to hand over West Point and George Washington to the British — and for this attack on his former home, an act seemingly beyond comprehension to his contemporaries. He could not know that this act of terror would be his last act of the war and that in less than two months the matter would be decided despite his efforts. The army that would decide it had marched just north of New London in June, and the fleet that would help had, the day before, already sailed into another bay to entrap the British general Charles Cornwallis.

The wind shifted at one o'clock, coming hard from the north. It would take nearly nine more hours for the first landing parties to row to the Connecticut beaches and begin their attacks, long after the sun had risen. But the delay between dawn and landing wouldn't matter.

By the end of the day on September 6, 1781, a prosperous seaside town would be ashes, and a terrible massacre would be enacted. This attack would not change the course of the war or turn the tide of American history. It would define the American soul.

The man on the deck was the dark eagle of the Revolution, Benedict Arnold, a man who could have been a founding father of America but instead became a national villain. Arnold's brutal attack on Connecticut epitomizes this transformation: the moment where his abstract idea of betrayal completes its evolution to the slaughter and destruction of his neighbors and their homes. Focusing on this significant but unfortunately forgotten incident addresses some of the major challenges of any discussion about this complex and confusing American figure. It also directly links Arnold's story with the stories of his friends and colleagues, something that has never been done before. The combination of these two approaches puts the focus on Arnold's effects rather than his motives, on the victims rather than the attacker. Moreover, it reframes his "treason" as "homegrown terror," a term that resonates with modern readers and whose definition echoes the eighteenth-century word "parricide," used by many contemporaries to describe Arnold's actions.

Those actions have historically presented two major challenges. First, Arnold's treason has primarily begged the question of "cause" from historians: How could his contemporaries so misjudge him? How could someone change allegiances so completely? The second challenge is much more complex and one that has occupied much of the discourse over the past several decades: Arnold's status in our national history. We could break this up into several questions or categories of approach. How could we present a full picture of a traitor who was previously a hero? Perhaps he was a Loyalist all along, as he claimed, and just a casualty of what was in some ways our first civil war? And is the word "traitor" appropriate? Could its legal definition be too narrow or could the expression have become too weak?

George Washington himself was among the first to speculate about the question of Arnold's motives. In a letter written less than a month after the initial plot was exposed, he mentions Arnold's "villainous perfidy" and states, "I am mistaken if at this time, Arnold is undergoing the torments of a mental Hell. He wants feeling! From some traits of his character which have lately come to my knowledge he seems to have been so hackneyed in villainy — & so lost to all sense of honor and shame that while his faculties will enable him to continue his sordid pursuits there will be no time for remorse."[1] Of course, if Washington was correct in October 1780, and Arnold was a sociopath who "wants feeling," then why had the usually perceptive commander in chief not noticed this fault before the shocking treason? Congress would ask that pointed question of Washington and many others during the aftermath.

Speculation about Arnold's motives ran rampant among his contemporaries. The same man, Joseph Plumb Martin, changes his opinion several times in his memoir of the war. On one page he marvels at the betrayal, "I should as soon have thought West Point had deserted as he," but a page later he waffles and writes, "I had been acquainted with Arnold from my childhood and never had too good an opinion of him." At another point he states more emphatically, "He looked guilty, and well he might, for Satan was in as full possession of him at that instant as ever he was of Judas; it only wanted a musket ball to have driven him out."[2]

For over two centuries Arnold's treason has been given explanations as diverse as greed and self-sacrifice. Surely, his Tory wife, Peggy, influenced him unduly? Perhaps it was jealousy of the other, less deserving generals promoted ahead of him? Perhaps he never believed in the revolutionary cause in the first place and fought only out of self-interest? Felt anger at the squabbling pettiness of Congress? A tragic character flaw? Mental health issues? Memories of his drunken father? Financial troubles? Midlife crisis? A whim? A blunder?

There is ample evidence for all the above. We can continue to analyze Arnold's psychology and actions, but there will never be a definite answer to the question, even if by some archaeological miracle a document written by him surfaces, explaining carefully and precisely his reasons.[3] But it is almost impossible not to speculate, and with such a fascinating figure as Arnold, no doubt the debate will continue.

Over the years a number of enthusiasts have shifted the debate to Arnold's status as both a traitor and a hero. His 1801 obituary unequivocally acknowledged Arnold's former patriotism, admitting, "there is no doubt, however, but he was, for some time, a real friend of the Revolution."[4] However, by 1901, the centennial of Arnold's death,

Connecticut Magazine pushed a more sympathetic image, including a laudatory article full of half-truths and outright falsehoods, honoring Arnold as the greatest of patriots, one who had merely made a small mistake.[5] More articles and books followed that described him as misunderstood, if admittedly flawed.[6]

During the 1976 bicentennial, Norwich historian Marian O'Keefe told a *New York Times* reporter, "if the British had shot higher at Saratoga, I could have sold medals," a claim repeated in dozens of popular culture outlets, including the *Tonight Show*.[7] Though not a champion of Arnold, O'Keefe was playing one of our favorite national games, imagining an alternate history. She was also echoing the habitually dour John Adams's endorsement for Arnold's valiance after the Battle of Saratoga:

> We could make a Beginning, by Striking a Medal, with a Platoon firing at General Arnold, on Horseback, His Horse falling dead under him, and He deliberately disentangling his feet from the Stirrups and taking his Pistolls out of his Holsters, before his Retreat. On the Reverse, He should be mounted on a Fresh Horse, receiving another Discharge of Musquetry, with a Wound in the Neck of his Horse. This Picture Alone . . . would be sufficient to make his Fortune for Life. I believe there have been few such Scenes in the World.[8]

And Saratoga was not a lone instance of this courage. Arnold had taken part in the capture of Ticonderoga; he was instrumental in securing the cannon that freed Boston. He had invaded Quebec after a long, often brutal march through Maine. He had stopped the British fleet on Lake Champlain. And when the British invaded his home state of Connecticut, he did not hesitate but galloped from New Haven to Ridgefield, where he fought again with undisputed fury and intelligence.

The bicentennial also saw Ellsworth Grant give what has come to be known as the modern "balanced view" of Arnold. In the *Hartford Courant* he stated that "no one can but admire the boldness, tenacity and brilliance" of Arnold's military career. He quoted historian Willard Wallace: "[Arnold] was a brilliant and daring soldier who accomplished a great deal of good for the young republic, probably even saving it. He was also a proud, imperious, avaricious individual who

Arnold's heroic march through Maine and attack on Quebec helped solidify his reputation as a capable military leader, as seen in this contemporary etching from 1776. Colonel Arnold, *Prints and Photographs Division, Library of Congress.*

hungered after power and glory and high social standing, a man who saw in every slight a blemish upon his honor."[9] With full knowledge of his military exploits, it is admittedly difficult not to admire parts of Arnold's life. Before his treason Benedict Arnold had been one of the Continental Army's bravest and most skillful field commanders; when the *New York Times Magazine* rated Saratoga as one of the most important battles of the last millennium, they gave Arnold his due.[10]

The matter of Arnold was just as confusing for his contemporaries. The Marquis de Lafayette wrote to a friend shortly after the betrayal:

> In the course of a revolution such as ours it is natural that a few traitors should be found, and every conflict which resembles a civil war of the first order (although ours is, properly speaking, but a war between nations) must necessarily bring to light some great virtues and some great crimes. . . . But that an Arnold, a man who, although not so highly esteemed as has been supposed in Europe, had nevertheless given proof of talent, of patriotism, and, especially, of the most brilliant courage, should at once destroy his very existence and should sell his country to the tyrants whom he had fought against with glory, is an event . . . which confounds and distresses me, and, if I must confess it, humiliates me, to a degree that I cannot express. I would give anything in the world if Arnold had not shared our labors with us, and if this man, whom it still pains me to call a scoundrel, had not shed his blood for the American cause. My knowledge of his personal courage led me to expect that he would decide to blow his brains out (this was my first hope).[11]

The confusion caused by Arnold's life could hardly be shown more clearly. Lafayette's humiliation and hope that Arnold would take the "honorable" way out stem from a real problem, caused not by the treason itself but by the preceding feeling of respect. In a contemporary diary Henry Dearborn, who had served with Arnold in Quebec and at Saratoga, expressed "joy" in seeing him at Valley Forge, then expressed alarm at his treason at West Point. And when news reached him of the attack on New London, he said, "it is said the Infamous Arnold headed the party that perform'd those brilliant exploits."[12]

This mixture of respect for his military prowess and moral disgust has been echoed by many thoughtful historians over the years. But in recent decades the mixture has unfortunately become muddled, leading some historians to respect Arnold as a man. Of course, it is important to give Arnold a historical due and to flesh out a demonized figure into a complex human being. Indeed, the complication of simple "truths" is always a worthy project, though sometimes this leads to a troubling ethical relativism.[13] But as we get further from an event, it becomes easier to forgive, and in the case of Benedict Arnold the balanced view has in some cases become a nearly complete amendment, to the point where many are not even clear *what* Arnold did, much less why he was so reviled by his peers.[14]

Another partial exoneration of Arnold has arisen out of the interesting reimagining of the American Revolution as our first civil war.[15] Assuming this is a valid point of view and that Lafayette's interpretation was incorrect, what is it that separates Arnold from the thousands of other Tories or Loyalists or Royalists, as they were variably called? Let's take a look at one of Arnold's Connecticut neighbors, Charles Jarvis of Danbury. He had been brought up as a Tory and during the war served in the British Army, fighting in Pennsylvania, New Jersey, South Carolina, and even within ten miles of his home in New York, burning property and shooting American soldiers. But he often derided the British officers and saw himself and the other Loyalist troops as liberating their country from the "rebels." On his return home in April 1783 to his father's house, he was harassed and finally emigrated out of the state to Canada.[16]

It is easy to see how and why Arnold does not fit the classic Loyalist mold. Jarvis never wavered from one side to the other, but he risked his life for a strong belief in his country's allegiance to England. Arnold switched sides during the middle of an armed conflict, after taking an oath of allegiance at Valley Forge in 1778, and he took money to do so. Previous to this, he had no Tory sympathies and in fact had often acted passionately against them. One Loyalist, Samuel Ketchum, had been pressed into the "rebel militia" commanded by Arnold early in the war. Ketchum recalled in his claims testimony that he was not doing his duty and that Arnold "ordered that he and a few more Tories should be shut up in a House and burnt."[17]

Of course, there were others who played both sides, who looked out for only themselves, who used both sides for their own purposes.[18] But none of Arnold's stature. What examples do we have of a successful and apparently enthusiastic general who fought valiantly for one side, then switched sides and fought for the other, attacking his own country-men, even his former friends and associates? It is an example without equal, to remain as Washington Irving said a few decades later, "sadly conspicuous to the end of time, as the only American officer of note, throughout all the trials of vicissitudes of the Revolution, who proved traitor to the glorious cause of his country."[19]

Another issue is the use of the word "traitor" itself. Over the past two centuries, very few Americans have been tried and hanged as trai-tors, as intended by the writers of the Constitution. Treason is defined narrowly in section 3 of Article 3 to prevent political misuse, the only crime specifically noted in the document.[20] When Chief Justice John Marshall freed Aaron Burr in 1807, he set a precedent that made secur-ing a treason conviction very difficult. In the case of Timothy McVeigh, a former soldier who bombed the federal building in Oklahoma City and killed 168 people on April 19, 1995, the prosecution was unable to use the treason clause of the Constitution due to its strictness, even though McVeigh had clearly broken the bonds of loyalty and moral attachment.[21] Nevertheless, by the Burr precedent set by Chief Jus-tice Marshall, Arnold would still have been hanged as a traitor. Unlike during Burr's conspiracy to create a new nation west of the Appala-chians, there was actual armed action to prosecute, and the Consti-tution covers both Arnold's initial "adhering to their Enemies" in his plans with General Henry Clinton and "levying War against them" in Virginia and Connecticut.[22]

Perhaps because "treason" has been so rarely used in its actual legal context, the word has become diluted by common use over the centuries. Political duplicity is almost laughable it happens so often, but that does not stop partisans from calling a politician "traitor," or "Benedict Arnold," for that matter. A quick search reveals thousands of merely political comparisons to Arnold in hundreds of newspapers, especially during elections and other tense moments of national dis-unity, everyone from John Adams to Theodore Roosevelt, from John F. Kennedy to Barack Obama. Abraham Lincoln and Jefferson Davis were both compared to Benedict Arnold in the same magazine, only one year apart.[23]

Despite Thomas Jefferson's fervent prosecution of Aaron Burr for the crime, he said himself, "Real treason is rare."[24] Unfortunately, we have watered down "real treason" to the point where the word, if not

This Civil War cartoon showing Benedict Arnold, the devil, and Jefferson Davis demonstrates the resonance of Arnold's betrayal on the American imagination. Burgoo Zac, A Proper Family Reunion, *Prints and Photographs Division, Library of Congress.*

the legal definition, is nearly useless for the purpose the writers of the Constitution intended. And the use of Arnold's name in so many lesser cases has diluted the seriousness of his own treason. That's why it is necessary to change the conversation about Arnold, and focusing on his "homegrown terror" attack on New London is a clear and effective way to do that. Whatever we judge now in calmer times, Arnold's treason and his subsequent attacks had a huge effect on the national psychology of early America. Those effects are worth exploring.

Some recent work has been more fruitful on this topic, putting the focus on the effects of Arnold's treachery rather than on his motives. Historian Charles Royster's study, "The Nature of Treason," argues that Arnold represented a "threat to public virtue," the self-sacrifice necessary for a civic society to exist, the public engagement that kept free people from being enslaved. Royster suggests that the citizens of the flowering nation hated him so fervently because he represented to them their own weaknesses by 1780: a loss of revolutionary fervor, traffic with the enemy for profit, and the corruption brought on by civic lethargy. He points out that his unambiguous treachery allowed the people to contrast their own supposed virtue, and not many could come out worse through comparison.[25] Sociologists Lori Ducharme and Gary Alan Fine build on this idea to examine the subsequent "demonization" and "nonpersonhood" of Arnold subsequent to his betrayal, documenting an "enduring degradation process" that transformed him into "America's greatest villain." They conclude that "Arnold provided a measure of social control against egotism, while simultaneously providing a counterpoint for the trill of patriotism."[26] By focusing on Arnold's life in Connecticut, and his attack on it, this book aims to show that just because Arnold was transformed into a symbol for evil does not mean he is an *inappropriate* symbol. The people he betrayed were very real: his peers and his neighbors, his family and his comrades in arms.

Furthermore, though some might point to the initial betrayal of Washington and West Point as the greatest crime, Arnold did not stop there, something that even the two excellent studies mentioned earlier fail to address. First, he attacked Virginia in a prolonged military invasion that threw the entire state into chaos. Then, more shockingly for the people of his home state, he burned New London, which suffered the highest percentage of destruction of any American city in the war. The coordinated Battle of Groton Heights had the highest percentage of casualties in what many called a massacre. These attacks changed Arnold's position from an arguably political traitor who broke an oath and sold military secrets to someone who carried out armed attacks on his homeland. That is an important distinction and one that could lead to a stronger conclusion. A 1902 reflection in the *New Haven Register* put it clearly: "To have been able to put his own countrymen to the sword showed that he was sunk even deeper than a political traitor."[27]

Focusing not only on Arnold's story but on the stories of those fellow Connecticutians he associated with and fought beside also shines particular light on the importance of trust and loyalty in a civic society. Arnold's world consisted of an interrelated network of friends and business associates serving together on the same committees or in the same battles. Jonathan Trumbull, Nathaniel Shaw, Silas Deane, Benjamin Tallmadge, William Ledyard, George Washington, Richard Varick, John Lamb, and many others befriended Arnold and bled with him before being betrayed; this is their story as much as his.

Biographers of men and women who knew Arnold tend to downplay their connections to him for obvious reasons, but it is these very connections that make his actions so indefensible. In his book on treason in American history, lawyer and historian Brian Carso states,

> in a republic, trust and loyalty do not spring solely from the external covenant of our constitutional order. The internal covenant between citizen and republic relies on matters of trust and loyalty being manifest in the constitutive elements of society. . . . Loyalty, as with other democratic virtues, begins its development in the personal and local memberships of daily life. Loyalty is rooted first in family and community, and learns expression through the everyday associations of local institutions.[28]

In the following narrative, we can see how Arnold turned his back, not just on his government or some abstract notion of America, but on his local associations, his community and daily connections, built before and during the war.

In doing so, he began a procession of Americans who used political violence against their own people, including Ted Kaczinski, Nidal Hassan, and Eric Robert Rudolph, to name just a few. Terrorism is defined today in the Code of Federal Regulations as "the unlawful use of force and violence against persons or property to intimidate or coerce a government, the civilian population, or any segment thereof, in furtherance of political or social objectives." If violence is being used for political intimidation, if the "rules" of war are broken, if civilian populations are bombed or burned, then "terror" seems the appropriate reaction, and perhaps an appropriate word. Of course, the choice of "homegrown terror" to describe Arnold's raid on Connecticut would be problematic from a strictly legal perspective; Arnold's actions took place during a declared war, after all, even though the attack broke the rules of war at the time in several ways. We can also find many issues with the way that "terrorism" is used by the media, while the term "terrorist" brings up many of the same issues as "traitor." Its definition is fluid and overused; even the FBI admits that "there is no single, universally accepted, definition of terrorism."[29]

Additionally, as security expert Bruce Hoffman has noted, "If one identifies with the victim of the violence, for example, then the act is terrorism. If, however, one identifies with the perpetrator, the violent act is regarded in a more sympathetic, if not positive (or, at the worst, an ambivalent) light; and it is not terrorism."[30] So if you sympathize with the American revolutionaries, Benedict Arnold could have been both traitor and terrorist. If you sympathize with the British king and his Loyalist allies, Arnold might have been a merely unsavory character with questionable methods and motives.

This book studies Benedict Arnold's relationships with his peers and neighbors, and therefore the term seems an appropriate one, focusing on the victims' reactions rather than the aggressors' actions. "Terrorist" should not be considered a legal term defining Arnold's official status or pigeonholing him into a category that will lead to a belated two-hundred-year-old conviction. Instead, it is intended to keep the focus on the people who suffered and died because of his actions. It was terror they experienced, and it was from one of their own.

"Terrorism" is also a term that brings into focus the results of Arnold's actions for modern readers in a way that "traitor" no longer does. Today, if a citizen blows up a building or shoots someone with a political objective, we would probably cry domestic terrorism before crying treason. It is another in a historical succession of terms we have created to define the boundaries of good and evil. Early Americans might have used the term "homebred evil" rather than "homegrown terror."[31] Another term Thomas Jefferson and others used to describe Arnold was a "parricide," a term that literally means "father-killer." But they were using the more metaphorical meaning, in the same way that "La Marseillaise," the French national anthem, defines the term, as a person who attacks his own countrymen.[32] Treason, parricide, war crimes, homegrown terror: no general phrase can be completely accurate in describing Arnold's actions, because what he did was so singular.

Moral evil was and is a difficult concept to codify in a democratic society, but it begins with broken trust. In a democracy we must put trust in people. We must assume others will hold our ideals and will be good. The idea of homegrown terror is so frightening for that very reason — because it is *home*grown: the neighbor you thought was a war hero coming back to burn you down, the mass murderer in your high school class, the spy at your office, the sociopath down the street, building a bomb in the cellar.

Many of the conversations and actions of the founding generation after Arnold's betrayal echo time and time again, with incidents like the bombings at the Boston Marathon and Oklahoma City and the assassinations of William McKinley and John F. Kennedy. Patriotic talk soars. Politicians call for stricter laws. Anger, despair, and confusion fuel attacks and arrests. Kidnapping plans are put into action. Spies are mobilized. Ordinary citizens debate the concept of a just murder. And finally, a free democratic society survives the worst type of threat.

The story of Benedict Arnold and the burning of New London will hopefully draw attention to a regrettably overlooked incident and its profound effects and help reassess Arnold and his place in American history. It will also, I hope, shine light on how Americans have responded and continue to respond to betrayal and terror.

* * *

Acknowledgments

I must first express my appreciation for Marian O'Keefe, local historian of Norwich, with whom I discussed the original idea for this book and who gave me help with sources on Benedict Arnold. I also want to thank Jim Campbell, Ed Surato, and Frances Skelton at the New Haven Museum's Whitney Library; Karen DePauw, Sierra Dixon, and Diana Ross McCain at the Connecticut Historical Society; and Alice Dickenson, Tricia Royston, and Marilyn Davis at the New London County Historical Society. Jeannie Sherman and Mel Smith were particularly helpful in guiding me through the extensive Connecticut State Library Archives.

I also want to thank Mary Witkowski and Elizabeth Van Tuyl at the Bridgeport History Center and Hamden Public Library's Phil Scott for his tireless work at the interlibrary loan on my behalf. The University of Bridgeport's Magnus Wahlstrom Library held a surprising number of published primary sources, as did many other Connecticut libraries. The Library of Congress, the New York Historical Society, and the Historical Society of Pennsylvania also held many important documents.

I am particularly grateful for the help from Parker Smathers, David and Trena Lehman, Michelle Calero, Alexis Dias, Katelyn Wall, Christopher Collier, and Thomas Juliusburger, as well as Carolyn Smith, Helen Vergason, Evan Andriopoulos, Edward Baker, Walter Powell, and other historians who have kept the burning of New London and Battle of Groton Heights alive in recent years. Also, thanks to Hans van der Geissen and Stephen Healey of the University of Bridgeport for suggesting and granting a sabbatical during which I completed the project.

And special gratitude as always to my wife, Amy Nawrocki, who taught me the meaning of home.

****

Homegrown Terror

* * *
On the Edge of Spring

FROM THE SMALL TOWN green of Norwich, Connecticut, paths ran in many directions. But when Benedict Arnold was born in January 1741, deep, suffocating snow snuffed all travel, shutting down the entire state and jailing all but the most foolhardy indoors. Bitter cold gripped the whole country, and every river from Connecticut's Thames to Virginia's York froze solid. Ice crackled out from the bays and coves of the coast, permitting one reckless man to travel by sleigh from Cape Cod to New York City. Half the sheep, two-thirds of the goats, and countless cows and horses simply gave up and died, despite families risking starvation to feed their terrified livestock. "God has sealed up the hand of every man," wrote John Bissell of Bolton in near despair, noting that no one had suffered this much privation since the early settlers a century before. By March three feet of snow still sheathed the countryside, and on April 1 the rivers could still be crossed on foot.[1]

Everyone must have been happy to see the spring through their leaded glass windows and to come out of their clapboard saltboxes into the mud. The work of the year could begin. Soon ox teams would plough up the soft earth, and the smell of baking rye bread in the house and odor of horse manure in the fields would replace burning tallow and beeswax. Built on five hills between the Yantic and Shetucket Rivers, Norwich had been granted by the Mohegan chief Uncas to the English settlers, whom he hoped would help him against his enemies, the Narragansett. Since 1667 it had grown from a few houses in a "pleasant vale" to one of the larger towns in eastern Connecticut, becoming a "half-shire town" in 1734, taking a long-desired share of the county court sessions from its neighbor New London. This required building a new jail and town house, as well as a whipping post and pillory.[2] Well-traveled roads ran east to Providence, west to Hartford, and north along the two rivers, following old Indian trails through sandy pine forests and rocky dells.

The road south to New London was a barely widened Indian trail, just broad enough to cart goods back and forth in a half-day's walk. It was far easier to make the journey by boat. The U-shaped glacial harbor that stretched between the two towns was the best in the colony; at seven miles long, one mile wide, and six fathoms deep, it was sufficient to hold a small navy.³ Docks and landings dotted the length at the bottom of a series of low, sloping hills at Gale's Ferry, Groton, Smith Cove, and all the way south to the bights at New London. Once called "Pequot Plantation" or "London" by the first European settlers, it had become part of the Connecticut Colony in 1646 and, because of its protected harbor at the east end of Long Island Sound, had quickly developed into one of its largest towns.

It had one disadvantage: its land routes to other colonial population centers were dreadful. So why not sail another seven miles up the harbor and save a half day of cart work? That is one reason why Norwich began to take some, though not all, of its neighbor's shipping business. Merchants could sail a few large ships to the new docks at the Chelsea waterfront where the Yantic and Shetucket Rivers met, a mile and a half from Benedict Arnold's house. And now, with spring in the air and the harbor open, men could go to sea and make their fortune in trade.

One of those men was Benedict Arnold Sr., who served as a captain for richer men, such as Hezekiah Huntington on the ship *Prudent Hannah*.⁴ Arnold Sr. had come to Norwich from Rhode Island and met a widow named Hannah King, formerly Waterman. He may in fact have been one of her late husband's shipmates, but that did not stop him from marrying her.⁵ They had named their first son Benedict after his father, but the child died at the age of eight months, along with a half sister named for her mother, both on the same day. In the custom of the times, the grieving parents named their next two children the same. The first Benedict Arnold Jr. was buried on the green, by the First Church of Norwich, where the deeply religious Hannah found comfort and faith.

The previous year, the "Great Awakening" had swept across New England, revitalizing the Christian church, which had waned in influence somewhat in the early decades of the century. During high summer of 1741 Jonathan Edwards preached his "Sinners in the Hands of an Angry God" sermon in Enfield, Connecticut, explicating Deuteronomy 32:35: *Their foot shall slide in due time.* With both reason and wrath he proclaimed that people "are liable to fall" and that "he that stands or walks on slippery ground needs nothing but his own weight to throw him down. . . . He cannot stand alone, when he is let go he immediately falls and is lost." The congregation was thrown into disarray, with "shrieks and cry" from the parishioners fearing they would go to hell.[6]

But despite the revival of Christian evangelism, this was no longer the society of the early Puritans. Other ideas were filtering into the public consciousness. A month after Arnold's birth, rivals Andrew Bradford and Benjamin Franklin published the first monthly magazines in the colonies. Franklin had already opened the first subscription library and started the first newspaper, though it would be at least another decade before the press fully reached Connecticut and thirty years before the state would open some of the first free public libraries in the country. In the meantime educated men argued in town halls and coffee shops, where this bitter drink was replacing hard apple cider or ale as the preferred refreshment at breakfast and lunch. Already in 1741 they discussed John Locke's theories of equality and the social contract between the ruler and ruled.

A young Connecticut man named Ezra Stiles demonstrated how these two apparently opposing worldviews could work in perfect harmony. In 1746 Stiles graduated from New Haven's Yale College at the age of nineteen and became a minister, while retaining a passion for intellectual liberty and reason. When he gave his master's degree oration in 1749, he said, "Tis Liberty, my friends, in the Cause of Liberty we assert—a Freedom from the Bias of a vulgar Education, and the Violence of prejudicate Opinions—a Liberty suited to the Pursuit and Enquiries after Truth—Natural and Moral. This is the Advantage of Education, and this the Emolument of the Liberal Discipline."[7] The deeply religious Stiles saw no contradiction in also being a champion of Enlightenment values: tolerance, education, reason, and freedom.

These ideas had not always necessarily been tied to representative democracy, but, mixed with the colony's unique voting system, they were radical. In a 1662 charter the king of England gave the full citizens, or "freemen," of Connecticut elected representatives twice a year and once a year nominated and selected the governor, deputy governor, and twelve assistants. This was a much different system from colonies where the royally appointed governors had veto power and could appoint judges, lawyers, and military officers with impunity. Not wanting to give up these rights, Connecticut thwarted an attempt by a less progressive monarch to confiscate the document in 1687. Despite a number of grumbling "King's men" who found all this republicanism heretical, the stability it brought was very difficult to argue against. Although the relatively small Connecticut had no large port, no readily exportable product, and few imported slaves or indentured servants, the social order remained fairly secure.[8] And the population boomed, from 38,000 in 1730 to 130,000 in 1756. Some of these were children, but more were immigrants from England and the southern states, including many Baptists, Quakers, and other dissenters.[9]

This population growth produced one of the first land crises in the colonies. By 1750 almost the entire state had been parceled out, and settlers looked to move west. This led to the simmering Yankee–Pennamite War in what is today northeastern Pennsylvania and eventually to the settlement of the Western Reserve in northeastern Ohio, as well as various other migrations and settlements, both legal and illegal. Like all populations that prosper and exceed their boundaries, eighteenth-century Connecticut exported its greatest resource — people. These migrations also signaled that the new nation was already far more fluid and cohesive than the parent country dreamed.[10] The inhabitants had begun to think of themselves as Americans and not just as residents of a colony or a town.

This mix of fluidity and cohesion marked Benedict Arnold's childhood. On the one hand, he was in the center of a close-knit community, with a fairly unified cultural and social life, especially for the children. They were all familiar with the sounds of long sermons in a cold church pew, sheep bleating from the hills, and the squeals of a hog butchered in the kitchen garden. They shared entertainment, like watching cats hunting mice in the corn and dogs chasing rabbits out of the grazing fields. They hunted deer and fished for trout. They pretended they were pioneers of a hundred years before, settling by "the rushing and picturesque cascade of the Yantic" under "rude ledges of towering rock."[11] They all had the same fears too — larger children probably warned them of "savage" Indians, like the remaining Pequots, who lived nearby at the source of the Mystic River.

Though little gray-eyed Benedict was not tied to the land as much as many farming families, he would have spent his share of the days heaping stones into walls and picking apples from the orchards, while older men heaped mowed thorns with pitchforks. But at the same time, his

One of two surviving Arnold children, Benedict grew up in this house in Norwich, which stood by the road between the center of town and the harbor docks. Courtesy of Marian O'Keefe.

father's position as ship captain must have seemed romantic and free, with the entire world to roam and conquer. And though his father was gone for months at a time, every day Benedict could watch cart horses pulling trucks full of salted fish and molasses past his window, struggling in the muddy ruts of the road, heading northwest to Windham or Hartford.

His mother continued to bear more children, and he would have been expected to help bring up these brothers and sisters. He had other family in Norwich too — his mother's relatives, like the Lathrops, had been there for years, and now some of his father's relatives moved in. Oliver Arnold joined his brother in Norwich by 1755 at least, with his two sons Oliver and Freegift, who looked up to their older cousin.[12] Benedict's uncle Zion may have moved into town from Rhode Island as well; he certainly visited at least. As his father's business grew in the 1740s, they moved into a large two-chimney house on the road south of the green, a signal that they had become part of the town's elite.

The Arnolds' pew at the Norwich Congregational Church was nearby the Lathrops, the Turners, and the Huntingtons.[13] In this way, young Benedict probably met Philip Turner and Jedediah Huntington, boys less than two years older. Jedediah was the son of Jabez Huntington, the richest merchant in town and one of the leaders of the colony. Unlike the Huntingtons, though, Benedict's father wanted little part in societal governance and remained at sea every summer. He was chosen for the grand jury in 1746 but refused to serve on it.[14] Philip Turner was the son of a father of the same name, who had moved to Norwich from Massachusetts. His parents died when he was young, and instead he was brought up by the kindly Dr. Elisha Tracy, who lived nearby.[15] Benedict learned his Bible verses and played on Sunday afternoons with companions like these, children of the rising middle class of the eighteenth century.

When Benedict was nine, his younger brother died, leaving him the only son. Two years later, in the fall of 1752, he trudged up the north road to Canterbury, following the Shetucket River. Along the way he must have passed through forests full of wild grapes and turkeys, where men cut down the straightest white pines for ship masts. He would have passed small cornfields, with interlaced rows of beans and squash. At last he reached the Congregationalist meetinghouse of Dr. James Cogswell, originally of Lebanon, who graduated from Yale the year after Arnold was born.[16] Benedict's schooling with Cogswell was clearly meant to prepare him for the revered teacher's alma mater.

While Benedict studied music and grammar upriver, a yellow fever epidemic paralyzed Norwich, where his mother said, "deths are multiplied all round us. . . . Your uncle Zion Arnold is dead. . . . John Lathrop and his son barnibus are boath dead."[17] His mother wrote him again on August 30, 1753, saying that his sisters Hannah and Marey were very sick, and "your father is verry poor; aunt is sick, and I myself had a touch of ye distemper. . . . Your groaning sisters give love to you . . . but I must not have you come home for fear that should be resumption."[18] His sister Hannah survived, but Marey died, leaving Mrs. Arnold devastated. Nevertheless, she did not forget to send her son a pound of chocolate, and the following spring sent him fifty shillings; she seems to have constantly worried about his health and welfare.[19] He must have seemed her hope for the future.

But after only two years of school, Arnold had to return to Norwich. It could be that he was a poor student, or more likely that his parents had overextended their finances. His father's business had been deteriorating, due mostly to an increasing problem with drinking. His mother alluded to these financial and health issues in another mournful letter: "I write to let you know ye situation of our family. Your father is in a poor state of health but designs, if able, to set out for New York on August 23, and if I can, I shall journey with him, and if Providence shall permit, we shall be back by ye middle September when I shall send for you home. . . . We have a very uncertain stay in this world."[20] The teenage Arnold seems to have spent time with his father at sea during the summer months, traveling to the Caribbean. Witnessing the sordid life of hardened sailors was one thing, but quite another if one of those sailors is your father. The boy might have also had to rescue his father from drunken sprees in New London, and stories proliferated in later years about this unhappy duty. This was followed by an arrest warrant for Benedict Sr. in November 1754, for debt.[21]

Presumably other relatives came to his rescue, because the elder Arnold was not imprisoned and remained a sea captain for the next few years. But the family was clearly in dire straits, and young Benedict's future as a college student was now impossible. Instead, his mother apprenticed him to her cousins, the Lathrops. Brothers Joshua and Daniel were the first pharmacists in the county and probably the first in Connecticut to keep "a general assortment of medicines." The Lathrops also sold fruit, wine, and miscellaneous merchandise, from painters' colors to Turkish figs. Arnold joined another boy named Solomon Smith as an apprentice and began to learn the trade.[22]

By now, Arnold had grown into a good-looking young man, strong and thin-lipped, with heavy black eyebrows and hair.[23] He could easily walk up the dirt track past the front of the Leffingwell Inn to the Lathrop store. But he may have actually lived in the large home of Daniel and his wife, Jerusha, since his bankrupt parents probably rented out rooms in their now too-large house. The Lathrops' three sons had died and no doubt they didn't mind the company. Besides, an apprenticeship was not just a day job; it was legally indentured servitude that led to expertise in a certain field. In this case, Arnold was not really learning to be a pharmacist; he was learning to be a trader in provisions. He went on innumerable short trips, like two miles away to grind corn at the mill, where "while waiting, he amazed the miller with sundry fan-

While apprenticed to Dr. Daniel Lathrop as a pharmacist at this Norwich shop, Arnold replaced the children the Lathrops had lost years before. Courtesy of Marian O'Keefe.

tastic tricks," such as holding onto "a spoke of the great mill wheel in its revolutions."[24] The Lathrops sent him on much longer trips too, to England and the Caribbean, trusting him as supercargo for exports and imports. In the tangled web of eighteenth-century international trade, having a man or even a teenager on the spot was vital.

In the 1740s and 1750s, currency in Connecticut depreciated, and the position of farmers, shopkeepers, and merchants was kept in a strange balance, with credit a flitting hummingbird that everyone tried to follow. One of the primary concerns was the honesty of customers, and the position of middleman was potentially prosperous even before the regularization and codification of finance laws. But business could also be potentially disastrous, and the entire credit system could break down when someone in the long chain of commerce did not pay. Many merchants were also farmers and shopkeepers, to hedge their bets, and a man named Jonathan Trumbull was one of them: driving cattle herds, salting and packing meat, running a flour mill, and selling imports and local farm goods out of his Lebanon retail store.[25]

A few miles northwest of Norwich, Lebanon had been built around a thick alder swamp, which slowly drained over the decades, becoming the largest town green in New England.[26] Trumbull had been born on October 10, 1710, into this frontier town, and grew into a robust five-foot-nine man with a hawk-like nose and large, drooping eyes. When he was in his twenties, the town began to grow rapidly, even though it was slightly off the confluence of paths from Hartford, New London, and Providence.[27] Trumbull had gone to school at Harvard, graduated at the age of seventeen, and returned home. But after three years of reading with the local parson, he returned to Harvard to get his master's degree, expecting to become a preacher himself. Meanwhile, his father had either built or bought a ship, called it the *Lebanon*, and Jonathan's brother set sail from New London for the Caribbean. Neither he nor the ship was ever seen again. And so Jonathan gave up the career in the clergy and became the "son" in Trumbull and Son.[28]

Trumbull's simple house in Lebanon was smaller than Arnold's in Norwich, with a central chimney, molded window cornices, and classical doorways. Much of it was built with wide pieces of pine, or "king's boards," supposed to be sent back to England—the Trumbulls had clearly ignored that command. It was a fine house to sit around the fire on straight-backed, rush-seat chairs, waiting for bread from a beehive oven while sipping a mug of good coffee straight from the Caribbean. But Trumbull himself had little time for such pleasures. He became Lebanon's deputy in the Connecticut House of Representatives, and then Speaker of the House at the tender age of thirty. He served as assistant to the council in the upper house from 1741 to 1751 and again from 1754 to 1763. He also served as a justice of the peace in Windham County, judge of the probate courts, and judge of the Connecticut Superior Court during those years. These were not vanity positions, but ones for which he continually performed difficult work.

Trumbull did it with the civil work ethic that characterized the people of New England at that time and that he epitomized. Other elected officials began to understand that they could count on the judicious Trumbull for anything.[29] Furthermore, by the 1750s Trumbull had become one of Connecticut's largest dealers in provisions, despite a consistent habit of giving too much credit to his customers and remaining in debt himself. This combination of skills served the colony well when war with the French loomed again.

A decade earlier, during the War of Austrian Succession, Connecticut troops had fought bravely during the siege of Louisbourg on Cape Breton Island, losing 150 soldiers. But when the British simply gave the fortress back to the French during peace negotiations, many were severely disenchanted with the mother country; even the pro-British governor called it an "unhappy experience."[30] Nevertheless, troops from New Haven, Hartford, and New London marched once again to assist the British against French forces in Canada. The Trumbulls, the Huntingtons, the Lathrops, the Williamses, and several other merchant families teamed up to supply the provisions of the state's troops.[31] One of those suppliers was a friend of Trumbull's named John Ledyard, who had a smaller mercantile business in Groton, a small town on the east side of the Thames River harbor, opposite New London. He imported goods to sell to the colonial armies, and then served in those armies himself.[32] Benedict Jr. actually served as supercargo on Ledyard's ship, along with another Ledyard brother named Youngs. Both brothers died within weeks of each other while at sea, and years later their supercargo was suspected of foul play.[33] John Ledyard's youngest surviving brother, William, was three years older than Arnold, but he did not head off to the war with his father. Instead, young William kept his father's business running, sending the Trumbulls molasses and other goods.[34]

Like John Ledyard, many Connecticut men also served in the locally dubbed French and Indian War, or sent their sons, like Trumbull's eldest, Joseph, four years older than Arnold.[35] At the beginning of the war, Arnold was too young, and perhaps his mother did not want her last surviving son to go. He was also busy. Lathrop sent much of his medical supplies to the Northern Army, and the war-disrupted trade made everything complicated and dangerous. Nevertheless, despite his indentured servitude to the Lathrops, once he turned eighteen Arnold seems to have immediately joined the New York Provincial Regiments to fight. It is unclear why he didn't join Connecticut's "voting" militia, which had always been "democratic," in the sense that officers needed to persuade their soldiers, and personal prestige and popularity mattered much more than military hierarchy. As early as 1709, an observer noted "an equality which is not so consistent with martial discipline."[36] This would have appealed to Arnold, who was not part of the aristocracy of the colonies by any means or even among the merchant elite that dominated his own state.

Arnold's service did not last long; he deserted in the spring of 1759.[37] His mother had taken ill, and it could be that he returned to see to her while her father spent the season at sea. She finally died that summer and was lowered into a grave by the town green by her grieving son and daughter. After that, young Benedict seems to have returned to the army the following spring but never saw any action. It is difficult not to read something into this double abandonment of duty, first of his apprenticeship and second of the army. But despite being punishable by hanging, desertion was not unusual and was almost common practice among the colonial militias.

Even with these regular desertions, Connecticut gave more than its share of provisions and troops for the French and Indian War, especially for the assaults on Canada that led to the capture of Quebec.[38] The war also created a network of veterans and merchants, and their leader was unquestionably Jonathan Trumbull, by the end of the conflict Connecticut's most respected public figure.[39] And Trumbull, along with almost everyone else who fought or contributed to the war, was disenchanted with the mother country. Military recruiters behaved dishonestly, British regulars demeaned colonial troops, and arbitrary imperial authority was followed by unpaid debts. It was not only soldiers that felt the brunt of this; families throughout the colonies had to quarter troops in their homes, and some towns such as Stamford and Norwalk were completely taken over.[40] Little did the troublesome British army know they were planting the seeds of rebellion.

Some Connecticut merchants also lost their fortunes during the war years. Arnold's father went completely bankrupt, perhaps because shipping became such a chancy prospect or perhaps because he became one himself. On May 12, 1760, a warrant was issued for his arrest, for the crime of losing "the use of his understanding and reason," a thinly veiled euphemism for public drunkenness and nuisance.[41] Shortly after this arrest, one of the Arnolds put an ad in the *New London Summary* for the sale of "a likely Negro boy to be sold cheap for ready cash or short credit."[42] Either this was a personal servant that the family was getting rid of because they could no longer afford one, or they had sunk to slave trading to try to pay the bills.

Whatever the case, Benedict Sr. died a year later, leaving Arnold and his sister, Hannah, orphans. Dr. Lathrop generously put up £300 to keep his apprentice out of debtor's prison and took back a mortgage so that in 1762 young Arnold could sell his parents' house for £700.[43] Lathrop also gave his apprentice an even larger loan of £500 to set up his own business. By now, Arnold was clearly no longer just an indentured servant but considered the childless Lathrops' heir. They even offered him a share in the business in Norwich, but he refused this kindness.

Perhaps there were too many graves in the cemetery by the green, or perhaps his father's dissolution had made the family name mud in the town of his birth. Perhaps Arnold simply wanted to establish a pharmacy in a new city, and since his fellow apprentice, Solomon Smith, was starting one in Hartford, he would start one in New Haven. He left Norwich and rode across the state with his teenage sister to start a new life.

Two decades later, a year after the burning of New London, Dr. Daniel Lathrop died. We can only imagine how he felt when from his old home in Norwich he saw the "whole southern horizon wrapped in the strange, flickering redness of a distant flame" and found out that it was his former apprentice who was responsible.[44] But his wife, Jerusha, lived to a ripe old age, long enough to radically change her opinion of the boy she had once offered her inheritance to. She told her tenant Lydia Sigourney a terrible and probably fabricated story detailing his cruelty to animals, with "dismembered birds" that she found lying around the yard.

Betrayal works on people in strange ways. It is no exaggeration to see Jerusha as a surrogate mother to the son of her husband's cousin. She had lost her own sons, and then trusted and maybe even loved a boy whose mother died young and whose drunken father was an embarrassment and a curse. And in the decades following his attack on

Connecticut, this woman had not created an abstraction or symbol of Arnold; he was still a real boy whom she had nurtured for seven years. But she had changed her memory so completely as to believe the most horrible things about the once-beloved teenager she now called "cruel Benedict Arnold."[45] No doubt she was hiding a lot of pain.

BENEDICT ARNOLD'S store on Leather Lane stood opposite the whipping post and town scales, where occasionally a slaver
would auction his wares. But Arnold did not sell slaves in New Haven;
he sold fantastic-sounding medicines, like Tincture of Valerian, Bate-
man's Pectoral Drops, and Francis' Female Elixir. He sold fever powder, rose water, cold cream, wall hangings, needles, watches, stationery,
mace, tea, and sugar. And it was not only the needs of the body that
Arnold catered to. He sold modern novels like *Tristram Shandy, Joseph
Andrews*, *Peregrine Pickle*, *Tom Jones*, and *Pamela*. Shelves sagged with
the poetry of Homer, Milton, Dryden, Plutarch, Johnson, Pope, and
Swift, and the essays of Aristotle and Locke.[1] His taste in stocking his
bookshelves shows that he may have even read some of them.

His sign read "Sibi Totique," usually translated as "for himself and
for all," either an attempt to unite the opposing poles of individual
and community or an attempt to advertise to the Latin-speaking Yale
students down the street.[2] Once established in New Haven, Arnold
quickly expanded his pharmaceutical trade to the more profitable
import-export business, becoming part owner of three different ships,
the *Charming Sally*, *Fortune*, and *Three Brothers*. They followed the
trade routes between Dublin and London and the smaller Caribbean
islands that formed the backbone of Atlantic trade. He often joined
these expeditions and became known in town as Captain Arnold. He
imported molasses and rum from the "sugar islands" and manufactured products from England, while exporting shingles, staves, corn,
flour, and barrels of pork.[3] He sometimes traded horses, bringing them
from Quebec to sell in the Caribbean.[4] He made enough money in just
a few years to permanently bring his sister, Hannah, to New Haven
and buy back his parents' Norwich home, though he eventually sold it
again for a healthy profit.

But aspiring merchants like Arnold were about to get a rude awaken-
ing. Despite the vital help the colonists had provided in defeating the
French in North America, the British government promptly levied the
Sugar Act in 1763, affecting colonies like Connecticut that were de-

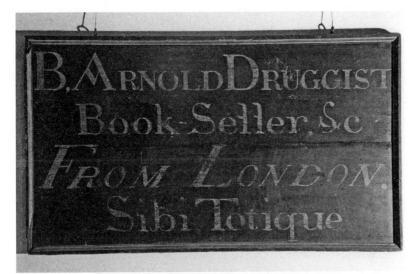

As merchant, bookseller, and pharmacist, Arnold became one of the richest men in New Haven, joining interconnected societies such as the Freemasons and Sons of Liberty. Courtesy of the Eli Whitney Library, New Haven Museum.

pendent on the Caribbean trade.[5] Americans were furious; they had a sense of entitlement to freedoms they earned, while the conservative wing of the British government, including the king, saw ungrateful dependence on the might of the British navy. Why not tax them more? Why not force them to buy duty to British goods and materials? The Sugar Act was followed by the Stamp Act in 1765, throwing the colonies into further disarray, with many in Connecticut protesting that the act violated the colony's charter.

New London, Norwich, Lebanon, and Windham rose up as a body, and by October 1765 the Sons of Liberty was formed. Merchants and shopkeepers were among the first members, secretly or openly. New Londoners burned the "stamp man" in effigy, and an anonymous protestor gave a long speech to attendees, protesting "the crown of all corruption, the ST−P M-N . . . an emblem of the molten calf." He appealed directly to the tradition of self-government, crying, "O *Connecticut, Connecticut,* where is your charter, boasted of for ages past" and "O freemen of the colony of Connecticut! Stand fast in the liberties granted you by your royal charter." But the citizens were clear that though their charter was "royal," they would sing for King George only "if we have liberty." They declared that those taxed have the rights of representation: "For being called Englishmen without having the privileges of Englishmen, is like unto a man in a gibbet, with dainties set before him, which would refresh him and satisfy his craving appetite If he could come at them, but being debarr'd of that privilege, they only serve for an aggravation to his hunger."[6]

Hanging in effigy was always a common practice, usually locally and haphazardly performed. But when Jared Ingersoll of New Haven agreed to distribute the stamps during the Stamp Act controversy, dummies with his name painted on it were hanged throughout the state, especially in eastern Connecticut. A group of five hundred men from New London and Windham confronted him on September 25, 1765, and forced him to resign his post.[7]

Governor Thomas Fitch had opposed the Stamp Act, but he would not go so far as to denounce the British parliament. He prepared to take the oath required to execute the act, and on November 1, 1765, he tried to force the members of the Council of Assistants to take the oath as well. One of those assistants was Jonathan Trumbull, now the Speaker of the House of Representatives. Fitch entered the chamber to find Trumbull and the other three members from eastern Connecticut protesting the decision. When Fitch did not change his mind, the four easterners walked out of the chamber in disgust, refusing to pledge to uphold the Stamp Act.[8] The esteemed French and Indian War veteran Israel Putnam also threatened Fitch, saying that if he didn't hand over the stamp tax papers, the governor's house would "be leveled with the dust in five minutes."[9]

Though these Acts had a trickle-down effect that hurt everyone, the ones hurt most directly were traders like Arnold. In New London the richest merchant in the state, Nathaniel Shaw Jr., complained of "the Stamp Act which has put a Stop to all Business."[10] Six years older than Arnold, the thin-lipped, strong-jawed Shaw had partnered with his sea captain father in 1763, after three of his brothers had been lost at sea.[11] Shaw Jr. expanded the business, trading with merchants in Boston, Philadelphia, and New York, as well as locally in Windham, selling molasses, flour, iron, paper, beaver hats, rum, coffee, and the occasional horse. He became rich enough to keep a private sloop called *Queen of France* to sail for pleasure and for coastal business trips, unusual in the eighteenth century. Shaw's father had been friends with Jonathan Trumbull and John Ledyard, and now the son kept his relationship with the younger relatives: doing business with Joseph Trumbull and his close friend across the harbor, William Ledyard.[12] He also became associated with two other merchants of his generation, Benedict Arnold and Silas Deane.

Silas Deane's father, also named Silas, ran a blacksmith shop a few miles from where Arnold grew up, in the northern part of Groton, and represented his town in the Colonial Assembly in 1752. Not wishing to follow in his father's footsteps, Silas Jr. graduated from Yale in 1758 and passed the bar, moving to live among the mills and tanneries of Weathersfield, just south of Hartford on the great road from New York to Boston. A good-looking, thin-nosed man with a receding hairline, he married a wealthy widow, but she died four years later after bearing him one child. He then married Elizabeth Saltonstall of Norwich, a beautiful woman with a delicate constitution.[13] Like Arnold, Deane ran a store that sold a variety of goods, from Barcelona handkerchiefs to Caribbean molasses to local hemp seed.[14] They met some time in the late 1760s or early 1770s, and Arnold began to win Deane's "friendship and confidence."[15]

In 1766 the cautious Governor Fitch was voted out, and a year later his nemesis Jonathan Trumbull noted that action taken by Britain would only increase strife, saying, "it is always to the interest of the Mother country to Keep them [colonies] dependent.... But if violence or methods tending to violence be taken to maintain their dependence, it tends to hasten a separation."[16] During the next few years, strife did increase, and men like Shaw and Deane joined in feeling and action with the progressive Trumbull, as the latter gained the governorship of the colony. Shaw preferred to take a quieter leadership position, joining the committee that approved the Boston resolutions of 1767 and acting as one of four delegates to the grand convention of the colony in December 1770. Deane, on the other hand, was more outspoken. On Christmas Day 1769, he took the floor at his Congregational meeting-house to condemn British taxes as "unconstitutional," and the rest of the town agreed, passing a resolution not to buy British goods. He was appointed to the Connecticut Committee of Correspondence, an innocuously named resistance organization.[17]

Arnold was certainly one of these radical Connecticut merchants. He joined the local Hiram Lodge of the Freemasons, a secret society dedicated to reason and other Enlightenment values, started in Connecticut by David Wooster. Born in 1711, Wooster was a veteran of the Louisbourg expedition of 1745 and had probably picked up Freemasonry from Gibraltar troops stationed there.[18] The Freemasons in America included such notables as George Washington and Benjamin Franklin, both of whom boarded at Wooster's father-in-law's house during the French and Indian War. In these years leading up to the Revolution, the Freemasons were instrumental in creating and supporting the paramilitary organization, the Sons of Liberty, in which Arnold soon became a leader. He was also eventually elected the captain of a more formal local militia organization called the Governor's Foot Guards.[19]

Often Arnold's values as a businessman and as a Son of Liberty coincided. After the British taxes and levies, many merchants turned to "smuggling," and local governments turned a blind eye to this practice. New London alone illegally exported 210,000 horses to the Caribbean in the decade before the Revolution. But there were always king's men ready to snitch to royal enforcers for not sending goods directly to England or for not paying taxes. On February 3, 1766, local sheriff Jonathan Mix arrested Arnold as one of the men who beat up a king's man named Peter Boles, who had also tried to blackmail him. Arnold and a few Sons of Liberty broke into the house of a local taverner "with Great Force" to get him and "with the same Force & Violence afs. then and there assault the Body of sd. Peter Boles then and there being in sd/ House in the Peace of God a& the King of him strip of his apparel & him tie & fasten to the Whipping Post in sd. New Haven & him did beat and abuse in a cruel shocking & dangerous Manner to his grievious Damage & against the peace & to the Terror of his Majestys good Subjects."[20]

Arnold was fined a few pounds for this brutal act.[21] Stranger than a respected businessman taking part in a violent beating was the fact that he and the other men were not jailed; the New Haven courts were clearly not sympathetic to Mr. Boles. Still, it was obvious Arnold had a temper, whether in politics or business. During a falling out with a New York merchant, Arnold began somewhat diplomatically: "I think I can convince the Whole World I have been a loser of Fifty Per Cent. on both voyages. . . . I cannot say what pleasure it is for you to keep the ballance due me in your hands; but can assure you it will give me much

Benedict Arnold's large house on Water Street in New Haven was later owned by lexicographer Noah Webster. Courtesy of the Eli Whitney Library, New Haven Museum.

pleasure to receive it, as it has been due three years and I want it very much."[22] But when the man replied with hostility, Arnold became insulting: "I assure you it is with the utmost indifference I observe all the unjust & False aspersions your Malice could Invent, both with regard to the Fortune's Cargo & our affidavits, as a Consciouness of my uprightness and Fairness in regard to our Concerns will never suffer the opinion of you or any other Blockhead to give me any uneasiness."[23] Arnold was having money issues at the time, having gone nearly bankrupt a year earlier, but this was probably not the way to go about getting it back.

Though he remained an active member of the Sons of Liberty, a year after the incident with Boles he tried to settle down into a respectable adulthood, marrying Margaret Mansfield, the daughter of one of his fellow Freemasons, New Haven County's high sheriff. He and Margaret borrowed money and bought a large clapboard house with a carved doorway, a cupola, and carvings of birds and other flourishes above the windows. In the yard was a barn with an attached store where Arnold sold his goods, a stable for a dozen horses, a coach house, and an acre and a half of land that included a hundred fruit trees.[24] In their sky-blue parlor they held dances and parties for the elite of the city and may have held Freemason meetings there as well.

Margaret bore him three sons: Richard, Henry, and, of course, another Benedict. The "loving husband" wrote often to his wife, asking about "our dear boys" and telling her not to neglect their education, that "it is of infinite concern what habits and principles they imbibe when young."[25] But politics kept intruding into their intermittently happy home. In the aftermath of the so-called Boston massacre in 1770, Arnold wrote furiously, "I was very much shocked the other day on hearing the accounts of the most wanton, cruel, and inhuman murders committed in Boston by the soldiers. Good God, are the Americans all asleep and tamely yielding up their liberties, or, are they all turned philosophers, that they don't take immediate vengeance on such miscreants?"[26]

Though his first home in eastern Connecticut was now also a center of seditious activity, Arnold could hardly have picked a better city to find radical politics, full of Enlightenment hallmarks like newspapers, coffeehouses, and an educated population. The largest city in the state, New Haven had boasted its first newspaper, the *Connecticut Gazette*, though it folded a few years after Arnold moved there. By then a number of other newspapers had sprung up, and folded, throughout the state, with the Green family starting most of them. Thomas Green started the *Connecticut Courant* in Hartford in 1764 and the *Connecticut Journal* three years later in New Haven.[27] But it was the presence of the state's only college that made New Haven such a hotbed of Enlightenment ideas.

The president of Yale College, Napthali Daggett, had been one of the first to attack the Stamp Act openly, in pages of the *Connecticut Gazette*. Daggett had, like Arnold, received "grammar instruction" from Dr. Cogswell of Canterbury, and now he trained many of the students who would go on to become ardent patriots during the Revolution.[28] The school was the largest of the nine colleges in the colonies in the 1770s, with approximately two hundred students.[29] It was located on the west side of the New Haven green, and in those days consisted of two buildings, Connecticut Hall and Yale College. Connecticut Hall was brick, modeled after Massachusetts Hall at Harvard, with large sleeping chambers that contained small study cells within them. Yale College was a long wooden building with six chimneys along the roof line, originally colored light blue.[30] Boys in felted hats and camblet gowns packed like ship cargo into uncomfortable rooms, studying logic, mathematics, languages, physics, oratory, and rhetoric. On good days they crowded into a thin dining hall and ate salted shad, corn bread, beans, peas, and onions, washed down with apple cider. In leaner times they were fed pumpkin and Indian pudding and drank boiled water. Of course, the wealthier students could be seen around town in their buckskin breeches, smoking tobacco and drinking coffee or, if they could afford it, a frothy mug of flip.

Two of the most popular and gifted students in those years were Benjamin Tallmadge and Nathan Hale. Born amid the soft green hills of Coventry in 1755 to a farming family, one of twelve children, Nathan Hale grew into a handsome boy with fair skin, blue eyes, and flaxen hair. By the time Hale reached Yale he was an athlete with a broad chest, solid muscles, and legendary jumping and leaping skills. He could kick a football "over the tops of the trees." He became a member of the literary Linonian Society and during his second year met a fifteen-year-old named Benjamin Tallmadge.[31] Tallmadge's father had been born in New Haven in 1725 and graduated from Yale in 1747, becoming a minister at Brookhaven on Long Island. That is where Benjamin was born, on February 25, 1754, and he grew into a good-looking, doe-eyed young man with a precocious intelligence. He was so talented, in fact, that President Daggett admitted him to Yale when he was only twelve years old. But his father wisely held him back three years until the autumn of 1769, when he crossed the Sound to New Haven.[32]

Their friendship became a touchstone in both their lives, with a witty repartee that hid genuine feeling. Tallmadge wrote during their junior year,

> In my delightsome retirement form the fruitless Bustle of the Noisy, with an usual Delight &, perhaps, with more than common attention, I peruse your Epistle. Replete as it was with Sentiments worth

to be contemplated, let me assure you with the strongest confidence of an affectionate Friend, that with nothing was my Pleasure so greatly heightened, as with your curious remarks upon my preceding Performance.

With his purposefully flowery, college-student prose, Tallmadge pontificates with a wink to his friend, taking issue with the smallest and most amusing points: "You intimated in your last, that my using the Comparative Degree was somewhat needless, alleging that the sincerity of my friendship would not be rendered more conspicuous by the use of the Comparative." He goes on like this for three pages, on the subject of what degree of language to put their friendship into and on a vague disagreement in a previous letter that is never made concrete, in the drollest rhetoric possible. In other words, he uses the highest and most formal language to say absolutely nothing: a classic college-student prank. At the end he jokes, "I have so far exceeded any design in treating upon the preceding Topicks, that I must omit many things, which I determined to have discoursed upon at this Time, to be considered in some future Paper."[33]

At graduation in 1773, Tallmadge spoke at the invitation of President Daggett, and he and Hale participated in a cutting-edge debate on the education of women.[34] The two young men left college and looked for employment. Hale first went to teach in East Haddam along the Connecticut River, but moved almost immediately to New London that winter, where he became the preceptor at Union School college preparatory academy and was befriended by one of its benefactors, Nathaniel Shaw. Tallmadge took a job as superintendent of a school in Weathersfield, where he was befriended by Yale alum Silas Deane. These young men had been educated in radical politics and now joined the network of merchants and politicians advocating resistance to British tyranny.

Tallmadge and Hale were not the only Yale graduates to take part in progressive politics. In the 1770s eight of the twelve assistants to the governor were Yale alumni, and, of course, Trumbull himself was a Harvard man. One half of the field officers of the Connecticut militia were Yale graduates, and a majority of the Council of Safety were also. Many of the graduates served as ministers throughout the colonies, and most of these promoted antimonarchist "Whig" policies from the pulpit and to their parishioners.[35] These networks were all merging and growing, with Freemasons, Sons of Liberty, and college graduates becoming interdependent and interchangeable. The Connecticut Committee of Correspondence had emerged as a shadow government and was populated by citizens from all these other networks. And they stretched outside of Connecticut, joining others, creating the vast root system that allowed the grass of a new nation to grow.

But people didn't have to have a college education or be part of these growing networks to understand that the British policy toward America amounted to tyranny. After all, the population of the American colonies was at least half that of England and twenty times that of Canada. That meant almost one-third of the so-called British dominions were ruled by a Parliament in which they had no representation.[36] These facts began to seep into the consciousness of the now vaguely united colonists, from the farmers and the craftspeople to the housewives and the innkeepers. This popular support meant governmental sponsorship; as early as 1769 Connecticut, New York, Massachusetts, and Pennsylvania had adopted the strategy of not importing British goods. Those who refused were often pressured by their more progressive colleagues and neighbors.[37]

The Tea Act in 1773 led to more protests and widespread dumping of tea by Americans, from the housewives who refused to serve it to their guests to the merchants who refused to import it. Nathaniel Shaw wrote in October, "In regard to the tea that is expected from England, I pray heartily that the colonies may not suffer any to be landed."[38] Many burned or discarded tea and other British-made objects in public demonstrations, and Labrador tea or coffee became the drinks of choice. Things seemed to be coming to a head, and Benedict Arnold could not help musing to his wife that winter, "how uncertain life is, how certain Death: may their loud & affecting calls awaken us to prepare for our Own Exit, whenever it shall happen."[39] He had created a new family from the ruins of the old, rebuilt his fortune twice, and now they were threatened by the simmering conflict, which may have been inevitable and just, but not welcome.

The Boston Port Act of 1774 was the fuse that lit the fire. The king and his supporters in Parliament had decided that their only options were capitulation to the American demands or war. Without reason to stand on, tyranny becomes the last refuge. And the Americans gave the king plenty of excuses to enforce that tyranny. When Boston was blockaded and put under military law by the British parliament on June 27, mobs harassed Tory politicians and demagogues throughout New England, while kidnapping, riots, and threats swept the land.[40] Special town meetings were held across Connecticut, most of which ended in a denunciation of England and a pledge of support for Boston. Shaw met with the New London town committee and vowed to adhere to the acts of the Continental Congress.[41]

Elected as a representative from Weathersfield two years earlier, Silas Deane sent a letter in June for publication in the *Connecticut Courant* that detailed the injustices of the British, asking, "Is there, my Countrymen, any other Alternative now left you but to submit, or prepare for resistance even to Blood? I declare I know of none. Our petitions dispised, our Liberties sported away, our private as well as public Interest invaded, and our lives at the Mercy of a General and his army!"[42] He was swiftly elected by his peers to serve in the upcoming Continental Congress in Philadelphia. The Massachusetts delegation, with Samuel and John Adams, reached Hartford in August 1774, on their way to Philadelphia. Deane and his stepson Samuel Webb rode up to meet them, and the following day they visited his house, where his wife Elizabeth served punch and coffee. A few days later, after settling his business affairs, Deane followed the delegation to Philadelphia, the second-largest city in the English-speaking world, to debate a course of action.[43]

Some in Connecticut could not wait for the results of the new Congress. Delegates from Windham and New London counties met in Norwich, condemning the "unconstitutional acts" and presence of General Thomas Gage's standing army in Boston, which was "too great to be given to any Person in a free Country . . . an Army not under the Control of the civil Magistrate! What Country? What State?" They lamented the possible "disagreeable necessity of defending our sacred and invaluable Rights . . . for, we could not entertain a thought that any American would or possibly could be dragoon'd into Slavery." Among the men at the Norwich meeting were Samuel Huntington, Nathaniel Shaw, William Ledyard, Jonathan Trumbull, and Israel Putnam. They all signed their names to this radical protest, two years before delegates from the entire country would sign a similar document, putting reputations and lives on the line for liberty.[44]

Not everyone was ready for rebellion. The reverend Samuel Peters of Hebron wrote a proclamation urging his flock not to take up arms, "it being high treason." The result, he wrote, was that "riots and mobs . . . have attended me and my house. . . . The clergy of Connecticut must fall a sacrifice, with the several churches, very soon to the rage of the puritan nobility." He pleaded for the Lord to "deliver us from anarchy."[45] The proclamation was not well received by the majority of the townspeople. A number of men arrived at Peters's house and found it full of his armed followers. They held a meeting outside, in which they argued about his use of tea, and during the argument Peters claimed there were no weapons in the house. The reverend started to "harangue" the crowd, when suddenly a gun went off inside. The men rushed inside to find loaded guns and pistols, swords, and two dozen large wooden clubs. After confiscating these, they let Peters go back inside to write a confession of what happened. He was not cooperative and the crowd grew "exasperated." Finally, the people seized him, took him to the green at the center of town, and forced him to sign a confession.[46]

According to Peters, admittedly not the most reliable witness, when he fled Windham County's mob rule to New Haven, he was met with more of the same from the local Sons of Liberty, including Benedict Arnold. At ten o'clock "Arnold and his mob came to the gate," and after Peters said he would not come out, supposedly "holding a musket" in his hand, Arnold told the mob to "bring an axe, and split down the gate." Peters replied, "Arnold, so sure as you split the gate, I will blow your brains out, and all that enter this yard to-night!" When Arnold retreated, the mob called him a coward, but he said, "I am no coward; but I know Dr. Peters' disposition and temper, and he will fulfill every promise he makes; and I have no wish for death at present." According to Peters, David Wooster showed up with another mob a half hour later, and these and other threats encouraged him to leave Connecticut altogether, heading for Boston.[47]

That autumn of 1774 people around the state quietly began to arm for a war many suspected would come, even though the first shots had not yet been fired. New military companies were commissioned, artillery was inventoried, weapons were repaired, and militia was trained. Connecticut called for a meeting of all the colonies to join forces and protest the Coercive Acts and even at this early date called for a more permanent union. The same year the monarchist Tories met in Middletown and tried to remove the radical Governor Trumbull from office. They were a dwindling minority, though, and failed. The council under Trumbull asked Nathaniel Shaw to send ships to the Caribbean to covertly buy powder and shot from the French. Arnold himself tried to gather muskets equipped with bayonets.[48]

In early 1775 a group of Tories in Stamford found out about a large shipment of gunpowder secretly entering Connecticut. They told a sympathetic customs officer, who seized the powder and kept it at his house. But the next day a large group of Revolutionaries, having heard of this incident, "proceeded in an orderly manner to the house where the powder was lodged, which they entered without opposition, and having found it, rode off with the casks." The Tories and their informers "hid themselves until all was over."[49]

Trumbull and the assembly also joined the new Continental Association. Every town but Ridgefield and Newtown publicly accepted their actions. These holdouts were promptly shunned by the rest of the towns in Fairfield County, who suspended all commerce dealings and connections from the inhabitants of these two villages.[50] In March 1775 Trumbull stood in front of the assembly and called the Tories "depraved, malignant, avaricious, and haughty," rallying for "Manly action against those who by Force and Violence seek your ruin and destruction."[51] By April Shaw had obtained powder and was trying to stock up on lead from Philadelphia.[52] He wrote on April 1 that "matters seem to draw near where the longest sword must decide the controversy."[53]

He was right. The first shots were fired at Lexington on April 19, and swift riders carried the word west across Connecticut. Hour by hour each town heard the news and sprang into action. In Brooklyn veteran Israel Putnam supposedly set down his plow and galloped to Boston.[54] When the news reached New Haven, class exercises were suspended, and Ezra Stiles's son, who had followed in his father's footsteps at Yale, left for Newport and arrived on April 26, surprising his father.[55] Norwich's Ebenezer Huntington, a senior at Yale, left class and marched directly to Boston to meet his brother Jedediah, who had graduated from Harvard a decade earlier. They and the other volunteers began to surround the city.

Twenty-one-year-old Jonathan Mix Jr., whose father had arrested Benedict Arnold nine years earlier, was a member of the New Haven

Cadets and had recently joined the Governor's Foot Guard under Captain Arnold. On April 21 a herald sent by Arnold banged on his door and called him out to the green, where he and forty others gathered and heard the news. They voted unanimously to march to Boston. The following morning when they gathered to leave, Arnold asked the Board of Selectmen for the keys to the powder house, since his small troop lacked gunpowder. Fellow mason David Wooster put up a cautious resistance, saying that they should wait for proper authorization, probably from Governor Trumbull. Arnold told him that they could give him the keys or he and his men would break in. Wooster gave him the keys. Arnold left his three sons and his sickly wife and marched to war, leading Mix and the small band of dedicated militia toward Boston.[56] Resistance had become revolution.

Meanwhile, the only colonial governor who supported that revolution, Jonathan Trumbull, called together his Council of Safety and began to form six regiments under new articles of war.[57] Few in the colonies were as ready as Trumbull and his allies for this moment. Men carrying letters and messages galloped around the state—between Trumbull in Lebanon, Samuel Huntington in Norwich, Nathaniel Shaw in New London, Thomas Mumford, Daniel Lathrop, Eliphalet Dyer, Benjamin Tallmadge, and William Ledyard—and circulated further on to those who had joined the army or were serving in the Continental Congress, such as William Williams, Oliver Wolcott, Roger Sherman, Jeremiah Wadsworth, Gold Selleck Silliman, Silas Deane, and Benedict Arnold. Shaw asked the Huntingtons for powder for the *Oliver Cromwell*. The Huntingtons sent flour and salt pork to the Trumbulls.[58] Forts were occupied, Tory assets were seized, and military plans were put into action. They had long since planted the seeds, and the grass had finally broken through the soil.

Resist Even Unto Blood

BENEDICT ARNOLD and his New Haven militia got as far as Massachusetts before they ran into a Connecticut patriot named Samuel Parsons. A member of the General Assembly, Parsons had ridden to Boston early and was coming back to report on the conflict. Arnold mentioned the cannon at Fort Ticonderoga at the southern end of New York's Lake Champlain, where the British garrison might not have yet heard the alarm of revolution. Parsons rode south and met his friend in the legislature, Silas Deane. Through a clever and possibly illegal financial maneuver, Deane and a few other legislators got the money and sent notice to Ethan Allen and his Green Mountain Boys, and an ambush, led by Allen and Arnold, was born.[1]

Events moved quickly. Recruitment began in Connecticut and Arnold and his allies moved across Massachusetts, collecting troops. Meanwhile, Ethan Allen gathered his own partisans, refusing to wait for the others. When Arnold heard this news, he was furious, through either personal ambition or worry that the entire operation would be blown. Riding alone through the hills of western Massachusetts, he joined former Connecticut man–turned-transient Allen and his Green Mountain Boys. The two egotistical men clashed immediately over command. But they both had enough presence of mind to put their differences aside and lead the motley soldiers through thick pine forests over the border of New York and sixty miles north past Lake George to the frontier outpost of Fort Ticonderoga.

In the dark early morning of May 9 they quietly crept within a mile of the fort. A small band of Americans padded through the forest along the cliff side and to the gate, where a lonely British sentinel stood guard. Before he could fire his flintlock, Ethan Allen knocked it to the ground and the band rushed the gates, scrambled across the courtyard, and ran up a flight of stairs to the captain's quarters. Allen pounded on the door and a lieutenant appeared holding up his pants with one hand. Allen told him to "deliver to me the Fort instantly," and the sleepy lieutenant asked what authority he had, apparently unaware of the situation in Boston. "In the name of the great Jehovah and the Continental Congress," Allen replied. The more diplomatic Arnold broke in, "Come, give up your arms and you'll be treated like a gentleman." Without much choice the British complied.[2]

Two days later they took the nearby lakeside fort at Crown Point. On May 12 the prisoners, including a major, a captain, and two lieutenants, were sent to Governor Trumbull. On their arrival, Trumbull immediately solicited the Continental Congress, pledging "support of the Grand American Cause" and urging for the "regular establishment of our Army around Boston." Inside, he sent a second, more circumspect letter, in which he told the Congress that the real message will be delivered by the carrier, one that told them of the Ticonderoga expedition, "an affair of so great Importance," and begged that Congress would "take it up."[3]

But Arnold moved more quickly than letters and slow-moving machinations of the Continental Congress. He cataloged the cannons and prepared them for transport to the siege of Boston, while Eleazar Oswald arrived at Ticonderoga. Oswald had been born in England and had been in America only since 1770, but he had married an American girl in New York City and believed strongly in the goals of the Revolution. After moving to Connecticut, he had joined the New Haven Governor's Foot Guard with Arnold, and now he brought more recruits and a sloop they had commandeered. With this ship at his disposal, Arnold rechristened it *Liberty* and sailed north across Lake Champlain with fifty men for almost a hundred miles, taking the Canadian outpost of Fort Saint-Jean just before the British had a chance to reinforce it.[4] He wrote to Trumbull that "had we been 6 hours later in all Probability we should have miscarried in our Design. . . . Providence seems to have smiled on us." They took everything portable from the fort, including prisoners, and sailed back down the lake.[5]

Left behind by Arnold, Ethan Allen had followed in slower ships and missed the spoils, though he was attacked by British reinforcements. Arnold reached Ticonderoga triumphant, proclaiming, "we are Masters of the Lake."[6] When Allen returned from Saint-Jean, the two men continued to argue. Arnold complained of the intolerable situation: "When Mister Allen, finding he has a strong party, and being impatient of control, and taking umbrage at my forbidding the people to plunder, he assumed the entire command, and I was not consulted for 4 days, which time I spent in the Garrison. And as a private person often insulted by him and his officers, often threatened with my life, and twice shot at by his men."[7] Arnold's ambitions had been satisfied by his success but were dampened by Allen's constant undermining of his authority and his accomplishments. However, the people of New York were more generous. Six hundred families subscribed to an address of praise for Arnold, "deeply impressed with a sense of your merit," after his part in the Ticonderoga raid and subsequent work in the region.[8] A troop of a thousand men finally arrived to reinforce the fort and secure the southern end of Lake Champlain. Arnold returned to Albany to give a report, where he learned that on June 19 his beautiful young wife Margaret had died.[9]

Silas Deane traveled to Weathersfield to visit his own wife, Elizabeth, but he was also needed in Philadelphia, pulled in different directions by love and duty. On one journey home he was joined by Arnold's childhood playmate, Philip Turner, now a talented surgeon who became the doctor for Connecticut's troops in the Continental army.[10] The previous summer in Philadelphia, Deane spoke of the "task before us, which is as arduous and of as great consequence as ever man undertook."[11] The camaraderie in the summer of 1775 continued to feed Deane's passionate patriotism, and even there at the heart of the Revolution, few matched him. He wrote back to Elizabeth in Weathersfield again, saying, "I have the fullest assurance that these colonies will rise triumphant, and shine to the latest posterity, though trying scenes are before us."[12] In another letter he continued even more firmly, "My principles are . . . to sacrifice all lesser considerations to the service of the whole, and in this tempestuous season to throw cheerfully overboard private fortune, private emolument, even my life — if the ship, with the jewel Liberty, may be safe."[13] This was no reckless youth with nothing to lose, but a man of nearly forty, whose success and family were much to risk and whose formerly mild temperament had brought him political position and success.

Deane tried to remain practical despite this revolutionary fervor, serving on various committees throughout the summer and debating with Thomas Paine and Roger Sherman on the positive necessity of clothing the soldiers.[14] When news arrived of Arnold and Allen's success, and his own part in financing the operation, his nickname in Congress became "Ticonderoga."[15] Then on June 14 Deane and a veteran of the French and Indian War named George Washington spent two days drafting rules and regulations for the army. The tall Virginian was preparing to ride to Boston and take command of the various New England militias and promised to stop in Weathersfield. Deane wrote to Elizabeth, "General Washington will be with you soon. . . . I have been with him for a great part of the last forty-eight hours in Congress and Committee, and the more that I have become acquainted with the man, the more I esteem him."[16] A few weeks later Washington rode through Connecticut, proclaimed in New Haven by cannons, drummers, and a Yale fifer named Noah Webster. The general stopped for lunch at Deane's house, meeting Governor Trumbull and Jeremiah Wadsworth. Elizabeth Deane set lunch and withdrew to sit with the house slaves, Hagar and Pompey, in the kitchen, while in the best room the three men talked of freedom.

Washington rode on to the siege of Boston, already over two months old. Within the week after the shots were fired at Lexington almost four thousand Connecticut men had marched to join the army assembling around Cambridge. Many of these men came back, since there was little food in April for the huge numbers rushing to defend their homeland.[17] But throughout the summer, recruitment for the war effort continued, and it increased with the arrival of Washington to lead and cohere the various militias and companies.

One of those inspired to join that summer was Nathan Hale, who felt restless teaching in New London. Every day thirty-two boys sat on benches at long tables and scraped their slates, staring out the wavy glass windows of the Union School while he taught them Latin and grammar. On Saturdays he taught girls, a practice for which he had been vilified by some of the more conservative people in town. But the trustees of the school, including Nathaniel and Lucretia Shaw, seem to have had no problem with this quirk, inviting him to meals at their huge stone house by the harbor.[18] After all, Hale was a respected teacher, "frank and independent in his bearing, social, animated, ardent, a lover of the society of ladies, and a favorite among them."[19]

Hale had joined the New London militia the previous autumn, and by the summer of 1775 was promoted to first sergeant.[20] But the battle was not at New London, not yet, and even though his contract was nearly up anyway, he decided he couldn't wait any longer. He wrote to his friend Benjamin Tallmadge about his conflicted feelings of responsibility, and Tallmadge wrote back, saying,

When I consider you as a Brother Pedagogue, engaged in a calling, useful, honorable, and doubtless to you very entertaining, it seems difficult to advise you ever to relinquish your business, and to leave so agreeable a circle of connections and friends. . . . On the other hand, when I consider our country, a land flowing as it were with milk and honey, holding open her arms, and demanding assistance from all who can assist her in her sore distress, methinks a Christian's counsel must favor the latter.[21]

Tallmadge's letter must have hit a nerve. On Friday, July 17, two weeks after Washington rode through Connecticut, Hale tendered his resignation, and as he left "gave [his students] earnest counsel, prayed with them, and shaking each by the hand, bade them individually farewell."[22] He joined the Seventh Connecticut Regiment as a lieutenant and recruited more soldiers from the area, such as Stephen Hempstead. A year younger than Hale, Hempstead lived in an old 1678 house a few blocks from the schoolhouse, at the bottom of a large hill. He idolized Hale and joined up as his sergeant.[23] Nathaniel Shaw gave his protégé Hale a gift of powder and shot before he left.[24]

At the siege of Boston Hale livened up the dull camp life with sporting events and games, but always meticulous, he carefully wrote down instructions for himself in his diary: "It is the utmost importance that an officer should be anxious to know his duty, but greater that he should carefully perform what he does know." He settled into a routine, drinking coffee in the morning and brandy at night, drilling his soldiers and preparing for the battles he knew would come.[25] Tallmadge visited the siege before returning to his job, where he weighed his options all summer and fall, aching to join up, but careful of his duties, unwilling to take his own advice.

Hale received many letters from friends he had made in New London; he had left behind many broken hearts. Gilbert Saltonstall wrote with tongue in cheek, "The young girls . . . have frequently desir'd their compliments to Master, but I've never thought of mentioning it 'till now — you must write something in your next by way of P.S. that I may show it them."[26] But Hale had left the pleasures of youth behind and was now on his way to becoming a man. Promoted to captain, he dined with Gen. Israel Putnam at headquarters several times, initiated fully into the circle of Connecticut Revolutionaries.[27]

Jonathan Trumbull, shown here with his wife, Faith, earned the respect of his contemporaries for his civil-work ethic and service in Connecticut government. Stuart, Life of Jonathan Trumbull.

The growing army needed to be supplied, and one hundred miles from Boston, safe in the New England interior, the hilltop town of Lebanon became one of the centers of the revolutionary effort. On the enormous, comet-shaped village green, livestock were gathered, soldiers billeted, and Governor Trumbull's country store became the "war office," where he would hold no less than nine hundred meetings of his Council of Safety during the course of the Revolution. Riders hurried to Lebanon from Boston and New York, and Trumbull remained one of the best informed figures in the war.[28] In fact, he may have been George Washington's most frequent correspondent, and the "the mutual friendship and esteem" that grew between the two men helped both.[29] Though the religious Connecticutian was twenty years older than the Virginian, they spoke on equal terms, and legend has it that Washington called him "Brother Jonathan," leading to the use of the term for the common Yankee soldiers during the war. Whether its origin is apocryphal or not, the term began to be used freely and proudly throughout the northern colonies.[30]

Trumbull saw the Revolution as something of a religious quest. He was also a born egalitarian, with a simple approach to everyday life that stemmed from his puritanical background. At one point he was mocked by Loyalists on Long Island for the baffling habit of getting shaved at the local barber shop, where he "stands among the rest, and among them takes his turn in the chair," rather than having a servant do this work.[31] This dated criticism reveals how strange and new these democratic ideas were, and how the class-conscious British society was easy for someone like Trumbull to reject.

His sons all graduated from Harvard, and like their father became devout advocates for the Revolution. Born in 1740, Jonathan Jr. supervised the family's Lebanon flour mill and East Haddam shipyard and now became the paymaster for the northern department of the army. The governor's youngest son, John, only nineteen years old, became an aide to George Washington, and his eldest, Joseph, took the greatest responsibility of all. Joseph lived in Norwich at the outbreak of hostilities and began serving as commissary general of the Connecticut troops in April. He was recommended to Congress by Silas Deane and had done such a fine job so far that they appointed him commissary general for the entire Continental army on July 19.[32]

The Commissary Department of the army immediately became the largest economic organization on the continent. Joseph siphoned grain from Virginia and salted pork and fish from Connecticut.[33] He sent and answered hundreds and hundreds of letters, requests, and orders.[34] His job was not an easy one and was praised by Washington, who said, "Few Armies, if any, have been better and more plentifully supplied than the Troops under Mr. Trumbull's care."[35] Having the governor of Connecticut as his father helped, and his mother, Faith, supported local charities, instituted clothing drives for the troops and kept up morale among the wives left at home.[36]

Under Governor Trumbull's zealous management, Connecticut became a model of a functional war state, with daily and weekly ration schedules for beef, pork, flour, molasses, milk, coffee, chocolate, rice, peas, beans, butter, corn meal, sugar, rum, beer, soap, candles, and tobacco. Clothing was supplied by establishing quotas in each town, and these efforts led to supplying not only the Connecticut troops but others throughout the colonies.[37] The state produced gunpowder at a far more rapid rate than any other, despite trouble importing saltpeter and sulfur. Muskets were put together by skilled craftsmen for five shillings a gun, enough so that almost all the Connecticut militia and troops in the Continental army were armed. The Salisbury foundry in the far northwest of the state produced cannon, grapeshot, and round shot for the fortifications around New York and along the Connecticut coast. Trumbull's operation became by far the most productive per capita of any colony.[38] While in New York, Arnold told his aide Richard Varick to get supplies directly from Connecticut, because his home state was so reliable.[39]

Governor Trumbull also supervised the daunting job of recruitment for the Continental army and local militia. Connecticut's population was about two hundred thousand, and one-fifth saw military service during the war, almost all men of military age. However, just as in every other state, there were many desertions. Trumbull offered bounties, though they still struggled to keep the Continental army recruitment up to a respectable level. Rather than lacking interest in the cause of liberty, the soldiers were frustrated by intermittent pay, inadequate provisions, and other problems that plagued the army.[40] Hale reported a private deserting to the enemy as early as October 1775, but it was rare enough to mention.[41] Two months later, though, when the Connecticut troops completed their initial enlistments, many chose to leave the siege of Boston and go home. Upon hearing about this disgraceful desertion of troops, Gideon Saltonstall wrote to Hale from New London, saying, "The behavior of our Connecticut Troops makes me Heartsick — that they who have stood foremost in the praises and good wishes of their Countrymen, as having distinguished themselves for their Zeal of Publick Spirit, should more shamefully desert the Cause, and at a critical Moment too, is really unaccountable — amazing."[42] Washington cursed the troops' "dirty, mercenary spirit," and despite the early valiance of Arnold, Putnam, and others, Connecticut briefly lost its reputation.[43] Indeed, when many of the militia returned home they found a hostile reception from their families and colleagues. Perhaps because of this pressure, many joined up again, and by the beginning of 1776 Connecticut's regiments were almost at full strength.[44]

Trumbull also commissioned two hundred privateers, which would capture more than five hundred enemy ships. But he had help with this job from an old friend's son, Nathaniel Shaw Jr. He was the richest patriot in the best harbor in the state, which Silas Deane proposed to the Continental Congress as the future home of the American navy.[45] Shaw himself owned several unarmed ships and an astonishing ten armed vessels, including the *General Putnam*, a privateer with twenty guns that took fourteen prizes.[46] He and the other owners or captains were able to auction off the captured ships and inessential supplies, while all the necessary food, clothing, and arms were sent to the army.

But Shaw did much more than this, keeping up the now-dangerous Caribbean trade to gather more supplies. On July 12, 1775, he told his agent to sell goods in Philadelphia and then take the ship to Hispaniola to purchase gun powder, and if there was none, then to bring back coffee and brown sugar. He tells him to burn the letter "for Fear of Accidents."[47] By January 1776 the prosperous businessman had felt the financial effects of war and moaned that "all our Trade is now at an end, & god knows whether we shall ever be in a Situation to Carry it on Again, no Business now but preparation for Warr, Ravaging Villages, Burning of Towns &c."[48] But he persevered, commissioning another ship to collect gunpowder and by the following June sent a supply of the precious powder to Washington, along with cases of guns and flints and cutlasses.[49]

Shaw was a businessman through and through and kept a clipped, professional attitude in his correspondence. His stark letters gave clear information, such as sending flour up the river to Norwich "as soon as the river opens," delivering powder to Providence, or informing others that "a great number of French troops are daily arriving."[50] But as the richer son of a rich man, Shaw had grown up with an opportunity for leisure that few in the eighteenth century had. He saved his emotions for hunting expeditions into the coves and bays of the Sound, searching for ducks and other waterfowl. Perhaps he considered these small holidays necessary for his effectiveness and came back to his huge stone house ready to make more money.

Trumbull's friend John Ledyard had died, but his younger brothers, William and Ebenezer, continued the family business. Though much less prominent in the interconnected Connecticut community, they were a vital part of the New London and Groton war effort. William and his brother sent supplies to the army, probably at a great loss, complaining once that "we don't mean to sell one article only to take some for the families. The remainder to lay by until we hear from the company. . . . We don't believe anything about Boston prices."[51] They also worried about the inefficiencies of government and the meanness of the common people at the same time, saying, "I must fear we shall ruin ourselves while we are striving to support our Liberties against our mother country we shall lose it among ourselves." Yet William and his brother kept faith, saying to Joseph Trumbull, "We hope and pray that union will increase throughout the Continent since on that our all depends."[52]

William Ledyard had married Anne Williams of Stonington, and together they lived happily on the large hill in Groton, giving birth to child after child. Ledyard was not as passionate as Silas Deane, as ambitious as Benedict Arnold, or as religiously devoted as Governor Trumbull. He had a classically moderate patriot attitude, desiring liberty from England but concerned about the cost and the consequences. He wrote to Joseph Trumbull that many of the "country people" were not Tories but felt as if "we have got between two fires."[53] Nevertheless he wanted "to hear of the welfare of our friends and Country Men" and told their overworked friend, "you have our best wishes for your health and prosperity and we hope that a kind Providence will preserve you in all your undertaking."[54]

Meanwhile, Benedict Arnold returned to his house on Water Street in New Haven, where his three motherless children and sister, Hannah, met him. His business had already suffered as well, even though Hannah had tried to take over, with the occasional help from their friend Silas Deane.[55] She never lost sight of her brother's welfare, sending him a horse on one occasion, "anxious" to have him know that she was looking out for him.[56] But Arnold was too passionate about the war to think of business anyway and could not sit idle for long.

There was not much opportunity to achieve distinction at the ongoing siege, but the American invasion of Canada offered a better chance. While the main invasion up Lake Champlain toward Montreal staggered under delays, Arnold proposed a new line of attack up the Kennebec River of Maine. He received approval on August 27, 1775, and put together an expeditionary force from the troops stationed around Boston, including his comrade from the foot guard Eleazar

Oswald, who continued his friendship with the newly promoted Colonel Arnold. By September 13 Arnold had gathered his troops and George Washington himself had given him instructions, saying, "you are entrusted with the command of the most consequence to the interest and liberties of America."[57]

Arnold and his troops struggled through the backwoods of Maine, heading for the fortress of Quebec City. He and Eleazar Oswald learned to depend on each other during this brutal, epic march over stubborn portages. By the time they reached Canada, they had lost at least a third of their men, and the rest were starving and frostbitten. They were joined on December 2 by Gen. Richard Montgomery, who had just conquered Montreal. In Montgomery's train were his young aide, Aaron Burr, and Capt. John Lamb of Stratford, another man who became great friends with Arnold. On the fifth, the combined force set up camp on the Plains of Abraham just west of the fortified city, above the icy Saint Lawrence River. The British troops stationed inside the citadel had much bigger cannon, and the Americans could not set up a proper battery to bombard the walls. So, on December 31, during a blinding snowstorm, they attacked.[58]

While Montgomery's troops scaled the bastion of Cape Diamond on the southwest corner of the city walls, Lamb bombarded the citadel with his mortars to give Arnold cover as he made a direct attack around the north side to the lower town. Cannonballs smashed through snow banks, and a musket ball smashed into Arnold's leg, bouncing off the bone and splintering it. His men tried to carry him off, but he concentrated on commanding their safe retreat while blood flowed down his leg. Finally, weakened by blood loss, he allowed his men to drag him to the makeshift hospital.[59] Oswald and Lamb attempted to keep up the hopeless assault, but grapeshot hit Lamb in the face, ripping his cheek bone and knocking him unconscious and destroying the sight in his left eye.[60] Though the soldiers continued assaulting the defenses, they were left without support and could not hold their gains. Lamb and a small band were captured before they could retreat.

From his bed, Arnold waited to hear the fate of his men. Meanwhile, his old Freemason master and the man who held the keys of the powder house back in New Haven, David Wooster, was coming with a relief expedition. Arnold wrote him, "In the attack I was shot through the leg and was obliged to be carried to the Hospital, ware I soon heard the disagreeable news that the General [Montgomery] was defeated at Cape Diamond."[61] It was worse than that: Montgomery had been shot on the walls of the citadel, and his men had fled in panic.

As the siege of Quebec dragged on, Arnold slowly recovered from his leg wound. As at Ticonderoga, Arnold made enemies among the other officers, but this time he also made friends, like he did with the paroled Lamb during their mutual convalescence. In battle, soldiers had to be sure their comrades had their back, and men like Oswald and Lamb had his.[62] One lonely midnight at the hospital Arnold penned a long letter to another friend, Silas Deane, saying, "I have often sat down to write you, and as often been prevented by matters of consequence crowding upon me, which I could not postpone."[63] Deane had become closer to Arnold after Ticonderoga, writing that the brave Colonel "has deserved much and received little or less than nothing."[64] And Arnold needed friends now, telling Deane that the fight for Canada looked more and more like a disaster. The American reinforcements under David Wooster did arrive, but they were not enough. When British reinforcements began arriving in May and June, Arnold and his comrades were pushed southwest back up the Saint Lawrence, and down into New York.

There was one piece of good news — Americans had finally dragged cannons from Ticonderoga across the snow-covered mountain paths to Boston, and the bombarded British had fled. But with reinforcements arriving on the continent, including tens of thousands of German mercenaries, unpleasant times seemed ahead for the Americans. If England was going to have this kind of help, the Americans needed help too. It was time to call on an old enemy, the French, who hated the British far more than the Americans did. The man they chose for the job was none other than Silas Deane, despite his previous lack of diplomatic experience. The thirty-eight-year-old man left for France in March 1776 and arrived with orders to get supplies, enlist men into service, and if possible involve France and other European nations in the war. He wrote a sorrowful farewell letter to his wife, saying, "It matters but little, my Dear, what part we act, or where, if we act it well."[65]

Once he settled into an apartment on the Rue de l'Universite in Paris, he met the French foreign minister, the Comte de Vergennes, and then Pierre-Augustin Caron de Beaumarchais, the French polymath who wrote *The Marriage of Figaro*. Deane appealed to Beaumarchais, who got his hands on 3 million livre, including 1 million from Louis XVI's personal coffers, to purchase one hundred cannons, countless guns, and twenty-five thousand uniforms. Eventually 6 million livre worth of supplies got around the British blockades in the early years of the war.[66]

Deane also recruited young French aristocrats for the American army, more for their money than their military prowess. But one would defy those expectations: the nineteen-year-old Gilbert de Motier, Marquis de Lafayette. He had learned military science and riding at Versailles and stood at the door of Deane's humble apartment on the Rue de l'Universite, asking to fight for human dignity.[67] Deane gave him the rank of major general to satisfy the young Frenchman's family, and he sailed for America.[68] Meanwhile, Arthur Lee of Virginia and Benjamin Franklin arrived. Franklin was already famous in Europe due to his popular *Autobiography*, and he began working on the more serious problem of involving the French government in the war.

While Deane was in Philadelphia and France, his brother Barnabas kept his Connecticut business going, connecting with Nathaniel Shaw and Governor Trumbull under the auspices of the Secret Committee of the Continental Congress. Letters flew to and from Congress and Lebanon, Weathersfield and New London. Shaw collected cargos from the port and distributed goods to his friends, who sent them on.[69] Shaw wrote to the Huntingtons in Norwich: "Must inform you that I have been oblig'd to supply the Continental Troops Quartered in this Town, from Newport who have almost consumed the whole, and I must be oblig'd to call on you for sum more [flour] also for sum work."[70] He had to balance the needs of the local people with the needs of Governor Trumbull and of George Washington's army.

Washington himself arrived at Shaw's granite mansion in New London on April 9, 1776, on his way from Boston to New York. He had been there twenty years earlier during the French and Indian War, while serving as a colonel in the British army.[71] He remembered old Captain Shaw well and was happy to meet his son, bringing seventeen bottles of wine and eating a huge meal on creamware dishes at the mahogany dining table, along with Gen. Nathanael Greene and Cdre. Ezekial Hopkins. Washington and the three men planned the naval war before the exhausted commander in chief retired to old Temperance Shaw's maroon and mustard bedroom.[72]

Norwich lawyer Samuel Huntington, now in Congress, had finally sent official instructions for privateers, giving them permission to attack British ships.[73] Shaw had already been arranging these expeditions for a year, but it was nice to have official permission from the new government. His job was to get supplies and take enemy ships, and these two duties often coincided. Jonathan Mix, now recovered from broken ribs received on the march to Canada, joined one of these expeditions out of New London during the spring of that year, joining the fleet under Commodore Hopkins. They sailed to the Bahamas, landed at Nassau, stormed the fort, and took the governor of the islands prisoner. As new British ships arrived, the American navy took them one by one, building up a store of supplies. When the ships were full, they sailed back to New London, slipping past the British fleet at the end of the Sound and depositing a huge supply of cannons, arms, and ammunition, which, as Mix said, "proved to be of great and timely use to our country."[74] Shaw used some of the captured cannons for defenses in Groton and New London, sent others to Newport, and shipped mortars and shells to Washington in New York.

Despite successes like this, Shaw settled in for a long war. He voted to restrict gunpowder use even for shooting game, to inoculate the populace for smallpox, and to provide for soldiers' families. He also secured the town records in the western hills, a move that kept them safe from the burning four years later, and at a full town meeting approved the Articles of Confederation "as being the most effectual measures whereby the freedom of said states may be secured and their independency established on a solid and permanent basis."[75] He often used his own money to supply the defense of the city and the troops and often went without payment from Congress.[76]

William Ledyard became Shaw's agent to Hartford that summer and discussed finances with Governor Trumbull, finally getting £300 recompense for his new boss.[77] He also was given command of the nascent Fort Griswold on Groton Heights for the first time.[78] Then, on July 10, 1776, Trumbull appointed Shaw agent of the colony for collecting naval supplies and taking care of sick sailors, another official sanction for a job he was already doing.[79] The Continental Congress followed, prompted by his friend Samuel Huntington, who recommended him, saying, "I had the pleasure of procuring you to be appointed Agent, being the most suitable person I could think of."[80] Of

course, this meant he was taking orders from both Lebanon and Philadelphia, like the micromanaging order from John Hancock to "deliver
Mr. Barnabas Deane any Continental Stores in your possession which
he may want for the up[keep] of the Frigate *Trumbull* now filling out
in your state."[81]

Shaw and Ledyard lived under constant threat of invasion from the
superior British navy. A "ship-of-war" ran a captured prize ship onto
the rocks by Fisher's Island, but luckily "armed men from Stonington" and Capt. Elisha Hinman in the *Cabot* took the supplies ashore.[82]
Next, on July 25 three British men-of-war, the *Rose*, the *Swan*, and the
Kingfisher, anchored outside the harbor to blockade the town. Shaw
kept his good humor, sending George Washington a report a few days
later and, along with it, an epicurean gift and joke: "as the Turtle was
Intended for the Support of our Enemys, we thought best to Send him
to head Quarters, to be Dealt with."[83] Washington thanked Shaw for
"an extreme fine turtle" and commiserated about a lost prize ship.[84]
Then, on August 5 and 6 nine ships and several other vessels arrived
but did not attack, being more interested in plundering Fisher's Island,
where they took over a thousand sheep, cattle, and other provisions.
On this occasion they paid the Tory owner but stole from other islands
like Gardiner's and Plum without paying.[85]

After this scare, Shaw wrote a more urgent letter to Trumbull the
following day, begging for help: "This town has been drained of men
already, so that there is scarcely a sufficiency of hands left to get in the
harvest."[86] Ledyard had already begun improving the land fortifications, saying, "no place lies more exposed than we do." Ships had appeared in the Sound as early as 1775 and "appeared to be beating in
but they came to Anchor off Fisher's Island." Ledyard "alarmed the
country," but so many people showed up to his signal that "we could
not agree on a plan to oppose [the raiders] till Monday morning when
they had got all the stock off." Ledyard was one of the people who lost
sheep in this raid.[87] Later that autumn a commission found "that there
is in Groton, nearly opposite the old Fort at New London, a hill or an
eminence. . . . It seems nature had prepared a place to plant cannon
for the protection of that port or harbor."[88] Now in 1776 the Groton citizens dug ditches and built fortifications around the harbor. At
Waterman's Point below Norwich, a small battery with four six-pound
cannons was also erected to receive a potential invasion. But the pro-

cess was slow. Acquiring the sledges, hammers, shovels, timber, and other supplies took ages, and every sight of sails would remind them that the work was incomplete. The lack of effective central government haunted small projects like this as much as it did George Washington's much larger needs.[89]

And Washington's problems had become very serious indeed. His army had gathered in New York, waiting for an invasion they knew was coming. One of the soldiers gathering with Washington was Nathan Hale, who had reenlisted on New Year's Day. His friend Benjamin Tallmadge had also decided to drop his job as high school superintendent and join the army. Perhaps one of Hale's hilarious poems of rhyming couplets had done the trick and inspired his friend, who was quite a fan of versified letters.

> Reviv'd a little by your letter,
> With hopes of speeding better,
> At length I venture forth once more,
> But fearing soon to run ashore. . . .
> For this I leave my wonted course,
> with you, and seek for aid from verse.[90]

Maybe it was a less poetic kind of aid Tallmadge thought his friend was asking for, because on June 20 he rode up the dusty track to Hartford, where Governor Trumbull gave him a lieutenant's commission.[91]

Only five days after Tallmadge joined up, British warships began appearing in New York Harbor. Throughout the hot, tense summer, more and more arrived, cutting off Long Island, spreading up the Hudson, just out of cannon range. Hale handed out new equipment to his men, preparing for an epic conflict.[92] Then, sometime in August, he switched to a company of Rangers to patrol the shores of Manhattan and Westchester. In doing so, he missed the biggest battle on the continent since Europeans had arrived.

On August 22, twenty thousand British troops landed on Long Island and smashed into the American lines, pushing them back across Brooklyn. Those troops not captured or killed barely escaped, retreating back against the East River. Tallmadge had just arrived in Brooklyn and remembered the retreat: "It was one of the most anxious, busy nights that I ever recollect, and being the third in which hardly any of us had closed our eyes in sleep, we were all greatly fatigued."[93] At last

Connecticut's front with British-controlled New York and Long Island lasted from 1776 to 1783, leading to dozens of confrontations. Connecticut and Parts Adjacent, Geography and Maps Division, Library of Congress.

they reached Brooklyn Ferry and crept across the river to Manhattan. It was one of George Washington's most skillful maneuvers, though there is little glory in retreat. Israel Putnam was astonished they had escaped from Long Island, saying the British commander "is either our friend or no general. . . . He suffered us to escape without any interruption."[94] Meanwhile, David Bushnell of Westbrook sent his *Turtle* submarine into New York Harbor, attempting to attach mines to the hulls of British warships, but this technological ploy was unsuccessful.

It was the beginning of a bad season. Throughout the autumn British troops whipped the Continental army off Manhattan and up through Westchester County. Stopped at the line of hills at the southwest corner of Connecticut, they pushed Washington and the main army across the Hudson River and into New Jersey. On December 7, 1776, another British force occupied Newport, Rhode Island, while a huge British fleet patrolled the Sound, effectively surrounding a panicked Connecticut on three sides.[95] Things must have seemed bleak indeed. But there was no turning back. These patriots had committed themselves now, through both declarations and blood, through fire and sacrifice. They were bound through comradeship and oaths, through the connections they had created before the war and through the ones they continued to make in the thick of the struggle. And each of them now faced an uncomfortable prospect: victory or death.

The Shadow War

GEORGE WASHINGTON needed information. No one could run a war without it, and now that the British had occupied Long Island, he needed to know what their next move was. He wrote to his generals on September 1, 1776, and told them he needed a "channel of information" through Tories willing to take a bribe, but "friends would be preferable, if they could manage it."[1] The officers filtered this request carefully down through the ranks, until it reached Nathan Hale, who saw in the job a chance to do something positive for the war. After all, he had yet to participate in a battle.

A college friend from Derby named William Hull was stationed nearby, and Hale asked his advice about the job of "assuming a disguise and passing into the enemy's camp." Hull argued against it, saying first that spying was "not in keeping" with Hale's "character," and then putting down the entire idea, calling this sort of action was "moral degradation." He asked, "Who respects the character of a spy, assuming the garb of friendship but to betray?" He insisted that it would end Hale's "bright career" and end in "ignominious death." Hale listened to this advice but decided that he needed "to be useful, and every kind of service, necessary to the public good, becomes honorable by being necessary."[2]

The faithful Sgt. Stephen Hempstead accompanied Hale, leaving Harlem Heights and traveling to Norwalk, Connecticut. Hale handed a "general order" to Captain Pond of one of the sloops there and silently slipped across the Sound with Hempstead. At Huntington, Long Island, Hale changed his uniform to a suit of plain brown, "assuming the character of a Dutch schoolmaster," keeping only his college diploma with him as evidence of his qualifications for that job. Hempstead sailed back to Norwalk, and Hale walked in disguise toward Flushing. He began drawing maps and taking notes on British positions.[3]

The following events are unclear, but Hale might have been betrayed by his cousin, who, though he denied it, fled to England. Nathan may also have revealed himself to Col. Robert Rogers, a double agent.

Whatever the case, he was discovered and brought to Sir William Howe. Now in possession of a smoldering Manhattan, Howe ordered the spy executed, and on the morning of September 22, 1776, Hale was brought to a makeshift gallows in Artillery Park. While waiting amid the haze of smoke from the fires, he was allowed to write letters to his father and commanding officer. Then he was taken to the gallows, where the provost marshal took the letters and destroyed them, refusing him either clergy or Bible. According to Frederick Mackenzie of the Welsh Fusiliers, Hale maintained his "composure and resolution." The hangman asked if he had any last words, which he did, "saying he thought it the duty of every good officer, to obey any orders given him [by] his Commander in chief; and desired the spectators to be at all times prepared to meet death in whatever shape it might appear." And then he offered a paraphrase from Joseph Addison's play *Cato*, probably learned in those more joyous hours in the Linonian Society at Yale: "I only regret that I have one life to lose for my country." Later that day, a flag of truce discussing the exchange of prisoners reached headquarters. George Washington, Alexander Hamilton, Israel Putnam, and William Hull received the messenger, who had witnessed Hale's execution himself and reported it to the group of American officers. A shocked Hull tried to hold back the tears in front of his superior officers.[4]

Hale's body was left hanging, and a few days later some mischievous British soldiers added a board painted with the words "General Washington" to the grisly scene.[5] His death was a reminder that despite the honor codes of war at the time, this was not only a war of gentlemanly conduct, parleys, and soldiers in formation firing at one another. It was dirty and brutal, and the methods by which it was carried out were just as horrific as or worse than any modern war. The casualty lists are deceptive, usually giving only the soldiers killed in pitched battle. People rarely died in battle — they died later of gangrenous wounds, of smallpox, of pneumonia. Men froze to death in winter camps and women suffered enemy soldiers' brutality.

It might be helpful to separate the war into three smaller wars, into actual battles fought by armed regiments, the struggle for money and supplies, and the shadow war of spies and prisoners fought in the back country, often by ordinary citizens, in which loyalty and courage was tested in a completely different way. Nathan Hale had been one of the

*Nathan Hale's reputation grew in the decades after his death as his story was
elevated to myth. Here, the British commander destroys documents before ordering
his execution.* Cunningham Destroying Hale's Letters, *in Benson Lossing,* The
Two Spies *(New York: Appleton, 1897), University of Bridgeport Archives.*

first casualties of that war, at which the British had long been experts.
George Washington knew that he had to improve his own chances,
and after Hale's death decided to set up a semi-official Secret Service
Bureau. There was a problem, however. Spying was thought the lowest
of the low, "ignominious" as William Hull put it. What man would
lead it? The answer was Benjamin Tallmadge.

Why would a promising young soldier in the dragoons decide to
become Washington's spymaster? Perhaps it had something to do with

his best friend's death. Perhaps he wanted to prove that such activity was not ignominious. But years later Tallmadge remained circumspect about his activities as George Washington's chief intelligence officer, stating, "I opened a private correspondence with some persons in New York (for Gen Washington) which lasted through the war. How beneficial it was to the commander-in-chief is evidenced by his continuing the same to the close of the war. I kept one or more boats continually employed in crossing the Sound on this business."[6] In such understated remarks he was referring to taking charge of the network of spies that Washington was using, primarily in New York City.

Tallmadge's career in the regular army is impressive, though not as impressive as Benedict Arnold's. In June 1776 he joined the army in New York to wait for the British fleet and took part in those awful battles in which the overwhelming force of British redcoats pushed General Washington and the American brigades off Long Island, then off Manhattan, and back to the heights of Westchester County. He was promoted to captain in December of that year by George Washington himself, having been one of the few to have fought bravely throughout the terrible campaign. During that winter, while the exhausted army rested in New Jersey, he returned to Weathersfield to train a regiment of dragoons. In the spring of 1777, at the head of his regiment, he marched from Weathersfield all the way to Morristown, where he joined Washington in that season's campaign. By July he had been promoted to major and became a field officer in the regiment. He took part in all the combat in Pennsylvania during that autumn, fighting at Brandywine and Germantown.[7] As commander of his light dragoon company, Tallmadge was praised by Congress.[8]

But he began doing much more. While Washington and his men suffered at Valley Forge, Tallmadge and detachment of dragoons spent their time galloping around the no-man's-land between the camp and Philadelphia, fighting off patrols of British light horses. This appears to have been largely cover for espionage work. On one occasion at least he rode to Germantown and met a female spy, who had ventured into Philadelphia on the pretense of selling eggs. As he was talking to her, a British patrol arrived, and he grabbed the woman and galloped with her for three miles before letting her off at a safe place.[9]

As the northern war settled into a standoff, he began his other work in earnest. By 1778 he corresponded with "Samuel Culper," the name assumed by the two chief spies in New York, Abraham Wood-hull and Robert Townsend, while his own code name was John Bolton or simply #721. He received constant intelligence as to British troop strength and position. They used invisible ink invented by John Jay's brother James, and by 1779 Tallmadge was even using a cipher code similar to ones used by the British. Pocket dictionaries with this code were used by his spies to decode and encode messages.[10] Meanwhile, he kept up an extensive correspondence with George Washington, keeping the commander in chief apprised of all the intelligence. Though not strictly written in code, this correspondence remained vague and indeterminate, with lines like "You will be pleased to observe the strictest silence with respect to _____ as you are to be the only person intrusted with the knowledge or conveyance of his letters."[11]

He had a difficult job. The British had the best secret service in the world in the eighteenth century, with professionals who stuffed messages inside hollow silver bullets that could be swallowed if necessary. But no matter how good they were, spies still had a dangerous job. Israel Putnam caught one and wrote to the Tory governor of New York, William Tryon,

> Sir—Nathan Palmer, a lieutenant in your service, was taken in my camp as a spy; he was tried as a spy; he was condemned as a spy; and you may rest assured, sir, he shall be hanged as a spy.
> I have the honor to be, &/C.
> ISRAEL PUTNAM.
> P. S. Afternoon. He is hanged.[12]

Luckily for the British, they also had a ready-made spy network in the colonies—the Loyalists. Of course, there was no neat and tidy separation between Loyalists and Revolutionaries. There were conservative Whig-Loyalists who tried to maintain power through the representative government that they nevertheless supported. There were religious neutrals, such as the Quakers, who supported the Revolution but did not participate. There were "rationalists" like the clergy who did not like the Calvinist leadership of the Revolution and could come down on either side, or neither. There were those who sympathized with the "Whig principles" of the Revolution but remained loyal to England, and so on.[13] However useful these political and religious distinctions are, we could also separate the people of the time into two different camps: those who saw America as their home and tried to do what they thought was right to preserve that home and those who were more concerned with self-preservation.

In Connecticut some simply did not believe in the cause enough to serve in the Continental army. Stephen Graves of Harwinton had paid for a substitute when the draft came through. After deserting from a second draft he was caught and brought back but still refused to serve, hiding out in the "Tory Den" near his home and sneaking back to work on the farm. His wife kept a conch shell on which she blew to warn him and the other Tories. Finally, one day a local captain caught her in the act and threatened her. She gave up the conch shell, if not her husband. Nevertheless, he was finally caught, tied to a cherry tree, and whipped with hickory sticks.[14] Leaders such as Gen. Nathanael Greene lamented these incidents, saying that "it would be the excess of intolerance to persecute men for opinions which, but twenty years before, had been the universal belief of every class of society."[15] Connecticut was at the forefront of this movement, offering pardons as early as 1777 for those who took an oath of allegiance to the new government. Another pardon act of 1779 stated that "very different motives and principles have influenced the conduct of the deluded few . . . some through ignorance . . . some through particular prejudice, prospects of reward and gain, or through timidity; others, deceived by the treacherous arts of subtle and secret enemies, have without deliberation given way to the force of various temptations."[16]

But there were others who openly served the British. Joel Stone could not "conceal my sentiments" from his neighbors and declined to sign an oath of allegiance. He could not join "in an act which I actually detested and which had been repeatedly deemed a rebellion." He tried to escape to New York before the "agents of Congress" could arrest him, packing his books and bills, leaving his house to his sister, and riding away on horseback in the night. But the "mob" broke into the house despite the sister's protest, and his possessions were confiscated. He escaped a "party of about twelve armed men with a constable" and finally reached Long Island, joining the king's army as a volunteer with other Loyalists. He served for two years in this capacity. Next, on May 12, 1778, Stone was surprised at Huntington, Long Island, by a "company of whale boatmen," who dragged him back to Norwalk and charged him with high treason. He petitioned Trumbull, who agreed to see him, but "the result turned out quite contrary" to Stone's wishes, and he was locked in a "truly dismal" prison. Only through the help of a bribe and aid from friends was he able to escape "into the wilderness."[17]

The majority of Americans, however, saw the Loyalists as assisting a foreign power against their homeland, no matter their ties of blood or finance to that power. And in many ways they were right, because they were often working against their own interests, against the place they actually lived. A Loyalist who had rejoiced at and assisted the British occupation of Philadelphia realized that they were leaving in 1778 and went in a panic to the officers. They told him he could take passage to England, but he said "what the Devil shall I do with my estate?" The British officer replied, "Damn you, why did you not stay at home and fight to defend it with your country?"[18] Much could be gleaned from this story about the unenviable but often contradictory position of the Loyalists.

In tandem with Washington's Secret Service Bureau, local governments set up their own systems of investigation. Steps were taken by the Connecticut Council of Safety to allow the detaining of people suspected of "Treasonable Practices against this and the United States" unless they gave bond or account for their suspicious behavior. Simeon Newell of Farmington became the "state detective" in charge of ferreting out spies, with blank warrants allowing him to secure suspects for "examination." Of course, Newell complained that the laws were not strict enough.[19] Governor Trumbull himself futilely asked Silas Deane, "Is it not high Time to find some Test, whereby to distinguish our Friends, from our Enemies; and provide suitable ways and means to prevent the Operations of their mischievous designs, and Machiavellian Policy in the midst of us."[20] It was a tricky business to balance people's rights and prevent espionage.

In the summer of 1776 openly active Tories in Connecticut were arrested and sent to the state's interior, so they could not help the enemy raiders. In August three full ships arrived with Tories from Long Island and New York and were sent upriver to Norwich and Windham. These detentions often lasted just a few months.[21] Some were arrested and promptly acquitted. Nevertheless, many continued to be convicted and jailed, like Moses Dunbar of Waterbury, who was convicted of enlisting men to serve the British army, from which he received a captain's commission. Reverend Roger Viets of Simsbury was convicted of helping prisoners escape and received a lighter sentence of a year in prison and a twenty-pound fine.[22] On at least two occasions men were hanged.[23] But Connecticut had a small percentage of Loyalists compared to most other states. For example, of the thousand Yale graduates alive at the time of the Revolution, fewer than twenty-five were Tories.[24]

The threat from Tory espionage was real, however, and many American soldiers and civilians did suffer because of their actions. Hale wrote to his brother of the menace: "It would grieve any good man to consider what unnatural monsters we have as were in our bowels. . . . Numbers in this Colony likewise in the western part of Connecticut would be glad to imbue their hands in their Country's Blood."[25] Tories helped the British during the raid on Danbury, where Rosanna Sizer, a "female Whig" only sixteen years old, wrote a poem on the subject:

> these Tories go creeping and skulking around, contriving
> to ruin both country and town. . . .
> When they are all hanged then we hope to have peace.[26]

A sixteen-year-old girl wanting to hang her neighbors gives a clear idea of the strong feelings provoked by those who helped attack their own country.

New York Tory Beverley Robinson went straight for the top and felt out General Putnam's willingness to "restore peace and legal government to our poor country" — a separate, private peace, of course. At the time Putnam lived in Robinson's confiscated house near West Point, and Robinson visited, soliciting the old general's dying wife. On receiving a courteous note from Putnam's son Daniel, Robinson tried to make a conference with the old general, leaving the purpose of the meeting mysterious.[27] Under the rules of a gentlemanly society, this sort of communication between enemies was quite common, and Robinson would later use it to approach Arnold himself. It worked both ways, of course. Yale president Ezra Stiles wrote to General Tryon after he attacked New Haven, politely inquiring if in the booty included certain mathematical and scientific papers and if so that they should be returned, appealing to the British general's "politeness and honor."[28] It was a way to bring civility to a barbarous business. But in the case of American officers like Putnam, who probably never considered turning traitor, it was also a special kind of trap.

Often the information given by Tories was used for even more dangerous operations, like kidnapping high-interest prisoners. Billy Silliman of Fairfield wrote, "our own countrymen and those whom we valued as friends are rising against us and concerting the most horrid and diabolical schemes for our subversion and entire ruin, while a British Army is on the borders of our coast."[29] Three years later he felt the truth of his warning when a group of Tory raiders crossed the Devil's Belt to Fairfield and pounded on the door of his father, Gold Selleck Silliman, brigadier general in the Continental army. After a tense moment in which Silliman tried to protect his pregnant wife, Mary, his valuables, and a trove of important documents, the raiders dragged him to British-controlled New York. The kidnappers had been commissioned by General Clinton himself and had targeted Silliman specifically, finding his current location from Loyalist spies. When no prisoners of similar rank were available to trade for the Fairfield general, Governor Trumbull authorized a similar raid, and twenty-five men slid across the water to Long Island. Their target was Judge Thomas Jones, who that night was entertaining guests at his house. The American raiders broke in, seized him and a guest, and dragged them down to their whaleboat, eventually trading him for General Silliman.[30] And while assassination of an enemy officer was off the table for the British army, who would have executed George Washington but never assassinated him, the local Tories were much more dangerous. A group in New York under the Loyalist mayor planned to kidnap him from his headquarters in the highlands and to stab or poison him if they could not take him alive.[31]

Connecticut felt these conflicts keenly because of its long front with the British throughout the war. The Loyalists on the south coast of the Sound and the Revolutionaries on the north stared at each other every day and played a dangerous game of "smuggling, marauding, plundering, and kidnapping." Men in Connecticut who were "lovers of money rather than lovers of their country" assisted, and the epithet "Long Island trader" became popular.[32] Many incidents of violence accompanied the occupation of Long Island, causing people who had no previous opinion of the British regulars to fear them. Approximately five thousand of thirteen thousand Long Island residents escaped to Connecticut as refugees, many of whom stayed there for the duration of the war. Benjamin Tallmadge's brothers John and Samuel fled Long

Island and served in the army.[33] Many also fled inland to be free of British coastal attacks. Arnold's friend John Lamb moved his family from Stratford to Southington to keep them safe.[34]

Women behind enemy lines were in danger of serious violence. On Staten Island in 1776, Francis, Lord Rawdon lightheartedly reported that "a girl cannot step into the bushes to pluck a rose without running the most imminent risk of being ravished, and they are so little accustomed to these vigorous methods [rape] that they don't bear them with the proper resignation."[35] A woman named Elizabeth Cain testified that two British soldiers had raped her and other women at gunpoint, then taken them back to camp for the other soldiers.[36] A French officer witnessed the aftermath of an attack on Jamestown, Virginia, by Banastre Tarleton's dragoons who "after pillaging a house, violated a young woman who was pregnant. After fastening her to a door, one of them split open her belly with a sabre, killing the infant, then wrote over the door the following inscription, which I saw 'You dam rebel's Whore, you shall never bear enny more.'"[37] William Ledyard's niece Fanny desperately wanted to move from Southold, Long Island, to Connecticut, and he had to obtain permission for her to bring her clothes, dry goods, and other personal items. Fanny "acted the friendly part towards" the British and Tories, but as her uncle said, "the difficulties attending her living on the Island any longer is so great owing to her fears of being illy treated by the British party."[38]

These incidents were mostly attributed to the British and German mercenaries, because both Loyalist and Revolutionary Americans were fighting on home soil — but when Arnold invaded Canada, Washington cautioned him, "While we are contending for our Liberty, we should be very cautious of violating the Rights of Conscience in others."[39] He was talking about plunder and rape, of course. Even speaking openly about rape was almost taboo, which hints that far more of these incidents were unreported, though the newspapers carried a few such tales anyway.[40]

Women often bore the brunt of the shadow war in other ways, having to take their husbands' share of work. Nathaniel Shaw's wife, Lucretia, spent her time tending to sick and wounded returned prisoners of war.[41] Connecticut farmer Betsy Foote "felt Nationly" when she did her chores, while Temperance Smith, a parson's wife, "never complained even in my inmost thoughts" despite having "no leisure for murmuring."[42] And, as usual, men's and women's roles often merged, with some women serving as spies or in a few cases even soldiers.

Unfortunately, not everyone was so stalwart in the face of the horrors of the war. Governor Trumbull's daughter Faith had married Jedediah Huntington, and while he was stationed at Boston during the siege, she visited him. She witnessed the carnage of Bunker Hill and the burning of Charlestown, and fear for her husband and brothers sent her into a state of shock. After returning to Norwich, her depression deepened, and she began to have fits and painful episodes. "She found herself surrounded, not by 'the pomp and circumstances of glorious war,' but in the midst of all its horrible realities . . . and it overcame her strong, but too sensitive mind."[43] Huntington brought her to Dedham, Massachusetts, where he could visit and have her treated by a doctor. Finally, on November 23, Thanksgiving Day, her husband failed to appear, concerned about a rumored British attack on Cobble Hill. He finally showed up in Dedham the following morning, and Faith seemed fine. But she was not. Less than an hour after he left she hanged herself in the bedroom.[44]

Women also took care of the Long Island refugees and British and Loyalist prisoners. As early as 1775 Trumbull brought in large numbers of prisoners into the state, keeping most in inland areas, some of which bulged to twice or three times their population. The metropolitan area of Hartford had a population of only five thousand, and the prisoners were often kept on their own "good word" in the houses of many citizens. But this could only last so long. The prisoners "often treated the citizens with superior disdain" and caused any number of problems, including constant escape attempts. The former governor of New Jersey was held in Middletown, where he promptly began a campaign of pro-British propaganda. Trumbull could have dealt with him harshly for this behavior but instead simply increased his confinement to house arrest.[45] Captured Tories were so numerous and sometimes so well known by their captors that it was difficult to keep them imprisoned for more than a few weeks; usually they were let go with a mere promise. Shaw tried keeping prisoners in a ship at New London Harbor, but it was too easy to escape and swim to shore, so they were sent to Weathersfield instead.[46] German mercenaries were often given to farmers to work, since they could not speak the language during an escape attempt. The most recalcitrant or famous prisoners were put into Newgate Prison in Simsbury, a former copper mine in which people were lowered by windlass into a lightless pit forty yards below the surface.[47] But, with a few exceptions, British prisoners were treated well in Connecticut.

The treatment of Americans taken by the British was another matter. Silas Deane's stepson Samuel Webb distinguished himself at Bunker Hill and Trenton but was captured in 1777 and spent almost four years as a prisoner of war. As an officer he did not spend his time in the infamous prison ships but at home in Weathersfield and with the army "on parole."[48] This gentlemanly idea of being a "prisoner" without being thrown in prison was part of the honor culture of the time, but a case like Webb's was the exception. Jonathan Mix, by then a captain in the Continental army, was captured and confined for six months under the most terrible conditions, where "the heat of breath and bodies nearly suffocated me," and he subsisted on weevil-ridden bread and stinking condemned meat. All but two of the men he went in with died on board the ship.[49] This was not unusual; those who made it out alive reported that men "confin'd in the different prison ships die daily."[50]

Hiram Stone of Guilford was captured during a whaleboat attack from Norwalk to Long Island and taken to the infamous "Jersey Prison Ship." During winter the British shoved him in a former sugar refinery, where he nearly froze to death. Finally, after an escape attempt, he was beaten, and the following day a "Refugee Lieutenant" offered to enlist him in the British army. He refused, and they threw him back into the miserable sugar house. On the way back to Connecticut after a prisoner exchange, he and half the other prisoners were poisoned by the bread given to them by the British, while those that ate no bread remained healthy. He spent the following year recovering from the poisoning.[51] Though this might have been a rare case of maltreatment, those who did make it back were almost always in terrible shape, often dying of starvation or fever. William Ledyard found one batch of returned prisoners "very low" and could not even move some to the hospital. Shocked at their condition, Ledyard exclaimed, "I don't expect to rest an hour."[52] In December 1778 five hundred frozen and smallpox-ridden prisoners were returned to New London. Many arrived dead, presumably from the rigors of the short journey from New York.[53] Benjamin Tallmadge's brother "literally starved to death" in one of the British prisons.[54]

These reports and encounters only hardened the patriots to the tyranny of the British and turned public opinion further toward independence. People began to refuse to keep British prisoners in their houses, and the Connecticut legislature took affidavits from those American captives released.[55] When the Tory governor of New York, William Tryon, sent Trumbull a feeble attempt at reconciliation, Trumbull was dismissive: "There was a day when even this step from our acknowledged parent state might have been accepted with joy and gratitude. But that day, Sir, is passed irrevocably." He cited the "barbarous inhumanity," "insolence," and "cruelty" of the British war efforts and asserted there was no recourse but "absolute and perfect independency."[56]

The shadow war continued overseas, with Silas Deane in Paris noting that "our enemies are near at hand and have an easy and quiet passage for any needs they choose to propagate, whether true or false, into this kingdom [France]." He received almost no mail from America, not from his brother, Trumbull, or anyone, and it caused him to "despair."[57] Much of it was probably intercepted by the British. He could barely go outside of the apartment he shared with Benjamin Franklin, saying, "Not a coffee-house or theatre or other place of public diversion but swarms with their [British] emissaries."[58] In a situation like this, it was important to know who he could count on. Tallmadge sent a letter to his friend and mentor in the autumn of 1777 that actually made it through the British net. He reported the intense fighting in Pennsylvania, providing some of the connections with America Deane needed.[59] Deane and Franklin also became close friends, living together for fifteen months, "the greatest part of the time in the same house," and Franklin thought him "faithful, active, and able."[60]

Unfortunately, not all the Americans were on friendly terms. The third emissary sent by Congress, Arthur Lee of Virginia, quarreled with Deane immediately. Through a series of lies and strange dealings, Lee also made a mess of the job they were both trying to do: get supplies from France. Lee's ambitious disdain for Deane would cause him to accuse the Connecticut man of things he himself was probably guilty of. But Lee's promises to the French had been specious, to

This drawing by John Trumbull shows a young Benjamin Tallmadge in his cavalry outfit, though his real job was as chief intelligence officer. Tallmadge, Memoir of Col. Benjamin Tallmadge.

say the least, and now, to protect himself and his ambitions, he threw blame on Deane and Franklin and their allies, calling them "dangerous men, and capable of any wickedness to avenge themselves on those who are suspected of counteracting their purposes."[61] These wild allegations were believed by his brother Richard Henry Lee, who was one of the most important men in Virginia and influential in the Continental Congress. Deane did not help his own case with his account books, which became a labyrinth of transactions that only he could find his way through.[62]

Lee was a political problem, though; his motivation seems to have been personal ambition, not disloyalty to his homeland. But American doctor Edward Bancroft was another story. He had been spying in England for Benjamin Franklin before the Revolution and as a younger man had studied law briefly with Deane. The old acquaintances met again shortly after Deane arrived in Paris, and Bancroft served as his interpreter and assistant in his negotiations with the French. Nevertheless, when he returned to England, ostensibly to spy for America, Bancroft contacted the British secret service and became a double agent. He cultivated his friendship with Deane and waited, reporting to the British on the activities of the American diplomats.[63]

Meanwhile, in the no-man's-land of Westchester County, Deane's other former protégé, Benjamin Tallmadge, snuck behind enemy lines to meet with his spies, handing them invisible ink and copies of his code dictionary. While stationed in White Plains, he was ambushed by the British, whose spies had targeted him and had "got information of my intended expedition, and threw a large body of infantry into a thicket on the road." Luckily, Tallmadge's spies were just as effective; he received a warning and escaped the trap.[64] It was a good thing, because if caught, he could expect the same fate as his friend Nathan Hale. The work of an enemy "chief intelligence officer" was punishable by death. Nor would this work be acknowledged or respected by most of his colleagues. It was simply not part of what made men heroes in the eighteenth century. But Tallmadge served anyway. There is courage in that, to do what is required no matter the sacrifice; whether toiling under a cloud like Tallmadge or even Loyalist Joel Stone, or giving everything like Nathan Hale.

Three years after he began working in the shadows, Tallmadge would help expose the biggest conspiracy of the entire war: Arnold's plan to give up West Point. It is not clear whether Arnold knew that his Connecticut comrade was the head of Washington's intelligence service. Regardless, he wrote to Tallmadge a few weeks later from British-controlled New York, trying to persuade him to switch sides: "As I know you to be a man of sense, I am convinced you are by this time fully of opinion that the real interest and happiness of America consists in a reunion with Great Britain." Tallmadge was on a raid of Oyster Bay at this time, and when he finally received the letter in January, he handed it to Washington, saying, "I have determined to treat the author with the contempt his conduct merits, by not answering his letter, unless your Excellency should advise a different measure."[65] The confused, humiliated Tallmadge "felt somewhat mortified that my patriotism could be even suspected by this consummate villain."[66] In Tallmadge's mind, a spy might pretend to be on side and belong to another, but his actual devotion never wavered. If Arnold's plot had one positive effect, it was that it made the distinction between loyalty and treachery very clear.

AFTER PARTIAL SUCCESS stopping the British on Lake Champlain in the autumn of 1776, Benedict Arnold returned to Ticonderoga, where his friend Richard Varick called Arnold's escape from the superior navy a "blessing from Almighty God."[1] After making sure that another friend, John Lamb, was officially "exchanged" as a prisoner rather than just being on parole, Arnold received a letter from George Washington, saying that Governor Trumbull had told him of a "large fleet" off New London, "without a doubt to make a descent." Washington ordered Arnold to take command at Providence, Rhode Island, to counter the British presence in Newport and "frustrate the intents of the enemy."[2]

Arnold made his way back to New England, stopping in New Haven to see his children and sister. He also visited Boston, where he met many young, eligible ladies, including Betsey Deblois, barely eighteen and admired throughout the city. Clearly in the market for a second wife, Arnold wrote to Gen. Henry Knox's wife, and enclosed a letter "for the Heavenly Miss Deblois" along with a "Trunk of Gowns" for the lovely lady. But he also asked Mrs. Knox for "some favourable Intelligence" on another "Miss Emery."[3] He also gave a loan to Lamb and Eleazar Oswald, who had been recruiting in Connecticut.[4]

While in Providence, Arnold missed Washington's ambitious attack on Trenton and Princeton; he wrote on January 13 to congratulate him the victories.[5] By the end of the month, he had ascertained that the British had no intentions of invading past Newport, but he could not gather enough militia to attack them either. He wrote to Washington again, calling the British "inhuman enemies." But more important, at this point both Arnold's and Washington's letters became very friendly, with a tone that implied more than just a working relationship.[6] Several weeks later Arnold was "unhappy" hearing that Washington was "ill with fever," saying, "my fears have not entirely subsided, I am still anxious for your safety and apprehensive your zeal for the public service will induce you to exert yourself before you are perfectly recovered."[7] Perhaps it was only the polite concern of a subordinate for his commander, but in Washington's mind it seems to have put Arnold on his side and may have been what gave him a "good opinion" of the man as well as of the officer.[8]

Though commended by everyone for his actions in Quebec and New York, Arnold was passed over for advancement by Congress. Washington slammed this "non-promotion," saying no one could find "a more active, a more spirited, and sensible officer." He used both "anxious" and "anxiety" in the letter, genuinely concerned.[9] He wrote to Arnold, "I am at a loss to know whether you have had a preceding appointment, as the newspapers announce, or whether you have been omitted through some mistake." He promised to try to "remedy" the error. Arnold remained unappeased and threatened to resign, though he said, "I shall certainly avoid any hasty step . . . that may tend to the injury of my country." Anxious not to lose a valuable officer, Washington wrote to Congress to try to fix the problem and told Arnold, "your determination not to quit your present command while any danger to the public might ensue from your leaving it, deserves my thanks, and justly entitles you to the thanks of your country."[10]

On the way to Philadelphia from an appointment in Rhode Island to investigate this "injustice," Arnold stopped once again in New Haven to visit family and old friends. There, on April 25, messengers rode breathlessly into town announcing that a large British force had landed near Norwalk and marched north into the state's interior. The British had been teasing the coastal communities for months, attacking with a small force near Darien and anchoring off Stamford "beyond the reach of cannon shot."[11] But now it seemed they had launched a full-scale assault, perhaps with the intention of flanking the Hudson River forts, perhaps as presage to a full-scale invasion of Connecticut.

Arnold's old friend and Freemason master, David Wooster, was in town. The failure of the Canadian campaign had led to a general investigation by Congress, and though Wooster was exonerated of culpability, they nevertheless stripped him of Continental command. Connecticut still had faith in him, though, and made him the senior major general of the militia. He called on Arnold and they rode west, gathering men as they went.

When the two thousand British soldiers under General Tryon reached the seemingly safe inland town of Danbury at two o'clock the next afternoon, the "handful" of Continental troops had to evacuate, taking with them only a fraction of their equipment. A Loyalist spy led the invading force to the barracks and storehouses, which they burned. But mostly the invaders met "scorn." A Danbury deacon refused the British offer of the king's pardon, affirming that "he was ready to die for his Country" and "his age was such he could not expect to live long, the General [Tryon] might kill him if he pleased." The invaders chose not to, and the brave man lived to tell the story to Benedict Arnold, who repeated it with pride.[12]

Meanwhile, hundreds of militia men gathered in the town of Redding, including Brigadier General Silliman, Wooster, Ebenezer Huntington, and Arnold's friends Lamb and Oswald. They marched north to Bethel in a pouring rainstorm, arriving at eleven at night and hunkering down for the night. The next morning the soldiers split up, with Wooster commanding a regiment that pursued the British out of Danbury, harassing them. During a fierce exchange of musket fire, Wooster went down, struck in the groin with a "mortal wound."[13]

Arnold and Silliman "used our best endeavours to collect our Troops" and built a barricade of logs, carts, and stones across the road outside of Ridgefield. Behind this Arnold and his five hundred men waited. The sound of marching feet heralded an oncoming column of red-coated British soldiers. They exchanged fire, and the Americans held the barricade until the platoon of infantry flanked the Americans. Arnold was on his horse shouting commands when some of the British who had advanced close by fired at him. His horse collapsed, and Arnold's feet tangled in the stirrups. He lay on the ground, at the mercy of the charging redcoats. An eager Tory ran toward him with a bayonet, calling, "Surrender! You are my prisoner!" Lying on the ground, Arnold drew his pistol and shot the man, remarking, "not yet." He escaped into a wooded swamp amid a hail of grapeshot, and his men regrouped outside of Ridgefield after inflicting heavy losses on the enemy.[14]

He led the small force to Saugatuck Bridge, where more militia and Continental army forces were gathering. Meanwhile, Ebenezer Huntington attacked the rear of the British column with another five hundred men. While the British desperately forded the river above the bridge, Arnold's force smashed into their flank and General Silliman's attacked their rear. John Lamb's artillery pounded the British, but he

This cannonball from the 1777 Battle of Ridgefield remains lodged in the pillar of the Keeler Tavern, a harsh reminder of the first of several British invasions of the state. Courtesy of the author.

was shot through the left side and stunned. The British continued to retreat, losing twice the number of men in each exchange. Elated, Arnold and Silliman's troops chased them down to the shore, where the "guns of some of their ships" at Cedar Point kept them back. The British embarked and fled across the Sound to Long Island.[15]

John Lamb recovered, the shot having missed his spine by a hairsbreadth. But David Wooster died five days later, another of Arnold's father figures gone. Despite this loss, the raid felt like a victory for Connecticut. After all, according to a list compiled by Arnold, almost a quarter of the invading force had perished. Ezra Stiles noted that "such Harrassings are equal to Victories. Witness Lexington and Bunker Hill."[16] A dramatic poem in General Tryon's voice was composed and distributed:

So thick, so fast, the balls and bullets flew,
Some hit me here, some there, some thro' and thro' —

And so by thousands did the rebels muster
Under Generals Arnold and old Wooster,
That let me, let, let me, let me but
Get off alive — farewell Connecticut.[17]

Arnold had a more practical response, worrying about the next attack. He told Trumbull that "I think it very probably [the British] have in Contemplation the Destroying the Continental frigate at Saybrook." He worried that "there is no Battery" at the mouth of the Connecticut River and suggested moving the ship farther up the estuary, even though it was apparently stuck on the sand bar.[18] Trumbull asked Washington for help, but the general had his hands full with the British plan to invade Pennsylvania.[19]

As a small revenge for the Danbury raid, Return Jonathan Meigs of Middletown, who had followed Arnold to Quebec, gathered 220 men in thirteen whaleboats at Guilford. They slipped across the Sound to Sag Harbor, forty-five miles away. At two in the morning the Connecticut troop attacked the garrison and burned twelve brigs and sloops. The next morning they arrived back in Guilford with ninety prisoners, without losing a single man.[20] After the success of this raid, Trumbull sent word to Shaw to help gather all the whaleboats in the state to New Haven, where they could be repaired and guarded for future excursions.[21]

Over the summer Arnold must have continued stewing about his lack of promotion to major general; he even handed in his resignation. But Richard Varick and other friends convinced him to stay, and the mollified Arnold wrote "no public or private injury, or insult, shall prevail on me to forsake the cause of my injured and oppressed country, until I see peace and liberty restored her, or die in the attempt."[22] He had his work cut out for him — the British were determined to put an end to the rebellion once and for all. In 1777 they simultaneously attacked Philadelphia and tried to split New England from the rest of the colonies.

Gen. John Burgoyne advanced toward Albany from Montreal, intent on controlling the entire corridor from Canada to New York City, a maneuver that the British thought would end the war. The army that they sent included some of the best troops and officers in the entire British Empire, a cadre of Loyalists, and numerous Native Americans.

They retook Ticonderoga without firing a shot.[23] Washington wrote to Congress, "If general Arnold has settled his affairs, and can be spared from Philadelphia, I would recommend him for this business. . . . He is active, judicious and brave, and an officer in whom the militia will repose great confidence."[24] He also assured Gen. Philip Schuyler that Arnold was the right man for the job, "the proofs he has given of [his bravery] have gained the confidence of the public, and of the Army." And Washington proclaimed to the troops that "general Arnold, who is so well-known to you all" would be taking command and that he had "no doubt" that the invaders would be repelled.[25] He trusted Arnold to do the right thing in the new nation's darkest hour.

Unfortunately, Congress voted down Arnold's promotion at this very time, and while commanding half the northern army, he offered once again to resign.[26] Luckily, General Schuyler and Richard Varick persuaded him to stay again. Arnold took charge of a division in the Mohawk Valley west of Albany and whipped the soldiers into shape, decreeing that "those who are found to have deserted their post in time of action may expect imminent Death." This was due to the "scandalous and irregular conduct of straggling from camp," behavior that made Arnold doubt that "the troops will act with spirit and firmness" despite fighting for "their just rights and liberties." He court-martialed a number of these fair-weather patriots. But he gave honors where they were due, later complimenting his soldiers on their "noble" behavior at the first battle of Saratoga.[27] He also found time in his busy schedule to write to his friends Oswald and Lamb on September 5, saying, "I wish the pleasure of hearing from you both often." He thanked Lamb "for the concern you express for my health and welfare; and you will not impute my silence to inattention of want of friendship." He blamed poor letter carriers for many missing letters and expressed condolences for Lamb's boring garrison duty. Then, he prophesied, "This month, I believe, will be very important in the annals of America."[28]

As they moved into more populated areas, the British, Germans, and their Native American allies began to inflict atrocities on the local inhabitants, and Arnold denounced the "robbers, murderers and Traitors, composed of Savages of America and more savage Britons."[29] Throughout August and September the armies skirmished in the Mohawk Valley and outside Bennington, with the Americans generally getting the best of the situation. Arnold forced the British into sending superior numbers to try to stop him but quarreled with Gen. Horatio Gates, the superior officer in charge of the entire northern department. Some of the conflict involved Gates's treatment of General Schuyler. The reason, according to a colleague of Schuyler's, "is simply this: Arnold is your friend."[30] He was also Washington's friend, and Gates was involved in an open conspiracy to replace the commander in chief. But they had little time to argue. British general Burgoyne finally attacked them on September 19, at Bemis Heights near Saratoga. At dawn, the two armies faced each other in two ragged lines from the Hudson River west across the densely forested hills. They maneuvered for position, skirmishing here and there, with Arnold smashing into the line at a place called Freeman's Farm. He nearly had them just then but was outnumbered and not reinforced, with Gates not even taking the field. A "blaze of fire" between the armies continued throughout the day, in one of the hardest and most closely fought days of the war thus far.[31]

In his reports Gates lied repeatedly about the encounter of the day, leading to Arnold's furious confrontation: "I found it necessary to send out the whole of my division to support the attack. No other troops were engaged that day except Colonel Marshall's regiment."[32] Now completely in Arnold's camp, Varick wrote in disgust, "This I am certain of: Arnold has all the credit of the action. . . . Had Gates complied with Arnold's repeated desires, he would have obtained a general and complete victory over the enemy."[33] Arnold threatened to leave again. Another soldier wrote, "I am much distressed at General Arnold's determination to retire from the army at this important crisis. His presence was never more necessary. He is the life and soul of the troops. . . . To him alone is due the honor of our late victory. . . . They would to a man follow him to conquest or death."[34] Arnold had not won the battle yet, but he had won supporters everywhere. He was making many friends and devoted comrades that would have followed him in war or in peace.

Arnold finally decided to stay, and, reinforced by General Lincoln, the American army began to look formidable to the invaders. On October 7 Burgoyne decided to attack before even more militia arrived, sending flanking movements to surprise the Americans from the west. The ploy did not work, and the Americans flanked them instead, using the forests as cover. They pushed them back across the farm fields, killing a commander and charging two fortified redoubts. Disobeying orders from Gates, Arnold rode into the fray, cheered on by the men, and directed the action as best he could. Upon meeting a regiment of Connecticut men, including many from his old stomping ground, he cried, "Ah! My old Norwich and New London friends. God Bless you! I am glad to see you. Now come on boys; if the day is long enough, we'll have them all in hell before night."[35] Riding between the two lines of rifle fire, he rode to the smaller redoubt, rallying the men. He drove a troop of German mercenaries from the center of the line, but his horse was ripped from under him, and he was shot in the thigh and crushed underneath the falling animal.

Arnold was carried into his quarters, having won the day. Burgoyne could only feebly retreat a few miles north to the town of Saratoga, where the victorious Americans surrounded him. By the 17 he signed the terms of surrender, and the British invasion from the north was over. Ten thousand soldiers had been killed or captured, and news spread quickly around the continent and across the Atlantic. A few months later, on February 6, 1778, Franklin, Lee, and Deane signed a treaty of alliance guaranteeing commerce and friendship between France and America, effectively bringing the French into the war.[36] It was largely due to Arnold's success at Saratoga.

Meanwhile, Arnold himself seethed in his sickbed, yelling at the doctors as "a set of ignorant pretenders and empirics." At last the wounded man jostled over the hills in a carriage to the Middletown, Connecticut, home of Comfort Sage, one of his old companions in arms, where his sister and sons were lodged with Sage's wife, Sarah.[37] He tried to recover from the wound as winter came on. It would be the worst winter since his birth, and outside of Philadelphia George Washington's army was in trouble, lacking shoes and blankets and, above all, food.

In his hour of need, Washington wrote to the reliable Governor Trumbull about the "alarming situation of the army on account of provision," saying that he had given up on receiving more from the southern and middle states, and

> there is the strongest reason to believe that its [the army's] existence cannot be of long duration, unless more constant, regular, and larger supplies of the meat kind are furnished. . . . I must therefore, sir,

entreat you in the most earnest terms, and by that zeal which has so eminently distinguished your character in the present arduous struggle, to give very countenance . . . to forward supplies of cattle.[38]

The new commissary general of the army, William Buchanan, had been plagued by the same problems that Trumbull's son Joseph had encountered. The logistical system buckled, and the Pennsylvania Dutch, who dominated southeast Pennsylvania, put more trust in the gold of the British who occupied Philadelphia than in Washington's paper money. The actions of some of the foraging American troops alienated them further. Meanwhile, Washington's army, failed by everyone from Congress to the local farmers, starved.[39]

Governor Trumbull sprang into action, doing what he did best, supplying armies. By March all the Connecticut troops had been fully clothed. Washington wrote, thanking Trumbull, "Among the troops unfit for duty and returned for want of clothing, none of your State are included. The care of your legislature in providing clothing . . . for their men in highly laudable, and reflects the greatest honor upon their patriotism and humanity."[40] But it was not just the Connecticut troops that Trumbull saved at Valley Forge. He sent his own stores of salted shad and pork without payment and ordered the collection of cattle throughout Connecticut. A herd of three hundred was gathered, and Col. Henry Champion of Colchester tasked with driving them. Champion and his son drove them through western Connecticut, across the Hudson River at King's Ferry, through northern New Jersey, across the Delaware River, and all the way to Valley Forge. The troops butchered them, roasted them, and ate them at a lightning pace. This would be the first of several emergency cattle drives throughout that cold spring, and it is no exaggeration to say that without them, the soldiers there would have deserted or perished.[41]

Trumbull still found time to give advice to old friends. North Havener Ezra Stiles had been forced from his new home in Rhode Island by the British occupation. Now he needed to decide between an offer to lead a congregation in Portsmouth or assume the presidency of Yale. He wrote Trumbull, saying, "I greatly distrust my abilities for the Presidency," calling it "an office full of weighty cares." So, he begged leave "to ask your council and advice, to request of you that Light, which your Knowledge and comprehensive view of Things will enable you to impart." Trumbull wrote back on March 15, saying that Stiles "would be of peculiar influence in producing that Harmony between the Government and the College so essential to the Wellbeing of the latter." And though his advice, he said, would "probably come too late," he hoped that Stiles's decision "will ever afford you internal Peace and Satisfaction of Mind."[42] On March 19 Stiles resigned his position as pastor and the following day accepted the presidency of Yale. While there, he encouraged the disputation on contemporary topics, and those students that were not fighting the Revolution argued about it during class time, debating events and outcomes.[43]

Stiles arrived in New Haven to witness the return of Arnold, who had been using his recovery time in Middletown to woo a potential wife. He implored one of the young girls he had met in Boston the previous year, Betsey Deblois, to return his "most sincere, ardent, and disinterested passion." He begged "a heart which has often been calm and serene amidst the clashing of arms, and all the din and horrors of war, trembles with diffidence and the fear of giving offense when it attempts to address you on a subject so important to its happiness." Twenty years his junior, Betsey apparently rebuffed him the first time, so he wrote her again:

> A union of hearts I acknowledge is necessary to happiness, but give me leave to observe that true and permanent happiness is seldom the effect of an alliance formed on a romantic passion when fancy governs more than judgment. . . . Pardon me dear Betsy if I called you cruel. If eyes are an index to the heart, love and harmony must banish every irregular passion from your heavenly bosom. . . . Let me beg of you to suffer your heart is possible to expand with the sensation more tender and friendship.

He ended the desperate letter, "in the most anxious suspense" and "unalterably yours."[44] Unfortunately, Betsey Deblois rejected him yet again.

By May Arnold's leg recovered sufficiently to allow a ride to his big house on Water Street. Governor Trumbull, Silas Deane's brother Barnabas, Samuel Parsons, and all the friends and companions of his New Haven days waited there to give him a welcome that most heroes never receive. He rode into town in the middle of a huge procession, which moved slowly across the green to the sound of cannons, the waving of flags, and the playing of fifes and drums.[45] Perhaps Congress had not given him the full approbation he wanted, but his community, his Connecticut, certainly did.

In fact, word of Arnold's deeds at Saratoga had spread, and far away in Europe Benjamin Franklin and Silas Deane answered questions from excited Europeans about the battle. George Washington wrote to Arnold, concerned about his health throughout the winter, and forwarded a gift: "A gentleman in France having very obligingly sent me 3 sets of epaulets and sword knots, 2 of which, professedly, to be disposed of to any friends I should choose, I take the liberty of presenting them to you and General Lincoln, as a testimony of my sincere regard and approbation of your conduct."[46] Washington's gift and Connecticut's celebration should have warmed Arnold's heart, though he still seemed to care more about what Congress thought. Nevertheless, there was no more talk of resigning. His leg had healed enough for travel, and he rode for Valley Forge a few days later, arriving on May 21 to find the army so recently saved by the exertions of Trumbull in "great joy" to see him.[47] There he signed an oath of allegiance to the American cause.[48] His leg was still not completely healed, and so Washington gave him the military governorship of the largest city in America, Philadelphia, which had just spent the previous winter occupied by the British. He would serve there for the next two years. The letters of this summer and fall show that Washington and Arnold have an even closer relationship than previously, perhaps due to Arnold's signing of the oath, perhaps due to his return after the wound at Saratoga.[49]

During those years his home state suffered. Governor Trumbull's family was having a difficult time. His oldest son, Joseph, had resigned from the commissary-general job in 1777, frustrated by the unhelpfulness of Congress. He did not resign from his part in the Revolution, though, and in November had accepted an appointment on the Board of War. However, he contracted a "cold" that winter, which paralyzed his left side and damaged his liver. He began to recover in the spring but relapsed and died on July 23, 1778, a man of great potential stricken by illness too soon.[50] Trumbull had now lost both a daughter and a son to the stresses of the Revolution. And there was more bad news. His younger son, John Trumbull, who had been serving as an aide to General Gates, resigned from the army after being passed over

In CONGRESS.

The DELEGATES of the UNITED STATES of *New-Hampshire*, *Massachusetts-Bay*, *Rhode-Island*, *Connecticut*, *New-York*, *New-Jersey*, *Pennsylvania*, *Delaware*, *Maryland*, *Virginia*, *North-Carolina*, *South-Carolina*, and *Georgia*, TO ————————

Benedict Arnold Esquire

WE, reposing especial Trust and Confidence in your Patriotism, Valour, Conduct and Fidelity, DO, by these Presents, constitute and appoint you to be ————

Major General

in the Army of the United States, raised for the Defence of American Liberty, and for repelling every hostile Invasion thereof. You are therefore carefully and diligently to discharge the Duty of *Major General*, by doing and performing all manner of Things thereunto belonging. And we do strictly charge and require all Officers and Soldiers under your Command, to be obedient to your Orders as *Major General*. And you are to observe and follow such Orders and Directions from Time to Time, as you shall receive from this or a future Congress of the United States, or Committee of Congress, for that Purpose appointed, or Commander in Chief for the Time being of the Army of the United States, or any other your superior Officer, according to the Rules and Discipline of War, in Pursuance of the Trust reposed in you. This Commission to continue in Force until revoked by this or a future Congress. DATED at *Philadelphia May 2d 1777*

By Order of the CONGRESS,

ATTEST. *Cha Thomson secy*   *John Hancock* PRESIDENT.

Benedict Arnold believed that his promotion to major general in 1777, just before the Battle of Saratoga, was long overdue. John Clark Ridpath, The New Complete History of the United States of America (Washington, DC: Ridpath Historical Company, 1905), University of Bridgeport Archives.

for promotion and headed to Europe to study painting. And the governor's good friend Israel Putnam had mismanaged the defense of the highlands in Westchester County, forcing Washington to remove him from his former duty.[51]

After the Danbury raid, the state lived in constant fear. Loyalist brigades attacked from Westchester into Connecticut on several occasions, and General Tryon led a force of 1,500 men into Greenwich, which the disgraced but never conquered General Putnam repulsed. Batteries and fortifications lined the coast at Greenwich, Stamford, Norwalk, Black Rock, Stratford, Milford, New Haven, Saybrook, Lyme, and Stonington. But New London was the most heavily fortified harbor, and for good reason.[52] In December 1776 a fleet of one hundred ships had anchored in sight of the town but attacked Newport instead. In winter 1777 British frigates *Amazon* and *Niger* blockaded New London off the west end of Fisher's Island with other vessels across in Gardiner's Bay. By 1778 William Ledyard had been appointed by Trumbull to the command of New London and the surrounding areas with rank and pay of major. He worried that the British "mean to make an excursion into some part of this State, hope we shall be prepared to receive them."[53]

On March 23, 1779, British forces again mustered across the Sound, and alarm bells and balefires signaled the militia. Ezra Stiles reported rumors that the attack would come at New London, and Trumbull agreed, saying, "New London Town and Harbor are threatened with an attack from the Enemy, with vigour and great force—have wrote to General Putnam for Continental Force to Providence on the subject—am calling for the Militia—part to go in forthwith—part to be in readiness on the shortest notice."[54] But the British were only responding to rumors of an American attack on Long Island, and after a week's worry nothing happened and everyone relaxed.[55] Alarms like these continued, and on July 5, 1779, Ledyard was informed that the British were attacking the Connecticut coast.[56] But it was not New London that would take the hit this time.

Thomas Painter of West Haven had served in the army and navy since the beginning of the war and in 1779 was in the company charged with the defense of New Haven. At midnight on July 5 he heard news of a "large fleet" sailing up the Sound, and he and some of the guards walked down to Clarke's Point, where they saw the fleet itself at anchor off Old Field Shore. Painter ran to his uncle's house with the news, and at first no one believed him. Finally he convinced them, and they warned the rest of the town. He buried his valuables, and with "what ammunition I had . . . waited until the Sun rose." Meanwhile, Ezra Stiles sighted the fleet from the Yale College chapel tower and rang the alarm, sending his diary and Yale papers north to the cliffs of Sleeping Giant with his younger children. He reported that "we were thrown into great Distress by the Approach of the Enemy in a Fleet of about fourty sail." The townspeople at first did not believe that the fleet would attack, and "all was Confusion." But as day broke, "all then knew our Fate."[57]

The huge ships began dropping rowboats for the shore. An hour later 1,500 British soldiers under Gen. George Garth, with artillery and field guns, landed at Savin Rock. Painter and the others with him fired on the landing parties and then ran back into West Haven in a hail of shots.[58] In New Haven 100 young men volunteered to slow the British advance to give the townspeople time to escape. As they crossed the West River, the aged former president of Yale, Napthali Daggett, rode "furiously" by them "on his old black mare, with his long fowling-piece in his hand ready for action."[59] He got it soon enough. The British surrounded the lone rider, and he had to surrender himself as a prisoner and beg for quarter. They responded cruelly to the old man. He wrote that "one of them gave me four gashes on my head with the edge of his bayonet, to the skull-bone," and after robbing him the company gave him "blows and bruises . . . with the heavy barrels of their guns."[60]

After the Americans' token resistance, the British soldiers had a comfortable breakfast on West Haven green before heading up to the bridges of the West River, driving the unfortunate Daggett with them, despite his blood loss. But Jonathan Mix and others had blown up one bridge and pulled up the planks of another, and the British lost time marching three miles farther to Westville, where under the shadow of the cliffs they unsuccessfully attacked a powder mill, then turned east toward the center of New Haven. Mix and about 150 men slowed them down, firing at them from a small hill, killing a number of the attackers. Unfortunately, another party had forded the river and, while Mix was riding down the road, ran at him broadside, firing their muskets. He miraculously escaped this certain death, though, explaining that he "had received one shot through the brim of my hat on one side turned up, another shot had grazed the skin on the back of my hand that I held the bridle with, and another shot had split the pommel of my saddle to pieces."[61]

At Ditch Corner a large group of militia from Mount Carmel and other nearby towns attacked, and the march into town became a running firefight all the way into the center square. Then, as Stiles wrote, "From the first Entrance till VIII in the Eveng. The Town was given up to Ravage and Plunder, from which only a few Houses were protected. Besides what was carried off great Damage was done to Furniture &c left behind."[62] Mix barely made it back to his house and gathered a few items, finding his strayed horse and riding off to join the bulk of the militia at Neck Bridge just as the redcoats marched onto the town green, ready to pillage.[63]

Mix's wife had fled with his children to North Branford, but his aged mother could not and remained in the house. The redcoats broke in and, as Mix recounts,

> robbed it of almost every article they could carry off and that they had destroyed every thing, breaking the furniture to pieces, scattering and destroying the beds and bedding. They had broken open my desk, where my two commissions were, and when they had found them they were more outrageous than before, calling my mother names and charging her with sending her sons to fight, frightening her so that she fled and hid in a neighbor's cellar till they went off.[64]

A man in a state of catatonia who had not spoken in six weeks was killed by an impatient British soldier with a bayonet thrust to the mouth. Another man named Kennedy had been a firm Tory and rejoiced at the soldiers' arrival. When they "plundered of his buckles" he protested, and they "stabbed him to death." Another old, infirm man who was "entertaining them in his own house . . . treating them with good wine and punch" was accused of having fired a gun out the window and was shot.[65] David Wooster's widow, then fifty years old, suffered abuse at the hands of the British soldiers, and everything in the dead general's house was carried off. Daggett wrote his account of the battle from his bed, from which he had "been confined . . . ever since."[66] Though he lingered for days, the old man finally died of his injuries.

While Garth's troops plundered the town, another division under Gen. William Tryon landed at Morris Point on the east side of the harbor. They marched north, burning houses, and attacked Black Rock Fort. The nineteen defenders and three cannons quickly fell to the overwhelming force, and the British continued northward to Beacon Hill, where they camped for the night. But militia from the surrounding towns flooded the area, blocking the British forces from joining together at Neck Bridge over the Mill River. Another thousand men, sailors mostly, came ashore during the afternoon but were sent back with a fear that drunkenness would ensue, a fear that became reality for many left on shore. By morning Tryon's forces were pushed off Beacon Hill by the militia, who grew "bold and adventurous," despite being fired on by the British war galley. More men from Derby, Cheshire, and Branford surrounded the town, firing at drunken soldiers with Brown Besses, muskets, and even old blunderbusses used for bird hunting. Facing huge resistance from all quarters, the British decided that their invasion had failed, or at least had done the damage intended, and evacuated the town from the Long Wharf, just past Benedict Arnold's house on Water Street, which somehow remained unharmed.[67]

After leaving New Haven the fleet sailed west along the Devil's Belt, passed the town of Fairfield, entered a thick fog, and secretly turned to the western shore of the town. At four in the afternoon they began landing troops, largely ignoring the fort at Black Rock and marching to the center of town, where they were met with all the resistance the few militia men present could give. Most people fled, except for a few women who had thought their "kind treatment and submissive behavior" would "secure them against harsh treatment and rough usage." They were "miserably mistaken." The German mercenaries attacked "Whig and Tory indiscriminately" and plundered the houses of the town. The attached Loyalist troops looted just as much but were not "so abusive to the women." Apparently no rape was committed, even by the most vengeful British troops, though it was reported at New Haven, much of it with Tory women who later understandably repented their Loyalist principles.

Beginning in the evening, houses began to go up in flames. Though General Tryon claimed to want to preserve the churches, at least, by night "all the town" was consumed when the rear guard, composed mostly of mercenaries, "tore Tryon's protections in pieces" and tried to burn everything in sight.[68] The British gave a different account, of course, with "[Brother] Jonathan cannonading his own town." They accused the people of Fairfield of setting the fires themselves, "uninfluenced by . . . gentle treatment, their hearts seemed hardened like the hearts of Pharaoh's servants."[69] But considering the established pattern of plunder and arson in New Haven, Norwalk, and later New London, not to mention other towns throughout the colonies, this account should be taken as mere propaganda.[70]

Tryon's fleet had not finished its reign of terror. Two days after leaving Fairfield, the British landed again on either side of the Norwalk River, marching along the coasts, burning houses under the covering fire of the warship *Hussar*. A small party of militia and Continental soldiers tried to stop them at Grumman Hill but were severely outnumbered and fled. The two columns of mercenaries, Loyalists, and regulars converged at the town green, not encountering the resistance they had in New Haven. They burned everything in town, including dozens of houses, shops, and barns. Benjamin Tallmadge ran part of his spy ring out of Norwalk, and he galloped there to try to defend it from General Tryon's forces. Unfortunately, his small party of dragoons was unable to hinder the superior numbers, even with the addition of local militias. He remembered, "The scene was awful — to see the inhabitants — men, women, and children — leaving their houses, and fleeing before the enemy, while our troops were endeavoring to protect them."[71]

After this brutal series of coastal attacks, American forces under Anthony Wayne counterattacked the British at Stony Point, taking the entire 670-man garrison prisoner. A month later another garrison fell at Paulus Hook, New Jersey.[72] Then at ten at night on September 5, 1779, Benjamin Tallmadge took 130 men from Stamford and landed on Lloyd's Neck, Long Island. He wrote that "our attack was so sudden and unexpected, that we succeeded in capturing almost the whole party — a few only escaping into the bushes, from whence they commenced firing on my detachment, gave the alarm to the garrison." Tallmadge and his force escaped back to Connecticut with numerous prisoners and "without the loss of a single man."[73] When it was clear that the state had not been cowed, the British thought them "the most ungrateful and insidious people on earth."[74]

But these revenges probably did not help the people of Connecticut feel better about their losses. In fact, most citizens worried about more attacks, and some proposed the heroic Benedict Arnold as commander for the state militia, to organize the defense of the sea coast "for the welfare of our Country."[75] No one expected that the next major attack would come from him.

✳ ✳ ✳
Villainous Perfidy

ON FRIDAY, June 19, 1778, Arnold's coach rumbled down Market Street into Philadelphia accompanied by a regiment of Massachusetts militia. Like New Haven, Philadelphia was a planned city, but it had grown much larger and grander, with a grid of streets spread between the Delaware and Schuylkill Rivers. Germans, Swedes, Dutch, both free and enslaved Africans, and Delaware Indians walked the wide streets speaking their own languages, while high-hatted Quakers and Mennonites chatted with Anglicans and Congregationalists, uncertainly feeling their way toward religious tolerance. Brick inns and taverns served hot flip, snapper soup, and dense black bread to merchants from the Caribbean and the Great Lakes, while farmers gathered in large squares to sell buckwheat and tobacco. And Arnold was now the ruler of this enormous city, not as mayor but as military governor, a position deemed necessary to keep the peace between the bitter Tories and the vengeful patriots who had recently suffered under the British armed occupation.

Arnold's fellow merchant, Silas Deane, had been recalled from France and replaced by John Adams. Deane arrived in Philadelphia with the French ambassador in July 1778, shortly after Arnold moved into the old Penn Mansion on Market Street.[1] Even though he was advised by others to look for lodging elsewhere due to Arnold's reputation as a hothead, he decided to board with Arnold at headquarters.[2] The two men had much in common — both had experienced victories and failures during the war, and since Elizabeth Deane had died the previous year, both had lost their wives.[3] They had been colleagues and comrades in the Revolution but now they became close friends.[4]

Like almost everyone during the Revolution, both Arnold and Deane mixed business with war in a way that looks suspicious to modern eyes and often did to the eyes of their contemporaries. This was a side-effect of having a volunteer army mostly officered by still-active shopkeepers, plantation owners, and merchants. Most were losing money every day and sought to recompense these losses with a casual disregard for where the money was coming from. And many were tried or court-martialed for this behavior, though often not the ones actually doing it. For example, the reliable Joseph Trumbull was court-martialed for defrauding the soldiers of provisions but was cleared.[5] Deane fell into Trumbull's category; Arthur Lee had seeded the Congress with rumors of Deane's transgressions in France and they had recalled him, though they couldn't even tell him exactly why. In fact, they took no action through the autumn and winter of 1778, leaving Deane literally outside in the cold. He sent dozens of appeals just to be brought before the body to speak or hear the charges against him.

The bitter personal conflict with his accusers in Congress spilled over into the newspapers, and unfortunately the writing talents of Thomas Paine were coordinated against him. That history would show Deane to be innocent of the charges of economic abuse was no comfort at the time. Feeling betrayed by these personality politics, he and Arnold no doubt had much to talk about. But if they thought they were alone, they were mistaken. George Washington, Benjamin Franklin, John Adams, and most of the generals in the Continental army had to face these insulting inquiries and investigations, though perhaps none so persistently and for as many years as Deane did. Personal politics and jealousy often divided the patriots into various camps, all intent on defending their own interests.

Fortunately, Deane had both facts and the French on his side. The ambassador Conrad-Alexandre Gerard attacked Arthur Lee and his allies in letters to Congress, forcing them to bring Thomas Paine into a heated conference and nearly removing Lee from office. Through his efforts Gerard actually prevented Franklin from being recalled for supposed misdeeds as well.[6] Pierre-Augustin Caron de Beaumarchais echoed Gerard's words and more to Congress in 1778, defending Deane in a letter.[7] Franklin sent a vote of confidence. Deane produced evidence. By now the otherwise patriotic Richard Henry Lee might have realized that by defending his younger brother he was creating a political maelstrom that could drag the entire Congress under. But rather than admit that Arthur Lee's charges had no merit, he and his allies preferred to continue the attack.[8]

During Deane's problems with Congress, he sent Trumbull a letter, hand-carried by Arnold's friend Eleazar Oswald, who had resigned from the army and set up a printing business in Philadelphia. Deane wanted it to remain private, since in it he ranted that he was almost "beyond all Patience" with Congress. He did not want to trouble Trumbull "or any of my friends with my particular affairs" since they paled in importance to the great cause they were all involved in. But he wrote "largely and freely" of the "state of the Nation" in much detail, complaining of various things, especially the recent agreements with France. "What has been the great Object of this war? Peace, liberty, and safety, which are only to be secured by our Independence." So, he posited, should we give up our dependence on Britain to become dependent on "another Power [France]?" This is the kind of morbid speculation that many were doing at this time, though in Deane's case it seems strange considering how much the French were helping him. He may have intelligently distinguished between revolutionary Frenchmen like Beaumarchais and the French monarchy, but that was a distinction lost on many Americans at the time.[9] This letter could mark the beginning of Deane's melancholy despair.

Meanwhile, the great battle commander Arnold was proving an unsuccessful military governor and quickly angered various factions. His seemingly contradictory actions regarding Loyalists pleased no one. Grace Growden Galloway, wife of a prominent Loyalist and civil commissioner of Philadelphia during the British occupation, said that she was "fright'd" of reprisals from American patriots and "wou'd Not have the lock taken off but went to Gen Arnold & told him how expos'd My house was & he kindly sent a guard Mrs Craige went with me he treated me with great Politeness & I went to bed in better spirits." Four days later Arnold hanged a man named George Spangler for being a British spy.[10] Of course, Arnold was judging each situation on its own merits, but it was a political disaster that infuriated people on both sides.

Rumors of his "peculation," or profiting from his position, spread.[11] They might have been true; he was certainly not as wealthy as he once was. Back in June 1777 Arnold had sent a job recommendation to Nathaniel Shaw for someone in Philadelphia and then a month later asked him for an eighth or sixteenth share in his ship *Putnam*, letting him know that his sister, Hannah, will take care of the payment from Middletown, where she was now living. But the following March he backed out of the deal, telling Shaw that it was more than twice as expensive as he thought, so "I must therefore decline," if "it would be no disappointment."[12] It may seem from this about-face as if Arnold was in financial trouble, but if he could afford even the lesser amount he was still a very rich man in 1777. Of course he was not as wealthy as Shaw, but few were.

Money would become a more serious problem two years later in 1779. He wanted to put his older sons in private school in Maryland. His allowance from the army was insufficient even for personal needs, much less public dinners like the one he threw for Deane's sailing companion, the French ambassador. And people expected the military governor to spend money lavishly on parties, especially since the British had done so the previous year. But the biggest expense would arrive in the form of a young woman with the same first name as his first wife, Margaret Shippen, known as Peggy. Everyone from Alexander Hamilton to Banastre Tarleton acknowledged that she one of the most beautiful women in America.[13] Arnold met her shortly after his arrival in Philadelphia, and his courting and marriage would cost a lot of money, far more than his stagnant New Haven commerce or military compensation could afford.

The previous winter John Andre had been one of the occupying British soldiers in Philadelphia and met the blue-eyed, blond Peggy Shippen, who lived only two blocks away. Whether they had a love affair or not is an open question, but they definitely struck up a correspondence. Before the British left Philadelphia they threw a huge party and faux knightly tournament called Il Mechianza, at which both Andre and Peggy were present, wearing "Turkish costumes" and earning the resentment of all the American patriots in town.[14] Her father had pleaded neutrality throughout the war, but her experience with these dashing British gentlemen must have pushed her politics toward full-blown Tory.

Like almost every man who met her, Arnold did not care what her politics were; in September 1778 he began to court her, asking her father's permission in a boastful note: "My public character is well known; my private one is, I hope, irreproachable." He then wrote a love letter to the young woman that almost completely rehashed the letters he sent to Betsey Deblois of Boston. "Your charms have lighted up a flame in my bosom," he wrote. "A union of hearts is undoubtedly necessary to happiness."[15] Unlike the letter to Betsey, however, this one was successful, though it took all autumn for Peggy to accept. By Feb-

Arnold overspent on this large Philadelphia mansion after marrying the beautiful young Tory Peggy Shippen, both of which may have contributed to his treason. Courtesy of Marian O'Keefe.

ruary Arnold had clearly won her over, writing her in familiar language and calling her "my dearest life" and "dear Peggy."[16]

Now that he was set to join a prominent Philadelphia family, he must have decided to make his permanent home in Pennsylvania, because he bought Mount Pleasant, a large mansion on the Schuylkill River that would have made Nathaniel Shaw envious. John Adams called it "the most elegant seat in Pennsylvania." A few weeks later on April 8 he was married to Peggy at the Shippens' house, supported by a fellow soldier during the ceremony, his leg still not healed completely.[17] Hannah and his youngest son traveled from Connecticut to join his new wife at the new house. Arnold's sister and wife seem to have gotten along, writing tender letters back and forth.[18]

Meanwhile, Arnold had angered one too many politicians. At the urging of state executive Joseph Reed, the government of Pennsylvania used Arnold's courtship of a Tory wife and his sometimes lenient treatment of Loyalists in general as an occasion to charge him with eight counts of misconduct and peculation. At the same time that Arnold was readying his mansion on the Schuylkill, Reed and the other elected officials of Pennsylvania put the charges against him in the newspapers, referring some of the charges to a court-martial. Arnold resigned his military governorship of Philadelphia in protest, after getting permission from a reluctant Washington, who had tried to pacify the younger man throughout the autumn and winter of 1778 to 1779.[19] But by May Arnold had enough of this sort of command and wrote to Washington,

> Believe me, my dear general, the whole is nothing more than a pretense and artifice to delay the matter, the final determination of which must make the President and counsel appear to the world in their true colors, as a set of unprincipled, and malicious scoundrels; they have prostituted honor and truth for the purpose of gratifying their private resentment against an innocent person. If your Excellency thinks me criminal, for heaven's sake let me be immediately tried, and, if found guilty, executed.[20]

This appeal to Washington may have been the last gasp of a dying patriot. He would begin his correspondence with the British sometime that month or the next.

Between his legal fight with the Pennsylvania government and his marriage with known Loyalist Peggy Shippen, rumors of his defection had already bubbled to the surface. One man wrote that he heard Arnold had deserted to the British as early as February 8, 1779.[21] British spies in Philadelphia heard of both the people's dissatisfaction with Arnold and Arnold's dissatisfaction with the people. And plans were made, though it is unclear who approached who. A flattering letter from the Loyalist Beverley Robinson may have arrived in May, 1779, that urged reconciliation, telling him that "united in equality we will rule the universe."[22] One British secret agent in Philadelphia later claimed that Arnold approached him and began the process of becoming a traitor in June 1779, only two months after his marriage to Peggy Shippen. Arrangements were made to use Peggy's relationship with John Andre as cover. Writing in a code he devised, Andre sent letters to Peggy's friend, who answered the letter but turned it over to Peggy, who gave it to her husband. He read the coded invisible ink in between the lines. Peggy's friend gave her the reply, to which Arnold also added lines in invisible ink before putting it in the mail. Thus, Arnold and British commander in chief Sir Henry Clinton carried on a correspondence filtered through Andre. Clinton was happy to receive any intelligence but suggested that Arnold "join the Army, accept command, be surprised."[23]

Though Arnold's grudge against the government may have produced quicker and darker results, his friend Deane's issues with Congress were much more serious, dragging on for over a year, costing him money, his reputation, and his former enthusiasm. Deane was still in the city, now living in a rented apartment and might even have attended his friend's wedding. That summer he probably heard an earful from the already faithless Arnold about the dim prospects of American victory. Finally in August 1779 the factionalized Congress adopted a resolution to allow Deane to return to France and settle accounts. Of course, they avoided actually ruling on his innocence or guilt.[24] When he returned to France, depressed by his wife's death, the political callousness of Congress, and the whispers of his friend Arnold, the weary Connecticut businessman had been softened up for double agent Edward Bancroft's attempts on his virtue.

Arnold's own hearings dragged on. He did not accept counsel and defended himself in court, leaning on his cane dressed in his military uniform, complete with the epaulettes given to him by Washington. He abundantly used testimonies from his friends and allies to support his case.[25] Finally, on January 26, 1780, the court acquitted him. But they recommended that his commanding officer reprimand him. Washington did the least he could, putting the reprimand in a general order:

> The commander-in-chief would have been much happier in an occasion of bestowing commendations on an officer who has rendered such distinguished services to his country as major general Arnold; but in the present case a sense of duty and a regard to candour oblige him to declare that he considers his conduct in the instance of the permit as peculiarly reprehensible, both in a civil and military view, and in the affair of the wagons as imprudent and improper.[26]

Arnold resented even this mild rebuke and wrote to Deane, complaining, "For what? Not for doing wrong, but because I might have done wrong; or, rather, because there was a possibility that evil might have followed the good I did." He even contemplated a career as a privateer.[27] His resentment was more than a little hypocritical; by the time he sent that letter he had been in secret contact with the British for eight months.

On March 19, 1780, Peggy bore Arnold a fourth son, Edward. George Washington sent a congratulatory letter, but Arnold busily conversed with the enemy, sending a coded dispatch to Andre, saying, "if I point out a plan of cooperation by which Sir Henry shall possess himself of West Point, the Garrison, stores, artillery, etc., twenty thousand pounds sterling I think will be cheap purchase for an object of so much importance."[28] Arnold began using the trust of his friends, and when Washington sent him a proclamation to the Canadians, Arnold promptly turned over the information to Clinton in New York.[29]

His Connecticut associates were not immune to this duplicity. Through ciphered correspondence, Arnold told Clinton that "Governor Trumbull is laying up flour and pork at Connecticut river for the French." In fact, he kept giving Clinton information throughout the entire second half of 1779 and first half of 1780, even while he traveled to Hartford to meet with Trumbull. While Arnold was there, the assembly voted to give him notes on the state treasury, an allowance that would make up for the deflation Continental currency was experiencing. Arnold went to Middletown next to pick up a small debt owed him and then continued on to New Haven, where he attempted to sell his house for a loss of £800.[30]

That year Arnold also tried to get the Connecticut legislature to give him money for his new rank, petitioning them that "most of the states have provided for their Major Generals, not only with respect to pay, but have furnished them with clothing and stores at the usual prices previous to the war." Some of his fellow Connecticut-born officers signed the petition and added their own plea for Arnold to it. Arnold was "relying on the wisdom and justice of your honorable house" to get paid and was making a reasonable request.[31] Reasonable, of course, if he had not been secretly corresponding with Andre and Clinton. Meanwhile, he kept maneuvering for the West Point command. Washington, who still trusted him sufficiently, worked to give it to him.

Unlike Ticonderoga, West Point was a new fortress, built by the Continental army over three years on the west shore of the Hudson River where it curved around a high hill. Designed by Polish engineer

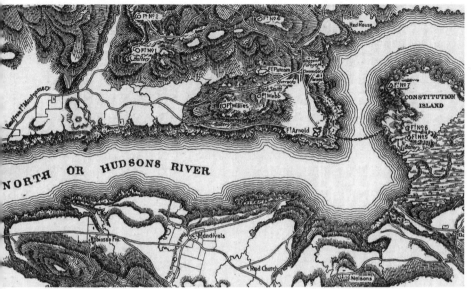

This detail from engineer Major Villefranche's map of the Hudson Valley shows Fort Arnold at West Point on the west (top) side of the river and the Robinson House on the east (lower left). Justin Winsor, Narrative and Critical History of America *(Boston: Houghton, Mifflin, 1888), University of Bridgeport Archives.*

Tadeusz Kościuszko for Washington, it included multiple fortified embankments, with cannons set up to rake any ship that traveled up the river. A thick iron chain stretched across the river below the fort, effectively closing off travel to the north. It was one of many forts along the river valley, but certainly the most important in deterring the northward progress of British warships. It also protected the roads between New England and the rest of the country. In 1778 West Point's main fort at the southeast corner of the jutting plateau had been renamed for the hero of Saratoga: Fort Arnold.[32]

The war went on, with the American army struggling in the south, but with new hope in the north when on July 10, 1780, five thousand French troops under Comte de Rochambeau landed at Newport, Rhode Island, which had been occupied for four years. Trumbull supplied them with flour and meat, gathered at Lebanon and sent east through Norwich. Shaw continually strained his vast resources toward getting supplies, often working around British blockades. He acquired flour and coffee, shoes and uniforms, gunpowder and shot. He dealt with the loss of his own ships and the acquisition of prize ships.[33] He tried to respond to urgent requests from Washington for supplies or information. In July, with the French installed in Newport, Washington asked Shaw to gather intelligence about the movements of the enemy on the Sound, and stated that he needed to have "expert and trusty pilots" ready to navigate the Sound "at a moments [notice]." He posted dragoons every fifteen miles from New London to West Point to get Shaw's intelligence as quickly as possible. A month later he told Shaw to send the intelligence to the French at Newport as well.[34] Shaw did the best he could, reporting on ship movements throughout August.[35] But Washington's summer 1780 plans would dissolve that autumn.

After intense petitioning, Arnold was finally given command of West Point on August 3, 1780. He rode up from Philadelphia and moved into the Robinson House on the east side of the Hudson River, used as the headquarters for the fort's commander. Israel Putnam had previously lived there, and Washington used it every time he traveled through.[36] Arnold found the fort on the west side to be in a bad state. A month earlier Titus Hosmer of Middletown, one of the signers of the Articles of Confederation, had pleaded with Groton's Thomas Mumford for provisions to be sent there, because "our necessities for an instant supply of salted provisions is greater than I dare tell you." He worried that the British could easily take the fort.[37] Recovered from his wound at Ridgefield, John Lamb had also been ordered to West Point with his old friend Arnold, though his artillery companies had been cut in half. He almost immediately saw the terrible state of the fort and told his friend, "Every method ought to be taken to prevent the enemy from knowing the real state of the post."[38] Six days later he wrote again, asking why soldiers were being sent away from the fort.[39] Of course, that was just how Arnold wanted it.

General Clinton had not been eager to pay for Arnold's defection. He told his superiors in England, "I was not at first, however, sanguine in my ideas of General Arnold's consequence, as he was said to be then in a sort of disgrace, had been tried before a General Court Martial, and not likely to be employed." But now that Arnold had been given command of West Point, he changed his mind. With the French fleet installed at Rhode Island, Clinton believed an attack on New York imminent. When the military situation looked most advantageous, he decided that the secret correspondence "should be rendered into certainty" and a "concerted plan" put into action to strike up the Hudson River at the linchpin of the Continental army. The reward would be a generalship in the British army and £20,000.[40]

Arnold now had to arrange everything else as quickly as possible, and he continued to try to gather money from his Connecticut concerns. In New Haven his accounts were a tangled mess, and the house still had not been sold.[41] Barely a month before his treason became known, he also sent a long letter to Nathaniel Shaw, trying to get money he said he was owed, asking Shaw "to inquire into the matter" for him as a "very particular favor." "I beg you will submit the affair to arbitration," he told Shaw, if he and the third party could not come to an agreement.[42] He still trusted his old colleague to do him justice in a matter of business and was using him even as he knew he was going to betray him. Furthermore, since Arnold was now Benjamin Tallmadge's direct superior, when the latter wrote to him asking for more horses, Arnold immediately granted them. Along with this sweetener, he added an offhand postscript about "a person I expect from New York," telling Tallmadge to send "James Anderson" up to West Point with an escort if he happened by.[43]

He wrote to Peggy, giving her careful directions to West Point, with instructions on which inns to stay at. "Let me beg of you not to make your Stages so long as to fatigue yourself and the D[ea]r Boy, if you should be much longer in coming."[44] Arriving in September, Peggy brought their infant son, Edward, and also brought her private cook, famous for her excellent cuisine. Arnold had also invited Richard Varick to join him in July 1780. Varick had just been about to retire to civil life but gladly accepted the invitation from his old friend to become an aide.[45] Only Eleazar Oswald was missing from the old gang, remaining in Philadelphia to run his new printing business.

But something was definitely wrong. Varick began to suspect that Arnold was using his position to increase his pocket, though he did not suspect him of anything greater.[46] When Arnold wrote to the British on the nearby ship *Vulture*, Varick thought that the letter "bore the complexion of one from a friend rather than one from an enemy" and made Arnold alter it. Unperturbed, Arnold inserted a private letter in the public one without his friend's knowledge, involving him in the conspiracy without thinking about the repercussions. Arnold was actually arranging a clandestine meeting with Andre to finalize the deal with the British. The first meeting went poorly, though, when "an un-lucky accident prevented the conference," namely the appearance of a gun boat that nearly discovered their subterfuge.[47]

Still trusting Arnold, Washington told him of plans to go to Hart-ford to meet the French, saying, "You will keep this to yourself, as I want to make my journey a secret."[48] Washington rode east to Hart-ford and on arriving was "saluted by a discharge of 13 Cannon."[49] From September 20 to the 22, Washington, Knox, Hamilton, Lafayette, Ro-chambeau, and Admiral de Ternay met at the Wadsworth Mansion in the center of Hartford.[50] At first they planned an attack on New York. But during the conference a message arrived, and as Rochambeau said, "our plans were soon frustrated by the arrival at New York of the En-glish fleet . . . which increased their numbers threefold."[51] The plans were scrapped immediately, and Washington began the trek back to West Point two days earlier than expected.

Arnold's plan, on the other hand, was moving forward. Now that he met Andre, he had a firm agreement for £20,000 and a British gen-eralship. He gave civilian courier Joshua Smith a pass and instructed him to take Andre south toward British lines. Andre had the plans for the fort hidden in his boot, something that Clinton had told him never to do. It could have been a last minute request by Arnold or it could have been Andre's proof of Arnold's treason, to keep him safely in the British camp. Or it could have been a thoughtless mistake. Smith thought that Andre was only a merchant pretending to be an officer and paid little attention to the project. Against Arnold's instructions, he and Andre spent the night in a farmhouse. Meanwhile, Arnold en-dured an uncomfortable meeting with Varick and his other aide, David Franks, both of whom upbraided him for doing business with Smith. They considered Smith part of a shady "commercial plan" with Arnold and agreed between themselves "to leave him [Arnold] if our doubts were confirmed."[52] They couldn't know that the suspected "pecula-tion" was actually treason.

On Saturday, September 23, the conspiracy broke apart. That morn-ing three "volunteer militiamen," in actuality highwaymen, stopped Andre and searched him, finding the papers in his socks. They took him to an American post and handed him over. The commander thought the papers a "very dangerous tendency." He sent Andre north toward Arnold but sent the papers postmarked to Washington.[53] At the same

The clandestine meeting of John Andre and Benedict Arnold led to Andre's death and Arnold's discovery as a traitor and became one of the most talked about incidents in American history. From an engraving by S. B. Stearns, in Writings of Thomas Jefferson, *vol. 7, University of Bridgeport Archives.*

time Benjamin Tallmadge returned from scouting duty and assessed the situation, being informed that a prisoner named John Anderson had been brought in that day. Earlier that month one of his agents had already uncovered that name as a possible spy and had urged his men to keep a close look out for this person. He immediately guessed that a serious plot was in the works and convinced the commander to bring Andre back for closer questioning. He also urged the commander not to inform Arnold, a plea which "strange as it may seem" was unfortunately ignored.[54] Tallmadge also discovered that "John Anderson's" real identity was Maj. John Andre and frantically wrote a letter to General Washington, becoming the first to fear that Arnold must be involved in something greater than illegally profiting from his position.

That night, thirty miles to the north in the dining room of the Robinson House, Arnold, Peggy, Joshua Smith, Lamb, and Varick ate a meal of salted fish together, and "there happened to be a scarcity of butter at the table." Peggy called for more butter and "was informed by the servant that there was no more." Arnold saved the dinner, saying, "Blessed me, I had forgot the olive oil I bought in Philadelphia, it will do very well with salt fish." When the servant brought the oil, Arnold bragged that it cost eighty dollars. Smith made a crack about how little Continental currency was worth, and Varick angrily attacked him for the slight. After dinner Varick confronted Arnold and was hurt that "he did not place that confidence in my repeated friendly assurances and advice" to get rid of Smith. Arnold assured his friend "of his full confidence" and admitted that Varick was correct: Smith was a "rascal," and he was sorry for "treating [Varick] with such cavalier language."[55] The two friends reconciled.

On Sunday morning Varick felt sick and remained so all day. On Monday he was still lying in a bed in Arnold's office. Arnold stopped in before breakfast and told him he would reply to letters from Tall-madge and Jameson himself.[56] Meanwhile, the meeting in Hartford had concluded, and George Washington, Alexander Hamilton, and the Marquis de Lafayette had ridden back most of the way to West Point on Sunday, lodging in Fishkill. On Monday morning Hamilton rode ahead with James McHenry and arrived at the Robinson House in time to meet Arnold for breakfast. Arnold opened his mail and left the breakfast table suddenly, confusing the other two men. Unknown to them, he ran upstairs, said farewell to Peggy, and slipped out the back, making his way to the *Vulture*, anchored downriver.

When Washington arrived, Hamilton reported Arnold's strange behavior, before the commander in chief rowed across the Hudson to West Point. Hamilton stayed behind with Varick, who walked upstairs and found Peggy in a bizarre state, babbling and asking him "Colonel Varick, have you ordered my child to be killed?" After witnessing Peggy's strange behavior, Hamilton and Lafayette began to suspect something amiss. Leaving Varick inside, they took a short walk to confer about their suspicions. Meanwhile Washington's long legs climbed the hill to the fort on the west shore, but he found only a surprised Colonel Lamb, who confusedly reported that Arnold was not there. Washington found the fortress itself barely defended and recrossed the river to the Robinson House, highly disturbed.

A packet of mail had just arrived that added to the pile of letters

Arnold had received before. Washington read the correspondence while Hamilton and Lafayette conferred outside. When they returned, he said in despair, "Arnold has betrayed us! Whom can we trust now?" He had read the letters about Major Andre, and

> from these several circumstances, and information that the General [Arnold] seemed to be thrown into some degree of agitation on receiving a letter a little time before he went from his quarters, I was led to conclude immediately that he had heard of Major Andre's captivity, and that he would if possible escape to the enemy, and accordingly took such measures as appeared the most probable to apprehend him.[57]

Hamilton sprang into action, riding himself to capture Arnold and sending orders to the Sixth Connecticut Regiment to reinforce West Point. But he discovered that his efforts were "too late" and that Arnold had escaped by boarding the *Vulture*.[58] As his first action on the British side, Arnold actually had the soldiers onboard arrest the two men who unknowingly rowed him out to the ship, after the bewildered duo refused to change their allegiance at his request. That same day, he wrote to his former commander,

> The Heart which is Concious [*sic*] of its Own rectitude, Cannot attempt to paliate [*sic*] a Step, which the World may Censure as wrong; I have ever acted from a Principle of Love to my Country, since the Commencement of the present unhappy Contest between Great Britain and the Colonies, the same principle of Love to my Country Actuates my present Conduct, however it may appear Inconsistent to the World: who very Seldom Judge right of any Mans Actions.

He then asked Washington the favor of protection for Mrs. Arnold, who is "Innocent as an Angel, and is Incapable of doing wrong."[59] This is as close to Arnold ever came to admitting that what he did was wrong, suggesting that, unlike his wife, he was not innocent. He need not have worried. Peggy Arnold maintained a program of feigned hysterics, giving a dramatic performance that fooled everyone and averted any suspicions she had been part of the plot.[60]

Washington could have begun a witch hunt and started hanging suspects, and no one would have blinked. But instead he followed up his question of "whom can we trust now" by continuing to trust. One of the first people Washington told about the treason was John Lamb, who was "overwhelmed with consternation." And though Washington knew the artillery colonel had been a good friend of the traitor, he still sent him that same day to take over at another post while the other commander traveled to consult with Washington about the treason.[61] Then, that night, Washington, Lafayette, Henry Knox, two French engineers, Lamb, and Varick dined together. "Never was there a more melancholy dinner," Lafayette said. "Gloom and distress seemed to pervade every mind, and I have never seen General Washington so affected by any circumstance." After dinner the melancholy Washington went on a walk with Varick, telling him the news of Arnold's certain betrayal. Washington then said he did not suspect Varick of complicity, "but that his duty as an officer made it necessary to inform me that I must consider myself a prisoner." Varick, "as politely as [he] could" agreed, saying, "it was what I expected. I then told him the little I knew."[62] The inquiries had begun.

That day Washington also began the troubling process of informing the troops, sending private letters that stated simply, "General Arnold is gone to the Enemy."[63] He also made a public announcement in his general orders to the army from the headquarters at Orangetown: "Treason of the blackest dye was yesterday discovered! General Arnold who commanded at Westpoint, lost to every sentiment of honor, of public and private obligation, was about to deliver up that important Post into the hands of the enemy." He continued, putting a positive spin on the event, "Great honor is due to the American Army that this is the first instance of Treason of the kind where many were to be expected from the nature of the dispute, and nothing is so bright an ornament in the Character of the American soldiers as their [*sic*] having been proof against all the arts and seduction of an insidious enemy."[64]

But trust was for the American patriots. The undercover agent John Andre was another matter entirely. Tallmadge brought the prisoner to the Robinson House, where Washington declined to see him. Andre and Tallmadge talked cordially on their travels, and Andre asked him if he would be regarded as a British officer. Tallmadge replied thoughtfully, telling him of "a much-loved class-mate in Yale College by the name of Nathan Hale." When he finished the story, he asked Andre, "Do you remember the sequel of the story?" "Yes," said Andre, "he was hanged as a spy! But you surely do not consider his case and mine alike?" Tallmadge replied, "Yes, precisely similar; and similar will be your fate!"[65]

Alexander Hamilton wrote a secret letter to the British general Clinton, suggesting an exchange between Andre and Arnold, with a postscript, "no time is to be lost." This suggestion, against all the rules of honor at the time, shows how far the Americans were willing to go to get back the traitor.[66] But Hamilton's letter would travel too slowly. A few days after he sent it, on September 29, a board of inquiry met at the little Dutch church at Tappan, with Gen. Nathanael Greene presiding, along with other officers, such as Lafayette and Ebenezer Huntington.[67] They tried Andre, found him guilty, and hanged him. Unlike Hale, the Americans gave Andre a decent burial. In fact, throughout his imprisonment and execution the British agent behaved so well that he won many supporters among the army. Tallmadge himself claimed to have mourned a little when Andre was hanged. Nevertheless, he pushed aside personal feelings for duty, saying, "enough of poor Andre, who tho' he dies lamented, falls justly."[68] And in another letter he wrote what everyone else was thinking: "I wish Arnold had been in his place."[69]

When Arnold heard of the execution of Andre, he wrote immediately to Washington, saying, "The wanton execution of a gallant British officer in cold blood may be only the prelude to further butcheries on the same ill-fated occasion. Necessity compelled me to leave behind me in your camp a wife and offspring, that are endeared to me by every sacred tie. If any violence be offered to them, remember I will revenge their wrongs in a deluge of American blood!"[70] It was as if Arnold was picking an imaginary fight to break from his past. Or perhaps this assumption of Washington's cruelty was Arnold's own guilt speaking. Washington did nothing of the sort and probably would not have even if Peggy had been rightfully arrested. Joshua Smith, on the other hand, was tried on the day after Andre's execution. Though acquitted, he was turned over to civil authorities for his financial mischief. After a year in jail, he would flee to England, blaming Arnold for all his troubles.[71] Varick and Arnold's other aide, Colonel Franks, requested an investigation of their own behavior to clear their names.

Despite this bold step, Varick made himself sick with anxiety. He said to Lamb, "my intellects are much deranged by indisposition. . . .

A little touch of fever in the night, has much debilitated me." When Eleazar Oswald heard of the treason while at his home in Philadelphia, he wrote in despair to Lamb, "Arnold's treachery was the principal subject of our last two letters. It will take up a small portion of this also, and then let his name sink as low in infamy as it was once high in our esteem. Happy for him and for his friends, it had been, had the ball which pierced his leg at Saratoga, been directed thro' his heart . . . but the remainder of his wretched existence, must now be one continued scene of horror, misery, and despair." He went on to describe his former friend's "prostitution" and doubted if the British would respect him for the treason.[72] As for Lamb himself, when a British officer under flag of truce presented Arnold's compliments to his old friend, the outraged Lamb replied, "Be good enough, sir, to tell General Arnold that the acquaintance between us is forgotten; and that if he were to be hanged tomorrow, I would go barefooted to witness his execution."[73]

Arnold allowed suspicion to fall on his best friends, involving them in an astonishing conspiracy without their knowledge. He put at risk all they had fought for, all they cared about. He had not betrayed his political enemies in Congress or even the rival generals he clashed with over the years. He had betrayed the men who had fought beside him at Saratoga, at Ridgefield, at Quebec, both the living and the dead. He betrayed Jonathan Mix and David Wooster, Eleazar Oswald and John Lamb, Richard Varick and George Washington. He betrayed all those who had believed in him and protected him, all those who had served with him and befriended him. But he would do even worse in the year to come.

***
The Scandal of the Age

THE CONTINENT buzzed with the news. When it reached Norwich, the angry townspeople gathered at the cemetery near Samuel Huntington's house and furiously smashed the graves of Arnold's father and older brother, both of whom shared the traitor's name. Samuel Huntington himself, now president of Congress, wrote to Governor Trumbull that "the treason of Benedict Arnold has been the Topic of much Conversation, and many of his scandalous trans-actions are brought to light that were before concealed."[1] Ezra Stiles traveled to Newport to visit his former "flock" there, now freed by the French navy, and on October 7 dined with Comte de Rochambeau and twenty-eight other Frenchmen. They conversed at the table in their common language of Latin, and all wanted to talk about Arnold's "flight from West Point." Two days later he dined with General de Chastellux and the Chevalier de la Luzerne, and again the topic under discussion was the astonishing treachery.[2] In coffee shops, farmhouse kitchens, and military camps, everyone gossiped and questioned and threw up their hands in confusion.

The scandal had plenty of dirt — treason, spying, tainted money, a near escape — and all at the highest levels of respectable society. Unlike imagined conspiracies that had floated through society earlier in the war, this was finally a genuine one, and one that had almost succeeded. As Lafayette put it the day after the discovery: "That same man who had covered himself with glory by rendering valuable services to his country, had lately formed a horrid compact with the enemy. And but for the chance which brought us here at a certain time . . . by a combi-nation of accidents . . . West Point and the North River would prob-ably be in the possession of our enemies."[3] Furthermore, most patriotic Americans clearly separated the sneaking, lying, "ignominious" Tory spies and the brave war heroes who would save them. No one believed these two qualities could exist in the same person — such a thing was unthinkable.[4] One of Connecticut's delegates to Congress, Jesse Root, talked to Trumbull about the "surprising conduct" of Arnold.[5] Even Tallmadge, used to the gray areas of the shadow war, wrote to Deane's son-in-law, Samuel Webb, saying, "You have doubtless heard before this of the rascally conduct of Arnold. He has gone to the enemy, where I think his misery, which must ensue, will be complete."[6] And like Tallmadge expecting that Arnold will regret his decision or feel guilty, Lafayette took it a step further, expecting Arnold would blow his brains out.

Those who had hated Arnold from the first began repeating a constant refrain of "I told you so," and many who had said nothing asserted supposed long-held doubts. Massachusetts firebrand Samuel Adams claimed "that I have long had my suspicions of this Traitor, & therefore you will not wonder that I am not so much astonishd as if any other officer had been detected. He has been gibbeted in the streets by the populace, anathematizd by the Clergy in the Pulpit, & his Name has with Indignation been stuck out of the List of Officers by Order of Congress."[7] Arnold's former army comrades and Connecticut supporters could not very well deny their previous opinions, but everyone else could, and did.

The discussion often focused on motives. Some thought that he was "corrupted by the influence of British gold."[8] In Paris Benjamin Franklin put the blame firmly on money, saying, "Judas sold only one man, Arnold three millions. Judas got for his one man thirty pieces of silver. Arnold not a halfpenny a head. A miserable bargain! Especially when one considers the quantity of infamy he has acquired to himself and entailed on his family."[9] Men who had served with Arnold focused on their "missed opportunities," like Joseph Plumb Martin, who reminisced years later that he had two opportunities to "put Arnold asleep without anyone knowing it" but of course did not have "the power of foreknowledge."[10] Ordinary men fantasizing about murder for the greater good was a quite common reaction.

Others began the process of demonizing Arnold, often quite literally. In Philadelphia a huge crowd "exhibited and paraded through the streets of this City, a ridiculous figure of Genl Arnold, with two faces, and the Devil standing behind him pushing him with a pitchfork. . . . Several hundred men and boys with candles in their hands — all in ranks; many Officers y Infantry, men with guns and bayonets . . . somewhere near ye coffee house. They burnt ye Effigy."[11] The citizens of New Milford, Connecticut, carried an effigy of Arnold sitting in a coffin throughout the town in a horse cart hung with "splendid lanterns."

REPRESENTATION of the FIGURES exhibited and paraded through the Streets of PHILADELPHIA, on *Saturday*, the 30*th* of *September*, 1780.

DESCRIPTION of the FIGURES.

A STAGE raifed on the body of a cart, on which was an effigy of General ARNOLD fitting; this was dreffed in regimentals, had two faces, emblematical of his traiterous conduct, a mafk in his left hand, and a letter in his right from Belzebub, telling him that he had done all the mifchief he could do, and now he muft hang himfelf.

At the back of the General was a figure of the Devil, dreffed in black robes, fhaking a purfe of money at the general's left ear, and in his right hand a pitchfork, ready to drive him into hell as the reward due for the many crimes which the thirft of gold had made him commit.

In the front of the ftage and before General Arnold, was placed a large lanthorn of tranfparent paper, with the confequences of his crimes thus delineated, i. e. on one part, General Arnold on his kneen before the Devil, who is pulling him into the flames—a label from the General's mouth with thefe words, "My dear Sir, I have ferved you faithfully;" to which the Devil replies, "And I'll reward you." On another fide, two ropes from a gallows, infcribed, "The Traitors reward." And on the front of the lanthorn was wrote the following: "MAJOR GENERAL BENEDICT ARNOLD, late COMMANDER of the FORT WEST-POINT. THE CRIME OF THIS MAN IS HIGH TREASON. "He has deferted the important poft WEST-POINT, on Hudfon's River, committed to his charge by His Excellency the Commander in Chief, and is gone off to the enemy at New-York."

"His defign to have given up this fortrefs to our enemies, has been difcovered by the goodnefs of the Omnifcient Creator, who has not only prevented his carrying it into execution, but has thrown into our hands ANDRE, the Adjutant-General of their army, who was detected in the character of a fpy.

"The treach`ry of this ungrateful General is held up to public view, for the expofition of infamy; and to proclaim with joyful acclamation, another inftance of the interpofition of bounteous Providence.

"The effigy of this ingrate is therefore hanged (for want of his body) as a Traitor to his native country, and a Betrayer of the laws of honour."

The proceffion began about four o'clock, in the following order:

Several Gentlemen mounted on horfe-back.
A line of Continental Officers.
Sundry Gentlemen in a line.
A guard of the City Infantry.
Juft before the cart, drums and fifes playing the Rogues March.
Guards on each fide.

The proceffion was attended with a numerous concourfe of people, who after expreffing their abhorence of the Treafon and the Traitor, committed him to the flames, and left both the effigy and the original to fink into afhes and oblivion.

'TWAS Arnold's POST fir Harry fought,
Arnold ne'er enter'd in his thought,
The fort is fafe, as fafe can be,
His favourite per force muft die,
His view's laid bare to ev'ry eye;
His money's gone—and lo! he gains
One fcoundrel more for all his pains.
ANDRE was gen'rous, true, and brave,
And in his room, he buys a knave.
'Tis fure ordain'd, that Arnold cheats
All thofe, of courfe, with whom he treats.
Now let the Devil fufpeÃ§t a bite
Or Arnold cheats him of his right.

Mothers fhall fill their children, and fay...Arnold!...
Arnold fhall be the bug-bear of their years.
Arnold!...vile, treacherous, and leagued with Satan.

After his treason, effigies of Benedict Arnold were hanged or burned all over the country, like this two-faced one in Philadelphia, being prodded by the devil. A Representation of the Figures Exhibited and Paraded through the Streets of Philadelphia, on Saturday the 30th of September, 1780, call no. Bb 612 R2997. Courtesy of the Historical Society of Pennsylvania.

Above him loomed Satan, "who seemed, however, ashamed of so unprofitable a servant," and on "the heart of the traitor was fixed a label expressive of his real character, the justice of his condemnation, and a bequest of his soul to the Devil." The townspeople hung the effigy with great formality while everyone hissed and lit off firecrackers, all with "the greatest decency and good order." Three cheers followed, as they buried the uniformed "body."[12] Other towns followed suit.

Some demonized Arnold more methodically. The *Boston Independent Chronicle* admitted that "robbers and assassins" like Arnold have "a certain species of bravery," but that this "can only serve to place [Arnold's] crimes in a stronger point of light." The writer went on to clarify and prove Arnold's nine crimes: treason, avarice, hypocrisy, barbarity, falsehood, mean deception, peculation, robbery, and, interestingly, ingratitude. Though Arnold would have hotly disputed the charges, if he read the article he might have listened to the following with alarm: "He aimed to plant a dagger in the bosom of his country, which had raised him from the obscurity in which he was born, to honor which never could have been the object even of his most sanguine hopes."[13] The author could have been writing a definition of "homegrown terror," and the reference to England's class system could have given the low-born "horse trader" a dark hint of the welcome would receive from many English aristocrats.

Fear was another common reaction. James Searle wrote to Benjamin Franklin on November 20, expatiating on Arnold's wrongs and warning his friend in Paris of other possible traitors: "Oh! My dear Sir I greatly fear there may be Arnolds Even in Paris, Natives of America. If there are any such, may your Attendant Angel keep them or drive them from your bosom, & from your Councils, that they may never tend to Cloud your Western Sun." Franklin wrote back, saying, "I hope your fears that there may be Arnolds at Paris are groundless. But in such time one cannot be too much on one's guard, and I am obliged to you for the caution."[14] And fear of Arnold himself became routine. Everyone in Connecticut was jumpy after they "received Intelligence from New York, in three different ways and in such a manner that we have great reason to think it may be depended on" that Arnold will attack Connecticut. In response, Trumbull "put our militia on the sea coast" and asked Washington for regular troops.[15] But the reports were false, at least this time.

Many put their feelings into literature. Some preachers wrote sermons incorporating Arnold into a lesson or used the discovery of the plot as proof of God's divine providence.[16] Some writers imagined letters or dialogues to and from Satan to Arnold.[17] Corruption by the devil was the easiest way for people in the eighteenth century to try to understand what had happened.

> Quoth Arnold to Satan, My friend do not doubt me,
> I will strictly adhere to all your great views,
> To you I'm devoted, with all things about me,
> You'll permit me, I hope, to die in my shoes.[18]

Some also wrote "epitaphs" for Arnold that showed up in the newspapers, like this one from New London:

An epitaph. In memory of the fugitive shade of Benedict Arnold, once a major general in the Army of the United States of America, who, with incredible fatigue, unparalleled sufferings, and all the obstinacy of perseverance, pushed his way to the gallows, from which his tormented spirit fled, at a day too black to be mentioned, into a state of disappointment, want, chagrin, and despair, the ghosts of 1000 murdered oaths cease not to harrow up his conscience; and the genius of his betrayed country dashes, with irresistible force and in thick succession, huge masses of solid gold full in his face, with one hand, while with the other she points him to a gallows at West Point, where hangs poor Andre. In this situation while he catches in vain at the gold, his poor, little, fickle, furious, dastardly, distracted shade, which once bore the name of a soul, stands an eternal butt for British ridicule. Alas, poor Arnold! May all who walk in his steps, do that service for their country which he did before, and at the time he eloped from life, and then share his present state![19]

This elaborate fantasy poses an interesting conceit, that Arnold himself is already dead, and that he walks the earth as a soulless shade, while his spirit is tormented by "disappointment, want, chagrin, and despair." Like Tallmadge and Lafayette, the writer of this tirade imagines these feelings to be necessary but separates the part of Arnold that could feel them from the husk that still walks the earth. Another poem in the *Pennsylvania Packet* solved this problem by changing his name: "ARNOLD! thy name, as heretofore, Shall now be Benedict no more. . . . And since of treason thou'rt convicted, Thy name should now be maledicted."[20] In the eighteenth century the idea of a person's character was less malleable than we believe it to be today, and it is telling that so much ink should have been spilled trying to reconcile the two Arnolds, rather than focusing on the dramatic possibilities of the event.[21]

Some did write more elaborate works, like the anonymous *Fall of Lucifer: An Elegiac Poem of the Infamous Defection of the Late General Arnold*, probably by a member of the literary group the Hartford Wits, like Timothy Dwight or the poet John Trumbull, cousin to the governor's family. The poet called the recent events "The Scandal of the Age" and dubbed Arnold a "fratricide" rather than a parricide, but the same connotation applies. The work is prefaced with the poet's claim of once holding the "highest esteem for the late [*sic*] General Arnold" but now "it must be confessed that, though Arnold, as a citizen, has eventually proved an execrable villain, his behavior, as a soldier, has indeed been heroical," as seen in "Quebec, Champlain, and Saratoga." This admission may be one reason the poem did not have a wider audience. Nevertheless, the anonymous poet states, "it is impossible to conceive what darkness and deformity mean, without having seen light and beauty, or to obtain adequate ideas of the character of a fiend, without first contemplating that of an angel."[22]

That sort of logic of the tragic fall made a lot of sense to the eighteenth-century readers, but few bought into the idea of Arnold as a tragic figure. He was to most early Americans wretched rather than tragic, vile rather than pitiable. Despite being fooled by Peggy Arnold's "wounded tenderness," Alexander Hamilton wrote well about the "baseness" of the betrayal, fitting words like "infamy," "effrontery," "farce," "despicable," "knavery," "prostitution," "dirty," and "fraud" in the space of one paragraph. "The history of his command at West Point is a history of little, as well as great, villainies," he wrote a few weeks after the discovery of the treason.[23] These kinds of comments were repeated time and time again by people from every walk of life.

We can clearly see the issues of defining and understanding Arnold in the evasive, ineffective October 1780 "Letter to the Inhabitants of America," written by William Smith from Arnold's notes, though with Arnold's name attached. The ghostwritten letter was published everywhere and was roundly denounced or ridiculed by both Americans and British. Even in this political document, designed from the outset to use half-truths and prevarications to achieve a desired result, there is a muddled narrative and specious reasoning, as if Smith himself could not quite get a hold on the logic or the heart of the matter. He begins by saying he is not "indifferent to your [the reader's] approbation" and says he cannot be "silent on the motives which have induced me to join the King's arms." But instead of a confession, the letter becomes an attempt to justify his actions. That is bad public relations in the first place, focusing on his questionable character rather than the reasons others should follow him. But the outright anger at the criticism he knows will come is off-putting even to those mildly in the British camp, many of whom questioned his actions themselves:

with respect to that herd of censurers, whose enmity to me originates in their hatred to the principles by which I am now led to devote my life to the re-union of the British empire, as the best and only means to dry up the streams of misery that have deluged this country, they may be assured, that concious of the rectitude of my intentions; I shall treat their malice and calumnies with contempt and neglect.

The rest of the letter is worse, getting tangled in "legality" and setting Britain and France against each other as monarchies to choose from — a straw man argument that all but the most nationalistic British or despairing American could see through. There are comically tortured equivocations such as, "And now that her worst Enemies are in her own bosom, I should change my Principles, If I conspired with their Designs. Yourselves being Judges, was the war the less Just, because Fellow Subjects were considered as our foes?" This cannot even be parsed logically, much less emotionally. Finally, the classic argument of the terrorist and the tyrant appears: "I was only solicitous to accomplish an event [the capture of West Point] of decisive Importance, and to prevent, as much as possible in the Execution of it, the Effusion of blood."[24] Spilling blood to prevent blood being spilt is always a questionable justification for war or violence, and the fact that he has to turn to this rationalization shows the insufficiency of his explanations. His justification assumes that the taking of West Point would have been a decisive blow to the American cause, thus shortening the war, rather than leading to further and greater bloodshed. Of course, an additional result could have been the death of his friends, including Varick, Lamb, and especially Washington, who would surely have been hanged.

And of course his plea for peace was another lie. At the same time Arnold wrote a letter to England detailing the "Present State of the American Rebel Army," information that would most likely lead to more bloodshed. He gave troop numbers and supply routes, suggestions on how to divide Congress from the army, and financial information on the colonies. His assessment was hopeful at best, a classic political document designed to appease superiors rather than a true account. Some of it may have been wishful thinking on his part, especially since he left out the French navy and only said of their army, "In the foregoing Estimate the French Troops at Rhode Island who amount to about 5000 Effectives are not included."[25] After all, he didn't want to worry his new superiors.

Arnold still hoped that people would come over to the British side. Rumors of a mutiny in New Jersey prompted him to write to Gen. Henry Clinton, "I'm happy to hear of the revolt of so great a part of Mister Washington's army. This event, I make no doubt, will be attended with happy consequences."[26] He would be disappointed when the brief mutiny led nowhere. The soldiers were angry about not being paid, not about the Revolution's aims. The inability to see the difference between those two may have been Arnold's greatest flaw. And it is likely that his appeals did more harm than good among the populace for the British cause. After all, who wanted to be associated with such a notorious turncoat? What Loyalist to the Crown wanted to see his own actions reflected in someone like Arnold?

Though Arnold's defection brought few people onto the British side of the war, Congress overreacted, beginning a process of arrests and investigations. Men who had known or supported Arnold all came under scrutiny: Varick, Lamb, Oswald, Trumbull, Schuyler, Parsons, and many more. The accusations against Silas Deane were renewed, despite his earlier acquittal. Even Washington had to defend himself from insinuations of disloyalty, due to his association with Arnold at the time of the earlier trial in Philadelphia. He wrote, "It was at no time my inclination, much less my intention to become a party in his cause; and I certainly could not be so lost to my own character as to become a partisan at the moment I was called upon officially to bring him to trial."[27] Political partisans used Arnold's treason to browbeat enemies who had served with him, dined with him, or even spoken to him once in public.

Some used Arnold's treason to push for their own agenda. The editor of the *Connecticut Gazette* wrote a long discourse he called the "alarm" about the evils of the whaleboat trade to Long Island. This was a very chancy prospect in a newspaper, since many of the readers were probably engaged in exactly that trade. Nevertheless, he wrote that the treason of Arnold had awoken the country, and "it is now high time to be up, we have had been dozing long enough. . . . The trade to Long Island is a pernicious trade, and ought to be stopped." They were "plundering us to feed and enrich our enemies, and, at the expense of our safety and happiness, keeping up a friendly and unnatural correspondence with them . . . in short, that they are plunging a fatal dagger into the bowels of their country." The writer compared the men who traded to Arnold himself, "lost to honor" and betrayers of a "public trust." He called for stricter enforcement, giving the classic argument that "none but the rogues are afraid of the law."[28]

John Adams made the same argument, but for military deserters rather than those who traded with the enemy. He wrote to Benjamin Franklin that "As long, as Congress and Courts Martial inflict So gentle Punishments upon flagrant Criminals, and then entrust them with Commands and Employments as if nothing had happened, So Long we may expect to see Examples of Treachery, Desertion, and every other Villainy."[29] This might demonstrate a disturbing effect on someone as influential as Adams, as he called for stiffer penalties and greater punishments. He balanced desertion, a very common offense in those days, with Arnold's more severe treachery. Washington remained lenient but left a door open to catch one man in particular: "I prefer permitting an escape to giving up; because doing the last would imply that we think we have no right to seize upon a deserter in all cases whatever and wherever we can find him, a point which I would always insist upon, more especially as it may one day be brought in question where a gentleman of high rank, who formerly belonged to us, may be the object."[30] Leaving the rule purposefully vague allowed for the hopeful eventuality of hanging that "gentleman," Benedict Arnold.

Some took a more optimistic view of the effects of Arnold's defection. Dutch biologist Jan Ingenhousz asked, "What impression has this event made in the minds of the Americans? It seems to me, that the attempt to bring back the colonies under the obedience to the mother country by bribery, treachery, and severity can not operate the desired effect, even if it could produce a conquest of the whole country; for it would alienate the minds of a nation subdued by such maxims."[31] Ezra Stiles also thought that the event would not have too large an effect on the Revolution. "Gen. Arnold is a Loss! But America is so fertile in Patriots, that we can afford to sell a Patriot or two every year without an essential Injury to the glorious Cause of Liberty and Independence]." He also predicted that not even the British would accept Arnold's action, writing to Benjamin Franklin that "Gen. Arnold has buried all his military Glory, & sends his Name down in History execrated with Contempt & Infamy. He will be despised not only by us in the United States but by all the Nations of Europe & in all future Ages."[32] Similarly, Virginia's Supreme Court chief wrote to James Madison, saying, "The story of General Arnold's corruption is indeed shocking to humanity." He asked Madison to reveal all to him, except for any state secrets, "to gratifie curiosity, and not because I feel any sure part or fear the keenest probe, as I hear some have done and taken themselves away." He hoped the deed would "rouse" all those wishing for "our just cause" from the "apathy from which alone our enemies can hope for success."[33]

Many of the British seemed to agree with this scornful assessment, though some conjectured in the press that the defection meant that many generals would go over to their side. A few of the British astutely thought the Americans saw in Arnold "distrust of themselves."[34] And, like the Americans, many of the British also questioned his motives. One British soldier acknowledged that "perhaps the real motive in which Arnold's conduct originated, will never be clearly ascertained." He then spent a page speculating on just that.[35]

Unsurprisingly, after Arnold's numerous services to the Revolution, many on the British side hated him outright. The German mercenaries in the British army had conceived a particular dislike for Arnold early on in the war, calling him "notorious," "horse-dealer," bankrupt," and "swindler."[36] A Connecticut merchant in New York under flag of truce, found that

> the affair of Arnold, Andre, and the intercepted Mail, were the principal Topics of conversation. As to the first, people of all ranks talk freely and unfavourably of Arnold; and however, (for obvious reasons) he may be countenanced by their leaders, yet I could not learn that the British Officers, nor the Generality of the Refugees approve of his conduct, or think him worthy of Trust than the people on our side *now* do. He has lost much of his merit by too late an avowal of his pretended principles, and not till he was detected in a plot, which left him no hopes of confidence or Security from his countrymen.

Even more embarrassingly, the merchant heard that a captain of a British ship had called Arnold "traitor," and when his commandant called him in for questioning, he said that "they must build more Gaols

Reconciling Arnold's treason with his former heroism has always been difficult for Americans; this monument to his wounded leg at the Saratoga battlefield is a clever way around the problem. Courtesy of Marian O'Keefe.

if they meant to imprison all those that made use of such epithets." He was discharged without punishment.[37]

General Clinton was very angry about the fate of his "valuable assistant" and "confidential friend," John Andre.[38] He blamed Arnold for Andre's mistake of changing his clothes and carrying writings "by which the nature of his embassy might be traced," though he ultimately blamed Washington for acting "in so cruel a manner" to put Andre to death.[39] Despite this loss and the collapse of the plan to take West Point, he nevertheless "thought it right to appoint [Arnold] Colonel of a Regiment, with the Rank of Brigadier General of Provincial Forces."[40] But by the end of the month, Clinton was having second thoughts about the "gain" of Arnold, finding that the "great advantages" that he expected had not materialized. In a letter to Lord Germain, he ruminated that because "the gaining over some of the most respectable Members of the Congress, or Officers of Influence and Reputation among their troops, would, next to the destruction of Washington's army, be the speediest means of subduing the rebellion and restoring the Tranquility of America, I was encouraged to make the attempt."[41] Unfortunately for Clinton, it became clearer and clearer that Arnold's defection had not brought anyone else of importance to the British side and had in fact inflamed many Americans to a renewed patriotism.

That fact was kept as much as possible from the supporters of war in England. News of Major Andre's death, however, was widely disseminated and lamented. And the British government took tough action in reprisal. Governor Trumbull's son John had traveled to London to study painting and had been living the high life with Maj. John Tyler, another former Continental soldier. While waiting for Tyler at his lodging, young Trumbull was startled by a knock on the door, which he thought was "some of his merry companions, for another frolic." When the door was opened, a "respectable looking, middle aged man" entered and said that he had a warrant for Tyler's arrest. Trumbull said, "I had for some time been apprehensive that he was spending more money than he could afford." The man replied, "You misunderstand me; I have a warrant to arrest the Major, not for debt, but for high treason; and, my orders are, at the same time, to secure your person and papers, Mr. Trumbull, for examination."[42] Trumbull was thrown in prison at Tothill-Fields Bridewell, as the son of a rebel governor and former officer in the American army.

Back in America a similar situation developed. Peggy Arnold returned to Philadelphia, but shortly afterward the executive Council of Pennsylvania kicked her out, sending her across New Jersey and the Hudson River to Arnold's new rented residence at 3 Broadway in Manhattan next to British headquarters, a few short yards from where Nathan Hale had been hanged. Hannah had refused to join her brother at West Point in September and now left Philadelphia to take Henry, Arnold's youngest son by his first wife, to Connecticut. Arnold's oldest sons had been attending school in Maryland and were sent to Connecticut as well.[43] Once there, they were kept under a loose watch. When Arnold requested that his eldest son be brought to him in New York, Governor Trumbull did not even stoop to respond himself. His son-in-law William Williams replied, "in the negative."[44] Arnold's family was not thrown in prison, however, and in fact was kept in relative luxury at the house of Sarah Sage in Middletown, where Arnold had recovered after Saratoga. When the citizens of Middletown burned him in effigy, Sage closed all the wooden window shutters so that the children should be kept in ignorance of the passing event.[45] No one ever questioned Comfort Sage's or his wife's patriotism, and when George Washington passed through Middletown years later, he paid special respect to the ailing Sage.

But there were other actions to take, and take quickly. Less than two weeks after the discovery of Arnold's plot, Congress voted to erase his name from all the registers.[46] They seized and auctioned off everything from his Philadelphia home, from looking glasses to curtains to mahogany bedsteads. Later in the week they auctioned off his chariot and horses.[47] Congress in Philadelphia and Trumbull in Connecticut seized his papers, searching for evidence of conspiracy.[48] Washington warned Tallmadge not to arrange any clandestine meetings, since "should an officer be taken under circumstances the least suspicious" they would probably be hanged.[49] Tallmadge cautioned him that "the conduct of Arnold, since his arrival at New York has been such, that though he knows not a single link in the chain of my correspondence, still those who have assisted us in this way, are at present too apprehensive of Danger to give their immediate usual intelligence." In New

York spy Robert Townsend wrote cautiously, "I am happy to think that Arnold does not know my name."[50] But the new traitor did his best to find the American spies anyway.[51]

Meanwhile, Tallmadge ignored Washington's warning and bravely crossed the Sound by himself to obtain intelligence. After returning with information, he gathered his best soldiers and on November 21, 1780, at four in the afternoon the detachment of dismounted dragoons silently pushed their boats off Fairfield Beach, crossed the Devil's Belt, and landed on Long Island. Caught in a driving rainstorm, Tallmadge and his men hid out for a night and a day, until the following evening when they marched all the way across the island. Reaching Fort Saint George at four the following morning, they crept up to the stockade and were within forty yards before they were spotted by a sentinel who fired on them. "Before the smoke from his gun had cleared his vision," said Tallmadge, "my sergeant, who marched by my side, reached in with his bayonet, and prostrated him." Tallmadge and his elite troops stormed the fort and demolished it, destroying their stores and weapons. Then, with a dozen men on horses Tallmadge rode and burned the unprotected magazine at Coram and rejoined his troops on their way to the north side of the island where their boats lay hidden. This remarkable expedition was brought off with no losses, though one man was badly wounded.[52] The war continued, no matter which side Benedict Arnold had chosen.

Washington himself was not idle. He wanted Arnold back, and not to give him a fatherly talking-to. He was stunned and outraged by the desertion of a man he had trusted. Less than a month after the discovery of treason, he secretly approached Col. Henry Lee in New Jersey with a plan to kidnap Arnold:

> The plan proposd for taking A———, the out lines of which are communicated in your letter . . . has every mark of a good one, I therefore agree to the promised rewards . . . with this express stipulation, that he A———d is brought to me alive. No circumstance whatever shall obtain my consent to his being put to death. The idea which would accompany such an event would be that Ruffians had been hired to assassinate him. My aim is to make a public example of him, and this should be strongly impressed upon those who are employed

to bring him of. . . . The most inviolable secrecy must be observed on all hands.[53]

Washington was very careful to stress that this was not an assassination, even though the ultimate aim was to hang the traitor. But, of course, anything could go wrong in a kidnapping operation. He and Lee chose a young Virginian named John Champe, a veteran solider with "uncommon taciturnity and inflexible perseverance." At the risk of his life and reputation, he pretended to desert the army at Passaic Falls, riding all night to Communipaw Bay, just beyond Bergen, where two British warships lay at anchor. Along the way he barely avoided an American patrol, which reported back. A captain woke Henry Lee to get permission for a pursuit party. But Lee told the captain that desertions were common enough and not to wake him up for this kind of story. When the captain persisted, saying that Sergeant-Major Champe had been identified, Lee slowly filled out long orders for his capture, all the while giving him time to reach the bay.

Fifteen dragoons galloped out of camp after the deserter, an hour delayed. Still, they nearly caught him before he reached British lines, where they were driven off by a hail of grapeshot from a warship. This close call only convinced the British of the truth of Champe's claims. By October 23 he was taken to Clinton's headquarters amid the burned houses of lower Manhattan, where he answered some questions truthfully and told the British what they wanted to hear, which was that "the soldiery [are] very much dissatisfied with the French." They offered him the chance to join the British army, but he convinced them this would be too risky. A few hours later, Champe met Arnold "accidentally" and was assigned to Arnold's "Loyalist Legion."

He watched Arnold's daily movements, finding that he returned home to 3 Broadway around midnight and that he rarely went to bed without visiting the little garden between the tall house and the alley. A plan was concocted. Along with several spies, probably in Tallmadge's network, Champe intended to seize and gag him while he strolled in the garden. They removed the nails in several of the fence posts and placed the posts back so that they merely leaned against the rails. In case they were challenged they concocted a cover story about transporting a drunken soldier. A small boat bobbed at a wharf on the Hudson River, ready to cross to the Bergen Woods in New Jersey, where a small troop of swift horsemen waited to carry the trussed Arnold back to American lines.

Champe set the date for December 11 and contacted American headquarters with the plan. The day arrived, but that afternoon he and the rest of the Loyalist Legion were ordered onto a transport. They were headed on a rare winter expedition to Virginia, commanded by Arnold himself.[54] George Washington and the soldiers waiting in New Jersey could only curse and moan the missed opportunity as once again the traitor slipped away.

A Parricide in Old Virginia

ON CHRISTMAS EVE 1780 a northwest storm battered Arnold's small fleet as it made its way south from New York. One ship almost sank, and another had to throw forty horses overboard to prevent it from swamping. Four ships were separated and not seen again for a week. Gen. Henry Clinton's orders were limited, allowing Arnold to destroy arms depots; to establish a base at Portsmouth, Virginia; and to gather Loyalists from the surrounding areas. Clinton told him specifically not to "make any excursions from thence" unless he could do so without danger. The British commander in chief also gave two other officers the authority to override Arnold if he took what they thought was an improper action, an order that was of course kept secret from the former American patriot. Under his dubious command were the Queens Rangers, the Eightieth Regiment of foot, an elite group of German mercenaries, and the Bucks County volunteers, an independent attachment of Loyalists. The fleet gathered at Cape Henry on December 29 and sailed the next morning past Hampton Roads to Newport News. Arnold wasted no time with limited orders and began a full-scale invasion of Virginia.[1]

Virginia's navy was insufficient, to say the least, smaller even than Nathaniel Shaw's New London one. And, unlike Connecticut, Virginia had no formal lookout system or fire signals along the coastline. Nevertheless, as Arnold's fleet sailed up the James River, it was spotted by one of the few naval lookouts, and the captain relayed the alarm. It reached Gov. Thomas Jefferson in Richmond, but unfortunately he believed it was only a foraging party and did not immediately call out the militia. Two years younger than Arnold, Jefferson had become a different kind of legend, primarily for his work at the Continental Congress and his authorship of the Declaration of Independence. Just after signing it, he left Congress to become a delegate in Virginia, then governor in 1779. He believed in and had argued for limited government for Virginia and for the new United States. On New Year's Day 1781, he was not as concerned with the British as with Indian attacks on the frontier, telling militia leaders to start "carrying the war into their own country."[2] But the poor state of Virginia's defenses was not all Jefferson's fault. The legislature in Virginia was even worse than the Continental Congress when it came to paying for arms and constructing defenses. And more significant, the tyranny-fearing planters had specifically created a weak governor and shunned a standing army. These views may have had admirable origins, but they were disastrous during wartime.

Arnold seized a small fleet of unarmed boats and their cargo of tobacco at Newport News and landed three hundred redcoats. They marched inland, taking prisoners as they went, and sacked the town of Hampton. By now the local militias were alerted, but it was too late to save the fifty-seven cattle and forty-two sheep that were roasted and devoured that night on the ships. One group of militia gathered on the north shore of the James River but was quickly driven off by Arnold's German mercenaries. Meanwhile, Arnold scooped up another five ships full of tobacco. During this encounter he sent a note to the people on shore, warning them not to interfere. It was Virginia's first notice that the traitor himself was commanding this invasion.

> Having the honor to command a body of his Majesty's troops, sent for the protection of his loyal subjects in this Colony, I am surprised to observe the hostile appearance of the inhabitants under arms on shore. I have therefore sent Lieutenant White, with a flag of truce, to be informed of their intentions.
>
> If they offer a vain opposition to the troops under my command in their landing, they must be answerable for the consequences. At the same time, I think it my duty to declare, I have not the least intention to injure the peaceable inhabitants in their persons or property; but that everything supplied the troops by them shall be punctually paid for.
>
> I am, Sir, your obedient humble servant, Benedict Arnold, B.C.[3]

In this letter Arnold put the responsibility for any hostilities on the other side, even though he was the invader. He also focused on whether or not the people will be paid for their losses, which although a concern was hardly the main one. Was this a last plea before Arnold had to do his "duty" or was he couching his deeds in the politest rhetoric? Either way, he was about to cross an invisible line from plots to deeds.

A messenger delivered Arnold's letter to Thomas Nelson, the head of the skimpy militia company at Williamsburg. Nelson asked the messenger if the author was "the traitor Arnold." Upon learning that it was, he asked if anyone ranked above him on the expedition, because he "would not and could not give up to a traitor." He would rather "hang him up by the heels, according to the orders of Congress." The messenger returned and delivered the message, causing Arnold to make a "very wry face." Whether Nelson's bravado worked or whether Arnold decided he had bigger fish to fry, the fleet moved on, using favorable winds to move farther up the James toward Richmond. By now Thomas Jefferson had heard more news and taken the alarm seriously, but his preparations were too late.[4]

Arnold's fleet of nineteen ships approached Hood's Point at a bend in the river, receiving intelligence from scouts that it had been fortified. The intelligence was correct, and the Americans promptly opened fire on one ship that poked its nose around the point. Arnold's ships returned fire, sending cannonballs smashing through trees, while his German mercenaries and Queens Rangers snuck on shore to attack the fortifications from the rear. When they reached Hood's Point, they found a rather pathetic, ill-prepared embankment, now abandoned by the skeleton crew of militia. If it had been a larger fort with a large garrison, as the German mercenary commander Johann von Ewald wrote, "this could very easily have prevented us from further undertakings." They were now within striking distance of any number of inland targets, like the arms depot at Petersburg or the governor's house at Richmond. At five in the morning on January 4, Jefferson was informed that Arnold had taken Hood's Point. He sent his wife and three daughters out of Richmond, along with important state documents, and at last began seriously raising militia to withstand the invasion.[5]

Arnold himself took up residence on the north shore of the James near Hood's Point, at a plantation called Westover owned by his wife's cousin, Mary Willing Byrd. His soldiers set up tents and occupied the forty buildings of the huge plantation complex, and suddenly to her alarm the old Loyalist widow watched her crops and livestock promptly eaten up before her eyes. Arnold told her that she would be compensated for her losses but gave no such assurance to her neighbor

Benjamin Harrison, a signer of the Declaration of Independence. The British sacked his plantation, destroying furniture, family paintings, and crops.[6]

Virginia had only recently moved its capital from Williamsburg to Richmond, since Jefferson thought that the inland location would be more secure. It was more a trading post than city, ten times smaller than Governor Trumbull's small farm town of Lebanon, without any real defenses other than being unreachable by naval warships. The arms depot at Petersburg was a much larger target, and the only reason to attack Richmond was symbolic: capturing the governor and destroying the capital would be a huge psychological blow. Arnold and his officers decided that Jefferson was the better objective and left Westover in a pouring rainstorm at two in the afternoon to retain the element of surprise. A full 900 of the 1,600 troops marched up the road throughout the evening hours, struggling to keep their powder dry, late into the night. Early on the morning of January 5 they rested at Four Mile Creek, only twelve miles from Richmond. A group of militia planning to stop or slow down the invaders was fooled by the Queens Rangers and entirely taken prisoner. This was the only resistance Arnold met until just outside town.[7]

Jefferson himself was preparing for bed at his modest wood-frame residence on Richmond's Shockoe Hill when a messenger banged on his door, telling him that the British led by General Arnold were marching toward him. Jefferson had no intention of being captured. Luckily, the Prussian-born volunteer Baron von Steuben, who had been training American troops since 1777, happened to be nearby. Jefferson ordered von Steuben to take command of the militia and rode to an arms factory at Westham, where he ordered the gunpowder moved to another location. Then at eleven o'clock he took the road to Tuckahoe to see his wife and daughters. The following morning he sent them even farther off and rode to a hill where he could observe Richmond with his spyglass. He could see Arnold and the British easily taking over the town, storming the small hills around it where militia had gathered. In a few minutes it was all over, and everyone in town but some of the slaves had fled.[8]

At Jefferson's townhouse on Shockoe Hill an officer, probably Arnold himself, knocked on the door with a pair of metal handcuffs and asked the slaves Jefferson had left behind, "Where is the governor?" They told him, "he's gone to the mountains" along with the keys to the mansion and the silver, which in reality they had hidden carefully. The soldiers made free with Jefferson's wine and rum collection and then continued to plunder the town.[9] They burned the foundry, the boring mill, the stores of armaments, and other buildings. Clothing, leather, tools, wagons, cannons, gunpowder, and at least three hundred muskets were destroyed. Arnold's experience as a field commander helped immeasurably, and in "less than 48 hours from the time of their landing and 19 from our knowing their destination they had penetrated 33 miles, done the whole injury, and retired."[10] It was a bold and swift raid, characteristic of Arnold. He was clearly not pulling any punches since switching sides.

Arnold blamed his soldiers and Jefferson himself for the extent of destruction, telling Clinton that "as Mister Jefferson was so inattentive to the preservation of private property, I found myself under the disagreeable necessity" of destroying what was left behind. Cold rain continued to fall every day, as Jefferson rode around the state trying to drum up support. Arnold returned to the Westover plantation, where he celebrated his fortieth birthday. His attack had been almost completely successful, although now militiamen were gathering in greater numbers, perhaps egged on by the news that the traitor was commanding the invasion.[11] Unfortunately, these part-time soldiers were often less than professional. One evening a group of 140 stuffed themselves into a tavern only six miles from the British, carousing and drinking. They were completely surprised and in their frightened retreat dispersed the rest of the militia in the area as well. Meanwhile 400 additional British soldiers arrived in Virginia, along with fresh supplies.[12]

The Baron von Steuben began skirmishing with Arnold's troops, nearly killing the opposing German commander, and surprising and seriously injuring the troops of Beverley Robinson Jr., the Loyalist whose parents' house Arnold had fled the previous autumn. But this was more Robinson's fault than the Americans' efficacy. Von Steuben complained that he had few supplies, little ammunition, and poor soldiers to work with.[13] The militia forces were also spread out "over a large tract of country" and could only respond slowly. Only 200 were near enough to Richmond to be called up before the earlier attack, not nearly enough to fight the regiment "commanded by the parricide Arnold."[14] Due to these issues, even after a month in the field von Steu-

ben was no more than an annoying insect to the British force under Arnold's competent command.

Some, like John Trumbull, put the blame for military incompetence on Virginia's government itself; he later favorably compared the small state of Connecticut's response of Danbury with the "feeble resistance" made by Virginia under Jefferson, even though Virginia had three times the quota of militia in a much more populous state. He noted that Arnold did more damage with only 1,500 men, even though 2,000 or more invaded Connecticut each time.[15] Many in Virginia agreed with this assessment, like a college chum of Jefferson, who said, "Arnold the traitor . . . has disgraced our country, my dear friend, so much that I am ashamed & ever shall be so to call myself a Virginian."[16]

Fellow Virginia planters such as Patrick Henry would use the weak response to the British invasion to cudgel Jefferson for the rest of his political life.

News of Arnold's frightening competence worried the British in New York as well. Frederick Mackenzie of the Royal Welsh Fusiliers noted that Arnold's

> success with so small a body of troops, will cause the Expedition under General Leslie, which was more numerous in troops and had the same object, to appear in a very unfavorable light. I am almost sorry, (If I may venture to say so) for the sake of the reputation of the British Generals, that such a man as Arnold should have executed with an inferior force, what a British General did not even attempt with a superior one. This is a strong proof how much success of an enterprise depends on chusing [*sic*] a proper person to command it. Arnold is bold, daring and prompt in the execution of what he undertakes.[17]

This was high praise from someone who did not particularly like Benedict Arnold in the first place. No matter what opinions were of the traitor's morals, his skill was never in question. Nevertheless, to avoid more embarrassment, the British decided to send another officer of the same rank to help restrain the political effect of Arnold, if not his aggressive tactics.

While the British in New York expressed astonishment at Arnold's success, he made few friends among his colleagues in Virginia, getting into a serious dispute with the naval officers over the division of booty. And he feared capture by the Americans more than death in battle. Every morning he put two pistols into his pockets, even though he was surrounded by British military might. Johann von Ewald said that whenever Arnold was in danger of capture he became "very restless" and believed that the pistols were not for defense but rather "a last recourse to escape being hanged."[18]

After his initial success, Arnold boarded his ship, sailed down the James, and turned up the Elizabeth River past the ruins of Norfolk. He and the bulk of the troops at Portsmouth began constructing a fort even though many other officers believed that Arnold was making a mistake, trapping his men on a peninsula and inviting a siege. Arnold met with local Loyalists, convinced many would join the cause. Von

Ewald remained skeptical, believing that the locals had merely put on a "good show" for the benefit of the conquering army. Only a few provided assistance, such as maps and supplies. This tactic of fortifying a peninsula would be disastrous for the British less than a year later at Yorktown.[19]

Jefferson remained on the run all that time, chased through the tobacco fields and swamp forests of his beloved Virginia by a man he once admired. Shortly after the sacking of Richmond, he planned a raid by a small elite force to sneak into the British camp and bring Arnold out alive, if possible, for 5,000 guineas reward. He suggested a possible trick by some western Virginians who could pose as friends and then drag him out in the middle of the night, "to undertake to seize and bring off this greatest of all traitors."[20] In March an American major attempted another kidnapping of the turncoat, watching his movements from an advance signal station and preparing to capture him on his morning ride. Unfortunately, British warships arrived at just the wrong time, spoiling the plan.[21] Jefferson raised the stakes and tried to kill Arnold using a fire ship filled with explosives, intending on floating it toward the flagship. But that plan also sputtered out.[22] This sort of officer elimination raid was completely against all the "rules" of war at the time, but clearly Jefferson thought Arnold's case a special one.

Nevertheless, Jefferson certainly appealed to the rules when it suited his purpose. In a letter from March 24, 1781, he wrote to Arnold himself, meeting threat with threat, saying that he had heard Arnold bullied unarmed citizens, telling them if they were found "in arms" they would be put to death, when the "law of nations" clearly states that "strict confinement" was the appropriate punishment. Jefferson warned that he would put to death all the British prisoners in Virginia's possession if Arnold began executing armed civilians.[23] Luckily, neither of these threats was carried out.

Arnold remained confident that many Loyalists in Virginia would join the British cause. There were certainly more than in Connecticut, especially in the southwest corner of the state. But Col. William Preston had done good work suppressing uprisings in that area. Virginia's Supreme Court chief Edmund Pendleton wrote to Preston just after Arnold's treason, saying, "I wish you good success in your endeavours to root the Tories out of your county, those parricides, who have kept their country from peace for some time past, and if they could be extinguished I believe we should soon Enjoy that blessing. General Arnold has lately topped all villainy of that sort."[24] From Pendleton and Preston's perspective at the time, there was little difference between Arnold and the Loyalists they were fighting. But ordinary Tories did not necessarily see it that way, and few came to the side of the British during this invasion.[25]

Meanwhile, one Loyalist in particular, Peggy's cousin Mary Byrd, made a big mistake while trying to play both sides. In her eagerness to have her forty-nine slaves returned by the British who freed them, she only cast suspicion on herself in the eyes of other Virginians. They began to suspect that her story was false and that she had collaborated with the British. Jefferson and other officials were sympathetic, though she was still eventually brought to trial. Somehow, she was able to keep her estate when the witnesses failed to show.[26] Her slaves, however, never returned. Like other Americans, knowledgeable slaves were divided on the war, but many went over to the British on the promise of instant freedom. Others hopefully thought the new country might lead to new freedoms. Both were destined to be disappointed.[27]

Unfortunately for those who trusted the widow Byrd, thousands of British troops would use her farm as a staging point once again in the coming weeks. In fact, reinforcements were on the way for both the British and Americans. Washington had first tried to send a French naval expedition from Newport, and after delays it had reached Portsmouth on February 13. But Arnold pulled his ships up the shallow Elizabeth River, safe from the larger French ones. After a "hard but doubtful combat" with the British navy, they were forced to return to Newport.[28] Then, on February 20 Congress gave Washington permission to send an official expedition to help Virginia, for which he chose his protégé, the Marquis de Lafayette. And he had a secondary mission, as Washington told him, "You are to do no act whatever with Arnold that directly or by implication may screen him from the punishment due to his treason and desertion, which if he should fall into your hands, you will execute in the most summary way."[29] The young Frenchman led a force of 1,200 men to the northern reaches of the Chesapeake at Annapolis, taking a ship himself to see von Steuben in Yorktown on March 13. They planned to assault Arnold's hasty defenses at Portsmouth, supported by an incoming French fleet. Unfortunately, a British fleet drove them off, leaving Arnold's secure. Then two weeks later 2,200 more British soldiers landed, forcing Lafayette to return to Maryland without bringing his forces by sea.[30] He would have to approach more slowly, marching south through Baltimore and across the Potomac.

The British sent Gen. William Phillips, who had coincidentally fought against Arnold at Saratoga three years earlier. He and his old adversary now planned a raiding party up the Potomac, primarily to destroy the properties of American leaders like George Washington. A small force sailed up the river to Alexandria, found no one opposing them, and anchored off Mount Vernon. They plundered the other side of the river; freed seventeen of Washington slaves, who fled to their ships; and terrorized Lund Washington, the general's cousin in charge of the estate. Contrary to Washington's orders, Lund gave in to the threats and supplied the ship with sheep and hogs.[31] The angry Washington wrote to his cousin, "that which gives me most concern, is, that you should go on board the enemy's vessels, and furnish them with refreshments." He said that he would much rather the British "burnt my house, and laid the plantation in ruin."[32]

Arnold and Phillips left a few hundred men at Portsmouth and, with the rest of the combined force, cruised up the James River, landed at Burwell's Ferry, and marched to Williamsburg. The fleet also destroyed the nearby shipyard, and once again the outnumbered militia fled.[33] The next target was Petersburg, with its store of arms and supplies. The militia under von Steuben stood their ground and put up a good fight, but the British numerical and firepower superiority was too great. The largest cities in eastern Virginia were now in British hands or destroyed, and Arnold and Phillips seemingly could do what they wanted with impunity. To prove it, Arnold sailed back to the James River to destroy the small remnant of the Virginia navy, which had bravely decided to stop the fleet from coming up the river toward Richmond again. Arnold cleverly brought four brass cannons onto shore and snuck them onto a bluff within a hundred feet of the small fleet. He rained cannon fire down on top of them from this safe position, and the defeated Americans set fire to their own ships to prevent the British from capturing them.[34]

Joined by Phillips, Arnold marched along the south bank of the James River to Richmond again. This time, though, he would be met by the Marquis de Lafayette, who had finally arrived by the land route. Of course, Lafayette wanted to capture or kill Arnold for his mentor Washington, but he also wanted General Phillips, whose father had killed his own in a European battle twenty-two years earlier. Nevertheless, he followed Washington's strict rules against assassination, something that "excited great dissatisfaction" among the other officers. But Lafayette was not without his own tricks. As the British approached Richmond, he spread out his modest force along the ridge of Shockoe Hill, fooling Phillips into thinking he was facing a huge American army. Phillips and Arnold retreated to Petersburg.[35]

As was customary, Arnold wrote to the commanding officer of the American troops. Lafayette refused to receive the letter from the traitor, and he said he would gladly put his motives in a letter if requested. In his note to the British he wrote, "In case any other English officer should honour him with a letter, he would always be happy to give the officers every testimony of his esteem."[36] Washington approved of this refusal, telling Lafayette, "My dear Marquis . . . your conduct upon every occasion meets my approbation, but in none more than your refusal to hold a correspondence with Arnold."[37]

After spending months masquerading as a British soldier after his failed kidnapping attempt in New York, John Champe managed to escape sometime in April. If he had been captured while fighting for the British he would have been executed, but now that he escaped his fate was hardly clearer. He had to contact Henry Lee or he could still be hanged and if recaptured by the British he would be hanged by them. Lee was now in the south, and Champe searched the dirt roads of Virginia and the Carolinas until he found the army camp on the Congaree River. Lee gave him an honorable discharge, and he returned to his home in Loudoun County, Virginia, forced to wait out the remainder of the war.[38] As for his intended target, during the campaign Arnold apparently asked an American prisoner of war what he thought the Americans would do if they captured him. The man replied promptly, "Why, sir, if I must answer your question you must excuse my telling you the plain truth; if my countrymen should catch you, I believe they would first cut off that lame leg, which was wounded in the cause of freedom and virtue, and bury it with the honors of war, and afterwards hang the remainder of your body in gibbets."[39]

Arnold's partner Phillips meanwhile fell ill on May 8 and was taken back to headquarters in a chaise. By May 13 he was dead, and rumors swirled around the British camp that Arnold poisoned him.[40] Arnold sat down to write a long letter to Clinton, bragging about how much damage he had done. On April 30, for example, he claimed to have destroyed twelve hundred hogsheads of tobacco, five hundred barrels of flour, several warehouses, a large ship, four other vessels, and "a large range of public ropewalks and store houses, and some tan and bark houses full of hides and bark." He also informed Clinton that Phillips is "reduced so low by a fever . . . that he is incapable of business." In fact, he was already dead, and Arnold concealed this fact either to fool possible spies or to serve his own purposes. Meanwhile, the Earl Charles Cornwallis marched north from his campaign in the Carolinas to meet Arnold in Petersburg, an event Arnold said would allow them "to operate as we please in Virginia or Maryland."[41] He arrived and met Arnold on May 19, 1781. The British now had seven thousand men on the ground in Virginia and seemed assured of victory.

That very day, far to the north in Connecticut, George Washington, Gen. Henry Knox, and Gen. Louis Lebègue Duportail "breakfasted at Litchfield, dined at Farmington, and lodged at Weathersfield at the house of Joseph Webb." The house was actually next door to Silas Deane's, and no doubt Deane's larger house would have been used if he had not been under a political cloud. Washington prepared the Webb House for another meeting with the French general Comte de Rochambeau, who had occupied Rhode Island the previous July and whose autumn 1780 plans had been so rudely interrupted. They attended church services at the Weathersfield meetinghouse, and that night Washington stayed upstairs in a room with huge, red castle-like raised flocked wallpaper and falsely grained wood that might have reminded him of the decor at Mount Vernon. He dined on salmon and shad and perhaps took a fortifying drink of port or Madiera from his own portable bar.

The following day Washington met with Governor Trumbull and Jeremiah Wadsworth at the Webb House to discuss strategy.[42] They were joined late in the day by Rochambeau, who had made a slow way over the rough roads of eastern Connecticut. That evening Trumbull, Wadsworth, Washington, Rochambeau, and the others attended a concert at the meetinghouse, and the French embassy lodged at Stillman's Tavern. The next morning the group gathered in the large front room

The Joseph Webb House in the foreground served as the meeting place for Washington, Rochambeau, Wadsworth, and Trumbull when the plans for Yorktown were made. If Silas Deane had not been under investigation by Congress, they would have probably used his house next door. Courtesy of the author.

of the Webb House, Washington in his blue and buff coat, with gold buttons and stars on the shoulders, and Rochambeau in black, gold, and red. The year before they had decided on a "combined operation," and the two leaders had resolved "to strike the enemy in the most vulnerable quarter." A "death-blow to British domination" was agreed on, but how to produce that?

The answer in 1781 seemed to lie in the French fleet under Admiral de Grasse reportedly on its way to the Caribbean. Washington wanted to attack New York and, as a "secondary object," considered an expedition against Cornwallis and Arnold in Virginia. Without deciding between the two they agreed to gather their forces together outside of New York and wait to hear of the news of the French navy. As Washington put it, "the point of attack was not absolutely agreed upon, be-

cause it cannot be foreknown where the enemy would be most suscep-
tible of impression."[43] They ate at Stillman's Tavern together, sealing
their mutual plan with wine and food.

Rochambeau left for Hartford the next day, and Washington stayed
on to write letters. "Fixed with count de Rochambeau the plan of
Campaign" he wrote in his diary of May 22. Meanwhile, his country-
man Lafayette sparred with the British in Virginia, despite being hope-
lessly outnumbered. The young Frenchman also made good the back-
handed promise to Arnold by opening communications with the new
commander when he arrived. Perhaps because of this insult or perhaps
because he always chafed under a superior officer, Benedict Arnold decided to return to New York, leaving Cornwallis to deal with the wily
Lafayette. His reasons were attributed by Cornwallis to "indisposition" and by others to fear or money.[44] He did need to secure his share
of all the prizes his troops had looted, and sleeping each night with two
pistols could have been wearing on his nerves.

It could also be that Cornwallis sent him back in order to secure his
own command, and Arnold no doubt found the hierarchical politics
of King George's army just as frustrating as Washington's. By June he
would be safely back in British-controlled Manhattan. But the success of his raid had led, somewhat unintentionally, to a full-scale invasion and occupation of Virginia. It was there that the British forces
in America would meet their ruin.

William Ledyard's Last Summer

WILLIAM LEDYARD was luckier than many during the Revolution, serving in a place where he could go home and see his wife, Anne, and their eight children almost every night. But they still didn't see much of him. Along with keeping his mercantile business afloat and supervising the militia around New London, he built the defenses of the Thames River harbor stone by stone, often without recompense. In March 1777 he began construction on Fort Griswold on Groton Heights, a 120-foot prominence with a level summit about 500 feet from the harbor's edge. The site was just uphill to the southwest of the Groton wharf, where it held the most commanding point for cannon, able to reach any ships sailing up to shell New London across the river or the smaller town of Groton below. The following year, from April 1 to November 1, he built Fort Trumbull on the small rocky peninsula just south of the Shaw Mansion in New London, opposite Griswold. It was a good site to place cannons to fire on ships coming up the harbor but offered no protection from the land side. Then, from April to October 1779 he built other defensive works around New London.[1]

All the while, he supervised the increase in Fort Griswold's size and effectiveness, which now had pointed bastions on the corners of the trapezoidal stone-walled fort, giving it the appearance of a five-pointed star. A deep ditch ran around the entire structure, and long sharpened logs projected over the ditch like a horizontal fence top. Leafless trees with sharpened branches also faced would-be attackers on the far side of the ditch, while in front of the gate a triangular hill of earth blocked it from direct cannon shot. On the parapets, cannons faced out in all directions from small platforms, while earthen or stone steps allowed defenders to reach over the high ramparts to shoot their muskets or to bayonet anyone who made it past the thicket of jagged logs. The stone outer walls were reinforced by a thick barricade of packed dirt, protecting a well, an ammunition magazine, and a long barracks for those on watch. A covered way led out a secret door and down to a small battery lower on the hill for a greater range across the harbor. The southwest corner of Fort Griswold commanded a view of New London west and

Fort Trumbull southwest, and on a clear day the whole prospect from the shore of Long Island to the hills of Norwich was visible.

As the war went on, the forts and fortifications around New London began to bristle with captured cannons, but otherwise construction remained slow, with innumerable delays and frustrations. The militia companies designated to defend the harbor were paid poorly and insufficiently staffed, with fifty official soldiers patrolling each side of the harbor at most, and usually fewer. And though two thousand men were technically available to muster in the surrounding areas, many of them were busy farming or sailing the Atlantic as privateers. Groton's men had also given more than their share to Washington's army.[2] Because of these losses, Ledyard had trouble filling his tiny militia companies and more trouble supplying them with flour and beef.[3] Not that he had much time for recruitment. Along with building forts, his time was taken up with irritations like sorting out lost cattle, and he found both the duties and restrictions of his military appointment frustrating and obscure.[4]

Disease thinned the available soldiers further; as Nathaniel Shaw complained, "We are in such a wretched state in this town by reason of the smallpox, fever and famine, that I cannot carry on my business."[5] It did not help that from 1776 to 1778 not a single prize was brought into port. In fact, Shaw worked himself too hard and by 1779 made himself sick, forcing Ledyard to take on even more responsibility.[6] In 1780 and 1781 these responsibilities included keeping track of ships sailing in the eastern Sound.[7] One alarm occurred in October 1780, when Ledyard was alerted to a small fleet of British ships crossing the New London Harbor. Foggy conditions made the number of sails hard to determine, but after questioning local fishermen, he was able to calculate thirteen. He reported directly to Washington and Rochambeau but continued to send intelligence to Governor Trumbull.[8] And, of course, it was not only for them that Ledyard stayed alert. Throughout the first months of 1781, the British fleet had blockaded Newport and Long Island Sound, sending shivers of fear through the Connecticut mainland. The Norwich light infantry company made the march down river to New London many times, often being stopped halfway and told that the alarm was over. But no attacks came, and two of the enemy ships were wrecked in a violent storm.[9]

Meanwhile, Ledyard's business was at a standstill. He was concerned what he would be paid for his time in charge of the port, since "being under an obligation to receive more or less company every day," he wanted to know what "allowances" he would receive. "My duty has been and still is very fatiguing," he said wearily.[10] He paid out of his own pocket for many of the fort's improvements and supplies, having to constantly keep ahead of the needs of defense, while hoping that the state would pay him back some time in the future.[11]

In addition to overseeing the militia and fortifications, Ledyard ran the hospital for the wounded and sick. He constantly tried to get Dr. Philip Turner to come down from Norwich to see the patients, at one time telling him, "one of the number is dead and the others so very low that I am afraid to move them — and since they are in pretty comfortable barracks it may be thought best to let them continue until they are better."[12] He did not often get results, waiting for the doctor ten days on one occasion, pleading that "Mrs. Halls continues very low."[13] Before Turner demobilized from Washington's army in June 1781, Ledyard and Shaw often turned to Avery Downer, a member of the militia assigned to Fort Griswold in 1779. Downer returned in 1781 as assistant surgeon of the Eighth Regiment, and his father, Joshua, acted as chief surgeon, though they lived even farther from the fort, east of Norwich in Preston.[14] Since New London and Groton had to call on these men often, it is likely that no qualified doctors lived closer by.

Luckily, Ledyard had some steady local help. Nathan Hale's old New London company garrisoned Fort Trumbull in 1777, including members of the Lathrop family and Ledyard's own relatives.[15] And more help came from Nathan Hale's former sergeant, Stephen Hempstead. While attacking the man-of-war *Asia* with fire ships during the Battle of Harlem Heights, Hempstead had been hit with grapeshot, which broke two of his ribs. He was sent back home and served in the New London militia for four years. The Hempsteads and Ledyards had been friends for decades, intermarrying and crossing the Thames to visit each other on holidays.[16] Now, he and Ledyard manned the two forts, staring across the Sound to the soft hills of hostile Long Island.

Leaders like Ledyard, Hempstead, and Shaw had difficult, thankless jobs. Ledyard had to take care of resentful British prisoners, pay for their upkeep, and ship them back and forth to New York.[17] At one point Shaw had to collect all the local firearms from local farmers and merchants and lock them up, due to "extreme necessity."[18] We can imagine the reaction to that. In New Haven Ezra Stiles was dealing with dysentery, lack of funds, and lack of students at Yale, forcing him to close the college time and time again. He kept up morale in April 1781 by conferring an honorary degree of "Doctor of Laws" on George Washington.[19] And yet another Connecticut leader had fallen: General Israel Putnam had suffered a paralyzing stroke in December 1779, forcing him to remain at home.[20]

But George Washington still relied on Connecticut's citizens, with commissary Jeremiah Wadsworth in charge of supplies. An "affectionate nephew" of Arnold's surrogate mother, Jerusha Lathrop, Wadsworth had also made his fortune in the West Indies trade and had become a practiced supplier.[21] Nevertheless, the competent and practical Wadsworth, like Joseph Trumbull before him, found Congress's delays too frustrating, and resigned in December 1779. Washington and his troops were wintering at Morristown, New Jersey, and again in dire straits, holding only paper Continental money that had depreciated so far that no farmer would accept it. Worse, the most damaging blizzard of the century hit Jersey, with six-foot drifts burying the half-built log cabins of the troops.[22] Washington turned again to Governor Trumbull:

> The army has been near three months on a short allowance of bread; within a fortnight past almost perishing. They have been sometimes without bread, sometimes without meat; at no time with much of either, and often without both. They have borne their distress . . . with as much fortitude as human nature is capable of. . . . Without an immediate remedy this evil would soon become intolerable. . . . We are reduced to this alternative, either to let the army disband . . . or . . . to have recourse to a military impress. . . . Our situation is more than serious it is alarming.[23]

Trumbull allowed the messenger who brought the letter to rest that evening, and in the morning sent him back with a list of provisions that Washington could expect, including the days and hours the food would arrive. He kept this promise, and Washington continued to request him for supplies over the next two years.[24] When Rochambeau arrived in Newport, Washington told Trumbull that his force of six thousand Frenchmen would need to be provisioned. At first Trumbull thought this new task would be difficult, but because the French

From the "War Office" in Lebanon, formerly his country store, Gov. Jonathan Trumbull directed the Connecticut war effort, including shipments of provisions to the Continental army. Jonathan Trumbull, ed., Lebanon War Office *(Hartford, CT: Case, Lockwood, and Brainard, 1891).*

had actual gold to spend, it turned out to be easy. Connecticut farmers competed to send supplies to Newport in return for actual coin, and Rhode Island filled up with grain and meat. Jeremiah Wadsworth even came out of retirement and helped the commissary.[25] Some of the French, including a legion of over two hundred Polish, German, and Irish hussars, wintered at Lebanon in 1781, building ovens on the long village green. During the early part of the new year, Trumbull collected money for soldiers, wrote to Benjamin Franklin, and tried to find supplies from abroad.

Trumbull did this in the midst of an economic crash in 1778, with American paper currency declining so much in value by 1779 that many feared anarchy. First the tenuous national government, then the states, then the towns went bankrupt, with illicit trade and demoralization following.[26] Trumbull tried to manage this as best he could, telling Jeremiah Wadsworth, "I do not permit any flower or wheat to be carried out of this state—and very small quantities of any other grain; I am fully sensible of the present distress—I much fear the people very injuriously withold their wheat and other grain."[27] After May 1780 Trumbull had to perform these tricky jobs without his steadfast wife, Faith, who had suffered and died from a mysterious dropsy-like condition. At least by summer 1781 he had some good news: his son John had been released from British prison and was in Amsterdam.[28] The governor struggled forward, trying to comfort and control a state full of suffering farmers and merchants.

Those in the army were no better off. Benjamin Tallmadge supplemented his below living wage with the occasional spoil of war, coming into a "little hard money" from the sale of a confiscated Tory estate in Hartford. But to arm his dragoons he needed help and asked friends Thomas Mumford and Nathaniel Shaw to front him £1000 worth of goods. With the confidence of his Connecticut connections he was able to purchase boots, swords, and saddlery for his troops.[29] Without legal authority or the ability to levy taxes for nationwide organizations like the Continental army, these sorts of local associations were often the only way to get things done, but in a haphazard and uncertain way.

In March 1781, to remedy the issue created when the thirteen colonies formally broke away from Great Britain, steps to ratify the Articles of Confederation were finally taken. Under the new articles Arnold's neighbor Samuel Huntington continued his job as the president of Congress. He kept simple habits, as religious and practical as his friend Governor Trumbull. In Philadelphia, the General de Chastellux said, "We found [Huntington] in his cabinet, lighted by a single candle." His wife, Martha, was a "good-looking, lusty woman, but not young, [who] did the honors of the table — that is to say, helped everybody — without saying a word."[30] The faith the rest of the fractious delegates had in him must have been a relief after the betrayal of fellow Connecticutian Arnold and the character assassination of Silas Deane. The politics of the Congress at the time seemed to have had less to do with regional disputes than with personality. Huntington felt the heaviness of his responsibility, saying a year earlier to Trumbull, "I find one consolation very necessary in public life: that is, to believe or at least act as if I did fully believe there are many wise men who can judge better than myself on important subjects, and I have the happiness generally to unite in promoting their determinations, as far as duty requires in any sphere I am called to act in."[31] Unfortunately, Huntington fell ill and in July returned to Norwich.

By that time everyone was working to coordinate the most complicated American strategic attack since the disastrous invasion of Canada. Benjamin Tallmadge snuck over to Long Island again in April 1781 to gather intelligence. He then met Rochambeau in Newport and traveled back to Hartford "to procure horses and accoutrements for our regiment, and while there the van of the French army arrived, on their way to our camp."[32] On June 4 Washington received positive news about the French fleet in the Caribbean, saying, "I shall be happy to receive a confirmation of the agreeable intelligence brought by Capt. Ledyard."[33] On June 19 Rochambeau's army entered Connecticut, crossing the Norwich-Boston turnpike at Plainfield on "very bad roads," then continued northwest to Windham and then Hartford, reaching it on June 22.[34] Three days later the French army left Hartford, and Tallmadge followed. The combined forces met with General Washington to make plans for the campaign to Virginia and to make sure that attacking New York wasn't the right strategy instead.[35]

In fact, nearly no one knew what the plan actually was. Washington took pains "to deceive our own army" to make sure no one but the commanders knew the next move.[36] By the summer of 1781 Col. Jonathan Trumbull Jr. had moved from paymaster of the Northern Department onto Washington's staff. He wrote in the "Minutes of Occurrences," "The attack upon New York from its first contemplation had been deemed eventual and contingent.... [Washington] took his resolution to abandon his first object, and to meet and cooperate with the fleet in the Chesapeak [*sic*] with a view to reduce the British army in Virginia."[37] But Rochambeau claimed later that the object was always Virginia, and people on both sides were fooled by "fictitious communication." According to Rochambeau, Clinton may have been accidentally deceived by an intercepted letter from Rochambeau's assistant, the General de Chastellux, in which he bragged that Washington had convinced everyone to attack New York.[38] Washington also made a feint as if to attack Manhattan by way of Staten Island and kept everyone in the dark until the march toward Philadelphia and the south.[39] The subterfuge paid off, though the British in New York may have been more confused than fooled. General Clinton wrote to Cornwallis, "I cannot well ascertain Mr. Washington's real intentions by this move of his army. But it is possible he means for the present to suspend his offensive operations against this post and to take a defensive station at the old post of Morristown, from whence he may detach to the southward."[40]

Meanwhile, Benedict Arnold stewed in New York with his reputation as a military commander intact, though his fellow British officers talked about his "love of money, his ruling passion," which had "been very conspicuous in Virginia."[41] Despite the fact that his wife, Peggy, was almost ready to give birth to their second child, Arnold suggested an attack on Philadelphia to seize Congress, but Cornwallis and Clinton shot it down. Arnold fumed at the "inactivity" of Clinton in New York, arguing that Washington's forces were too weak. He "despair[ed] from the defect of the spirit of enterprise and indecision. He can get nothing done."[42]

Arnold's immediate family remained in Middletown for the moment, but his uncle, Oliver, long an invalid, died in 1781. Though Arnold had sent his uncle a small stipend in previous years, his two cousins now expressed their hatred for their turncoat relative, putting their patriotism above family loyalty. His former friends and neighbors in Connecticut were still talking about him too. In February William Ledyard wrote to Trumbull to report on the refugees in New London and mentioned that he had heard that "Arnold made his escape up the river [in Virginia] in a small vessel."[43] He remained a source of gossip and focus of their attention, if not of any new kidnapping plans.

The war of attrition on the long front of the Devil's Belt continued all through that summer. In July seven boats of Tories from Lloyd's Neck landed in Darien and snuck up on the local meetinghouse, surrounding and capturing Rev. Moses Mather and forty praying parishioners.[44] Governor Trumbull commissioned privateers to attack the fleet in New York and arranged an attack on Lloyd's Neck, but it went astray. Several small attacks were made by whaleboats, but none succeeded. Then, on July 31, Capt. Dudley Saltonstall of the *Minerva* captured the *Hannah*, a British cargo ship full of £80,000 worth of gunpowder and other goods bound for New York. After a long, dry season, it was the most valuable prize taken by a Connecticut privateer during the entire war, and the sailors rejoiced.[45]

On August 9 Governor Trumbull left for Danbury to be closer to the forces surrounding New York and within a day's ride of George Washington, who was headquartered at Dobbs Ferry. At this point it was still possible the Continental army would attack New York City, and Trumbull wanted to be near the action in case his firm leadership was needed. He took bodyguards with him, a necessary precaution, since according to him one man he met in Newtown "said he would kill me as quick as he would a Rattle Snake." On the eighteenth he was able to see his son Jonathan Jr., probably to give him advice before the campaign. Meanwhile, Washington's forces slowly and secretly moved across the Hudson and New Jersey.[46] By this time, even the most ignorant soldier knew what was happening. They were headed to reinforce Lafayette, who continued to play a dangerous game of cat and mouse with General Cornwallis in Virginia. The British still thought that their naval superiority would allow Cornwallis to escape at any moment, but they reckoned without the French.

The summer of 1781 had been full of ups and downs for William Ledyard, with his eldest daughter married in July and another daughter dying shortly after.[47] But his happiness surely increased when his wife, Anne, gave birth to their ninth child, a boy named Charles, on August 27, coincidentally the same day Benedict Arnold's wife gave birth to their second son, James. It was not a time for thinking about combat. The war had moved south and the Connecticut coast had not been attacked in force for two years. A few days later, on the final day of August, a British excursion landed in West Haven, captured sixteen men, and stole horses and cows.[48] But these sorts of attacks had little effect on morale. Most left behind in New England did not know what was happening with Washington's army yet, though Ledyard was one of the few who had intelligence about the French fleet in the Caribbean. He had certainly been thankful when the first French fleet had taken Newport the previous year. The pressure had been relieved from a flanking attack on Connecticut, and now that Rochambeau had marched west, Rhode Island was a much more likely target for renewed British incursions.

On August 29 Washington and Rochambeau met nearly two hundred miles to the west in Princeton, New Jersey. They rode together to Philadelphia and were "received by crowds of people with shouts and acclamations. All wonder at the design of this visit."[49] British spies in the city frantically tried to get word to General Clinton in New York, who was still in the dark about Washington's plans. Clinton's own plans were confusing, to say the least, especially his order to General Cornwallis to establish a fortified base. Despite advice to the contrary, Cornwallis had done so, bringing all the British troops onto the narrow York peninsula, expecting that the British navy could supply and rescue him at any moment. Clinton had also asked Cornwallis to send any troops he could spare to New York, in case Washington and Rochambeau attacked. Even when it became clear that Washington's army had left for the south, Clinton dithered, though he knew the French fleet was coming. Then, sometime during the last days of August someone suggested an attack on Connecticut to "distract" Washington from his march.[50]

Finally Arnold's wish for action had been answered. On September 1 Frederick Mackenzie noted, "An Expedition is immediately to go against New London under the Command of Arnold, to destroy some shipping, and a quantity of Stores there. It is a remarkable place for Privateers." The decision was a strange one, even discounting the fact that Arnold's son was only five days old. First, there were a number of other targets that made more strategic sense, either for the long-term war or the short-term distraction of Washington's army. Second, Arnold was no stranger to the violence and chaos of military assaults, and yet he asked for the mission to a place where people he knew would likely be, where he ran a serious risk of killing or ordering the killing of old friends or acquaintances. Furthermore, his sister and two of his sons were still living as potential hostages in Middletown. Either he was willing to sacrifice them to the possible vengeance of the Americans to establish his new allegiance, or he trusted the essential humanity of the people of Connecticut even while he terrorized them.

Even more strangely, by the following day of September 2 the British had figured out that the American army "intend turning their utmost force against Lord Cornwallis's Army."[51] Yet neither General Clinton nor Arnold himself decided to change the mission, to better use the two dozen ships and two thousand troops to try to head off the impending catastrophe. The mission continued, mustering in the western reaches of the Sound. Two days later, on September 4, Ledyard wrote to Trumbull about the capture of two provisions ships and news that a large fleet of fifty sailed off the capes of New Jersey and Maryland.[52] Spy Daniel Bissell of Windsor had just snuck into New York pretending to be a deserter and enlisted as a supply sergeant under Arnold. When the expedition was announced, Bissell frantically tried to get the information back to the Americans but could not get word out.

Then, on September 5, another American spy named David Gray appeared in New London and told Ledyard that Arnold was coming and that at last report he was in Huntington harbor with a large navy, intending to attack New London. Ledyard knew Gray, having talked with him the year before about a net of Tory spies that reached from Canada to Connecticut. Now Gray stopped again with more immediate news.[53] Though it was late in the evening, why not call the militias from surrounding towns as soon as this news arrived? It may be that they had cried wolf too often and feared to do it again. At any rate, if Gray's information was acted on, it was only in limited ways. Gray was also too late to stop the overworked Nathaniel Shaw, who had taken a small hunting party out for a little midweek sport, heading east along the coast, searching for ducks.

The same day Trumbull received a letter from George Washington that contained troubling news. He instantly convened his council and reported that "the movements and designs of the enemy in New York" led many to believe there would be a "hostile attack upon or invasion of this State." They began planning defense measures, ordering the militia to be reviewed and readied, with "detachments to be sent to the seacoasts, and valuable effects there deposited to be removed to interior parts."[54] At the same time, riding south of Philadelphia, Washington received the news that the French fleet had arrived in the Chesapeake, and he rode back to "rejoice" with Rochambeau.[55]

On the morning of Thursday, September 6, Washington and his secretary, Jonathan Trumbull Jr., ate breakfast at Christiana Bridge in Delaware, while at Hartford Governor Trumbull received a report of the enemy skirmishing off of West Haven, throwing the city into "alarm."[56] General Clinton wrote Cornwallis from New York City, telling him to expect reinforcements, even though he knew that the substantial force under Arnold was heading in the wrong direction. This hopeful but terribly flawed order may have stalled Cornwallis, who was being urged by his officers to escape the trap against the weaker American force. The commander of that force, Lafayette, was celebrating his twenty-fourth birthday nearby.

There were no celebrations in New London County that morning. Arnold had anchored a fleet that included the *Lively*, *Amphion*, *Recovery*, and *Beaumont* on the Long Island side of the Sound at two in the afternoon of September 5, and he waited until dark before moving toward the harbor at one in the morning. The wind shifted, and they struggled to sail in. But by then the British ships had been spotted. Rufus Avery was on duty at Fort Griswold, and at three o'clock, when the first hints of daylight cracked in the east, he saw the fleet past the lighthouse, thirty-two ships by his count, and immediately sent for Capt. William Latham. The captain rode up to the fort from his home in Groton, saw the fleet, and sent messages across the harbor to Ledyard, who was spending the night in New London. Latham and Avery loaded two large cannons and fired them off. But as they gave the alarm, Benedict Arnold, knowing the signal, fired another from one of his ships. Three cannons shot meant good news or a prize, and many people turned over and went back to sleep.[57]

William Ledyard, however, did not. On receiving the message, he moved immediately, sending expresses to both forts, to all the militia captains, and north to Norwich and Lebanon. As Rufus Avery said, though, "few came: their excuse was, that it was but a false alarm, or for some trifling alarm."[58] Luckily, some immediately believed the news. Fourteen miles away in Preston, Dr. Joshua Downer and his son, Avery, heard the shots and, after some confusion, saw the smoke from New London. They mounted their horses and rode for the town.[59] Walter Buddington woke and told his wife that he had a dream of a man lying across their garden wall, and there would be "bloody work" to do that day.[60] Stephen Hempstead jumped out of bed and ran to Fort Trumbull, just south of the Shaw house. Hempstead's cousin John heard the signal from his bed and "turn'd out," asking his wife to "git Breakfast." He climbed Prospect Hill and saw the fleet "in a line acrost" the harbor and returned home to eat a quick meal. Telling his son to run into town and help his grandmother flee, he took his musket and cartridge box and rode toward town. His wife called out and he turned around, asking what she wanted. "Don't let me hear that you are shot in the back," she told him.[61]

Ledyard must have longed for the help of his friend Nathaniel Shaw. But Shaw floated helplessly a few miles to the east between Fishers Island and the mainland in his duck hunting boats, watching in frustration as the daunting fleet blocked his way home. Trapped by circumstance, he and his hunting friends slipped into a creek mouth east of Groton to wait out the attack. His leadership would be missed, and

Nathaniel Shaw's impressive stone mansion served as Connecticut's Naval Office during the Revolution and survived Arnold's burning expedition. Pre-1923 postcard. Courtesy of the author.

Ledyard had to make the best of a bad situation.[62] Minutes counted now, as the first gunshots cracked on the southern beaches.

Ledyard ordered storekeeper John Holt to ferry nine hundred pounds of gunpowder and twenty-four pounds of pickled beef across the harbor to the fort, preparing for a long siege. Ledyard also tried to save as many ships and boats as he could, finding many sailors willing to escape upriver with them, but few willing to come with him to the fort. In one of the barges, he sent his wife and newborn child. Then, after vainly trying to get more of the frightened townspeople to come with him to defend Fort Griswold, he stepped off the New London dock into a small ferry to cross the harbor to Groton, just out of range of the British warship guns. As he left, he said, according to those who witnessed it, "If I must lose honor or life today you who know me best can tell which it will be."[63]

THE STREETS OF New London pulsed with fear. Men loaded their muskets and flintlocks, rushing this way and that, leaderless. Pale-faced women dragged bags and pillowcases full of valuables or drove their livestock before them. Others, holding their children in their arms, ran for the edge of town, forgetting food or silver in their rush to escape. Mattresses and clothing draped over horses and socks full of money and home deeds draped over shoulders. Those with carts frantically filled them with furniture, glancing over their shoulders toward the south. Family dogs wandered through the chaos, howling and trembling. All sought the quickest roads out of town, and most fled north along the Norwich road.[1]

Reliable John Hempsted sent his horse north with his servant, and on his way to muster he was joined by two other captains. The three stopped at the house of Col. Joseph Harris. With Nathaniel Shaw absent and Ledyard across the river, Harris was the chief remaining officer. Unfortunately, he was holding a petty grudge for being recently censured and refused to stir. Hempsted continued to the shoreline by the lighthouse, where forty other armed New Londoners stared out at redcoats clambering down the sides of warships into the landing crafts. Hempsted saw "one man drest in red," possibly Arnold himself, standing in the stern of a boat, brandishing a sword and calling, "God dam you, pull away!" As the boats started for shore, the British warships *Association* and *Colonel Martin* fired sprays of grapeshot from their cannons to clear the beach.[2]

A few miles north fourteen-year-old Jonathan Brooks mounted the family horse behind his father, while his seven- and five-year-old brothers drove the family cow out of town. His father intended that Jonathan would bring the horse back to the house and protect both from burning or plunder, treating whatever soldiers arrived "civilly." They rode down to the lighthouse south of town but found the British landing craft scraping the beach, "so near in, that we could see the soldiers plainly, and hear them converse." The warships continued an artillery barrage to clear the beaches and nearby areas of any American skirmishers, and landing soldiers began to fire their muskets. Brooks and his father fled back over the low hills to the west and promptly got stuck in a swamp.[3]

At ten in the morning Benedict Arnold stepped onto the sandy beach, along with the Thirty-Eighth Regiment, the so-called Loyal Americans, the American Legion Refugees, and sixty sharpshooting German mercenaries called Yagers, who swiftly cleared the immediate area of New London militia. Arnold was hours later than he wanted to be. But with his usual decisiveness, he put his men into order and marched them off the beach up Town Hill Road toward New London. John Hempsted and the others fell back, "exchangen shot." By eleven Arnold had approached within a half mile of Fort Trumbull. He sent four companies of the Thirty-Eighth Regiment to attack it.[4] He didn't need that many; only twenty-three men had assembled at the fort under Capt. Adam Shapley, including Stephen Hempstead and a number of his other relatives. As Arnold's force marched up the road from the south, the tiny garrison at the fort knew they were doomed. They fired a round of grapeshot that killed four or five redcoats and then spiked their cannons and piled into three small boats to cross the harbor. Arnold's advance force reached the landside fortifications and shot at the retreating men, but all missed. Unfortunately, one of the boats was too close to the shore, and the redcoats splashed into the water and captured it at bayonet point. The escaping Shapley and Hempstead rowed across the harbor toward Groton Heights, just out of range of the ships at the harbor mouth.[5]

Back in town at the crossroads Jonathan Brooks met one hundred armed volunteers under Capt. Nathaniel Saltonstall, a cousin of Silas Deane's wife. The useless Colonel Harris rode up and told the men assembled, "You must excuse me, gentlemen, as I have a violent sick headache this morning and can hardly sit on my horse." This enraged the gathering so much that a few almost shot him as he rode away. The solid columns of British soldiers could be seen on the road now, and though the men wanted to fight "at any odds," Saltonstall decided to harass the soldiers instead of directly confronting them, being outnumbered almost ten to one. He divided his company into two, using the stone walls along the sides of the dusty cart path for shelter.[6] They began a running firefight into town, carrying away their wounded, such as Samuel Hempsted, shot in the thigh.[7]

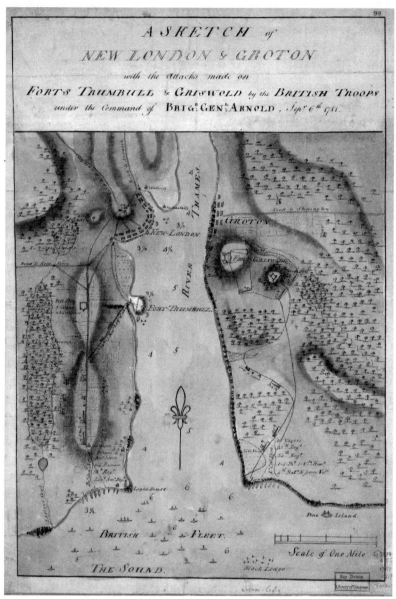

This contemporary sketch by Loyalist Daniel Lyman shows the routes of British attack on both sides of New London harbor. A Sketch of New London and Groton with the Attacks Made on Forts Trumbull and Griswold by the British Troops under the Command of Brigr. Genl. Arnold, Sept. 6th. 1781, *Geography and Maps Division, Library of Congress.*

Arnold's main force marched up the road toward the redoubt on town hill "vulgarly called Fort Nonsense," under occasional fire from Captain Saltonstall's men. The retreating John Hempsted was caught between the cannon shot of the fort and the British. He and his soldiers retreated crossways around the fort, where he saw his cousin William at the door to his house, drinking a case of Holland gin with other officers, including Saltonstall. John asked if William was going to leave the gin for the British. To save it they carried it to a potato patch and hid it among the weeds before heading back to work.[8] Little Jonathan Brooks, sent home by his father, found himself instead at Fort Nonsense, really just a small barricade on the hill to the southwest of the town. He climbed a sycamore and saw the redcoats dragging their cannons toward town. He ran again, encountering "a great booby of a boy whom I knew," crying from being thrown by his horse. He helped the weeping boy and then rode home, telling all who he passed that the enemy was close by.[9] He was just in time, because Arnold's men surrounded the fort.

John Hempsted hid in a corn field nearby and watched a British banner waving above the stalks until the soldiers were only six rods away behind a stone wall. Hempsted fired, hastily reloaded, and fired again into a huddle of soldiers, until "two men with grene cotes and long feathers," German Yagers no doubt, jumped over the wall to kill him. He fled, barely missed by their shots, one of which hit a "potato hill" by his feet as he fled toward an orchard. Arnold and his force took the small fort easily. Reaching a hill just to the north, Hempsted encountered a gathering of one hundred New London volunteers, though many were unarmed. They did have two field cannons, which they fired at the marching redcoats when they appeared. But most people fled, while Hempsted and two other captains hid the cartridges and tried to spike the guns. Forced to flee again, Hempsted decided he would retreat to his house, where he could possibly save the books and papers his father had left him when he died.[10]

Meanwhile, Jonathan Brooks had also returned home, where his mother gave him a sack of papers to take out of town. He had not gone far when he "heard the musketry going crack crack, on the whole westerly side of the town." He rode to the head of the cove near the wharves and straight into a huge crowd of women and children slowly dragging their goods out of town. "They will be among you within five minutes if you delay," he told them, and they threw away their sacks and ran. At the corner of Post Hill, northwest of the commercial district, bullets whizzed over Brooks's head just as he cleared the edge of town.[11]

The men shooting at him were soldiers under Lt. Col. Joshua Upham of the New Jersey Loyalists, who had been ordered to the hill north of the church, "where the rebels had collected, and which they seemed resolved to hold." Upham took the hill with only one man killed and one wounded" and remained there, under a "constant fire" from neighboring hillsides, as well as from across the bay, though at that distance accuracy with smoothbore muskets must have been impossible.[12] Five hundred men gathered three miles north at Quaker Hill, a small rise at the next cove in the harbor, though many were without weapons. One officer rode up and asked, "why the Devel don't you go down and meet the enemy?" But the men, scared and poorly armed, would not.[13]

The two forts taken, Arnold marched in full force toward the center of New London. At the edge of town he passed Nathaniel Shaw's house, with the captured *Hannah* drifting at the end of Shaw's dock. Arnold burned it to the water, and then his soldiers set fire to the large stone mansion. In addition to the main stone house, a large wooden structure had been built on the north side, and served as Shaw's office and store-house. Arnold's men set fire to this part of the house, and though Lucretia Shaw and the servants had rescued many books and papers, the chest containing Connecticut's naval office papers went up.[14] After Hempsted stopped home and hid his father's papers in the swamp, he returned to town and saw the roof of "Mr. Shaw's stone house" on fire.[15] Luckily, a neighbor had hidden in his own home, and after the soldiers marched away, he snuck into the mansion and "finding a pipe of vinegar in the garret, he knocked in the head, and dipping from this fountain poured the convenient liquid from the scuttle down the roof till the fire was subdued."[16]

Arnold and Upham had now effectively surrounded the city, and the troops moved into the center of town, starting fires as they went, "scouring the whole Point, destroying the battery, shipping, warehouses." They piled branches and paper against the wooden walls of buildings and lit them. Along Main Street many of the seventeenth-century family homesteads were lit, including the old Saltonstall house. Nathaniel Saltonstall had not expected the entire town to be burned and left his home without many of the papers of the court of probate,

later mourning this additional "dismal misfortune."[17] Stephen Hempstead's house was destroyed, after his wife and children fled six miles
into the forests. Though Arnold would later claim that most houses
went up accidentally, the systematic nature of the burning made it
clearly intentional, as the troops moved up each street and fired houses
far from the wharves and warehouses. Whether Arnold ordered this
action or simply could not control his soldiers, those who want the
honor of command also get the blame when things go wrong. Credit
goes to honorable victory and also to devastation and massacre.

Nathaniel Shaw had brought the first fire engine to New London
from Philadelphia in 1767.[18] But there was no one to run it, and it
would not have done much good against a fire of this magnitude. A
few houses survived nevertheless. The "widow's row" was spared, along
with individual houses here and there. The daughter of Guy Richards
was lying ill in her home, and an officer allowed her to stay and spared
the house. Stephen Hempstead's sister-in-law had been preparing the
midday meal with her young children, but when they saw the British
advancing, they fled. When they returned to the house it was not
burned but the dinner had been eaten completely. She conjectured
that their enjoyment of her cooking saved her house.[19]

She was one of the lucky ones. The British and German soldiers
threatened to burn some women and children inside their houses if
they did not leave, though in some cases seem to have accepted money
for leaving property alone. There were the usual plundering raids,
though Arnold's orders had supposedly forbidden them, and not
only the houses of the rich suffered. Many poor fishermen who lived
near the harbor mouth found their all the furniture stolen from their
houses.[20] One German mercenary captured near the end of the battle
was found to be carrying in his pack "3 small pieces Holland, a small
piece of scarlet broadcloth, a common prayer book, a checked linnen
handkerchief, a comb and a pair of scissors" as well as "sundry articles
of plate and jewelry" and an "American Ensign." And of course fatal
mistakes happened regardless of intention. Another old man had hidden himself in his garden and was standing in the bushes leaning on
a cane when a redcoat, probably thinking he was an American soldier,
shot him dead.[21]

Not all the invaders behaved badly, and less rape occurred than in
some other battles during the war. The women who stayed in their

houses to protect them were apparently treated with respect, even if their houses were not. Officers stopped enlisted soldiers from plundering on several occasions. One anecdote speaks of a woman who stayed with her aged, infirm father, dragging him into the garden when she became afraid that her house would be burned. An officer watched over her and made sure she would not be harmed.[22]

Abigail Hinman had stayed in her house, anxious about her husband's safety. She had previously lived in Norwich and was "well-acquainted with Arnold, as he had often dined at her house, and had been a friend of her husband." From her doorway she watched the British arrive in town, and saw Arnold ride up. He saluted her and told her that he would spare her house. She lied and told him that several of her neighbors' houses were also owned by her husband. Then, while Arnold supervised the battle, Hinman watched from her roof, becoming angrier and angrier. She clambered down and found a musket in a closet, pointing it through a window at her former friend and pulling the trigger. Unfortunately, it misfired and Arnold heard the loud snap, turning and asking her what the noise was. "With great presence of mind," she dropped the musket below the window frame and told him, "it was the breaking of a chair."[23]

Meanwhile, at a farm outside town, a ravenous Jonathan Brooks gathered peaches while waiting for his brothers and mother. Finally his mother appeared and became alarmed when she found that his little brothers were missing. "Get up the horse and look for them; go here, go there, go everywhere," she said breathlessly. They thought perhaps the small boys could not drive the cow properly and had returned to town, to "be burnt in the house." Brooks rushed to Quaker Hill along the Norwich road and encountered the incoming Norwich militia under Col. Zabdiel Rogers, now taking charge of the huge crowd of sullen New Londoners. Brooks tried to turn his horse for town, but they grabbed him off his horse, telling him he must not go into town. But when Rogers decided to ride to a nearby hill to scout the enemy's position, he allowed Brooks to tag along. While the men were busy, the dutiful Brooks urged his horse into the north end of New London.[24]

By the time Brooks made it back into town, the center was entirely consumed in flame, including the Episcopal church, the jail, and the courthouse. In fact most of the town could not be seen, "owing to

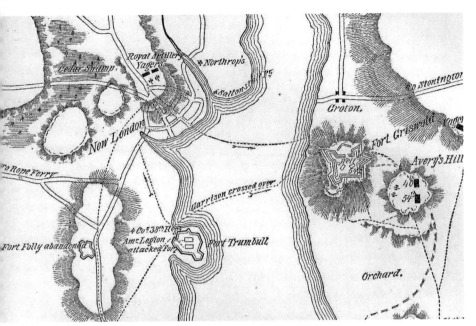

This detail from Col. Henry Carrington's map of Arnold's attack clearly shows the action of September 6, 1781, including the attacks on Fort Folly (Nonsense), Fort Trumbull, New London, and Fort Griswold. Henry Carrington, Battles of the American Revolution *(New York: Barnes, 1876), University of Bridgeport Archives.*

the density of the smoke." He did see a store explode, throwing smoke and fragments, "which fell around [him] in every direction." He carefully rode home and discovered his little brothers not there. Near the printing office he found a British soldier lying on his back, drunk, and grabbed his gun and threw it over a fence. He rode back out of town, not knowing that his father was with other militia men in the midst of the smoke-filled parade, trying to stop the fire. Other than the drunken solider, he had seen nothing alive, "except one singed cat, that ran across the street when the store blew [up]."[25]

Some of the less savory townspeople, either Loyalists or criminals, had looted the storehouse that contained the *Hannah*'s prizes.[26] Others helped the enemy openly. Thomas Fitch was caught trying to drive a flock of sheep to the British ships and was held in a house at bayonet point.[27] A few of Arnold's old friends "had held secret intercourse with him and officiated as counselors and guides in this expedition." But the soldiers under Arnold did not spare the houses of their supporters, knowing that this would only bring down more severe revenge from the Revolutionaries. Arnold dined at the house of an old friend on Bank Street, either James Tilley or Jeremiah Miller, "but even before they rose from the table the building was in flames over them."[28] The Loyalist legion accompanying the expedition included Capt. Nathan Frink of Pomfret, who acted as an aide to Arnold and a guide for the British soldiers, having visited New London many times to see his sister Lucy. This relationship did not stop him from burning out her friends and neighbors.[29]

Twelve American ships did not make it out of the harbor in time and were burned, along with thirty-seven storehouses on the docks full of powder and foods from Europe and the West Indies. Fifty cannons, the battery, and the wharves were destroyed as well, and these military targets gave Arnold and the British all the excuse they needed. But the destruction was far greater than any military attack of the war. The printing office, the jail, the town mill, the customhouse, 18 shops, twenty barns, and 65 dwellings were all burned. "Hogsheads were knocked in; sugar and coffee lay in heaps; and rum and Irish butter, melted in the fire, trickled along the street and filled the gutters."[30] A total of 143 buildings were destroyed by flames on the west side of the harbor alone, leaving a precious few, like Nathan Hale's former schoolhouse.

While Zabdiel Rogers gathered the incoming militias, trying to find a plan of attack, attention turned to the swarms of refugees. The Miller family on the Norwich road opened their dairy and larder to feed the refugees, servants carrying "milk, cheese, and bread, or porringers of corn-beans" out to the people.[31] The Winthrop family, descendants of the founders of the city, gave "wine, coffey, tea, and chocolate for the sick and rum for the whole."[32] And one hundred women and children had gathered at John Hempsted's farmhouse when he returned from his day of sweat and blood.[33]

After Benedict Arnold had taken the center of the town with his troops and ordered its destruction, he limped up to the old church on Post Hill, which Lieutenant Colonel Upham had taken earlier in the day. Now, a few hours later, Arnold stood at the little cemetery near the grave of Nathaniel Shaw's father, just below the lip of the hill, where he was safe from gunshots from surrounding hills. With a little spyglass he watched the burning town below and looked across the harbor to the fort on the hill opposite, where battle had now been joined. The afternoon sun slanted from behind him, lighting up Groton Heights and the water, but the black haze from the burning town below obscured his view. But what he did see disturbed him.

> From information I received before and after landing I had reason to believe that Fort Griswold, on the Groton side, was very incomplete; and I was assured, (by friends to government) after my landing, that there were only 20 or 30 men in the fort, the inhabitants in general being on board their ships, and busy in saving their property. . . . On my gaining a height of ground in the rear of New London, from which I had a good prospect of Fort Griswold, I found it much more formidable than I expected.[34]

He also felt the favorable wind and saw many of the American ships escaping up the Thames, beyond the reach of his field cannons. He claimed later to have sent an order across the harbor to stop the attack, but this was probably another fabrication. Taking the fort was still necessary if he wanted the warships to pursue those escaping boats and to protect his men from cannon fire while they burned Groton. It was also necessary for a victory that he could report to his new superiors.[35] He stayed on the hill and watched as one of his childhood haunts burned to the ground. How many times had he been here on errands for his father or the Lathrops; how many times had he sailed into its harbor? And now, seeing it wreathed in flames, what was he thinking? He had seen other American towns under the torch, some that he defended and some that he destroyed. Could he see how much worse this was?

In fact, the column of smoke reached high into the heavens, and as the sun set, the blazing fires reflected off the clouds. Almost thirty miles north in the town of New Scotland, Arnold's elderly teacher Dr. James Cogswell, three decades after his pupil left his care, gathered his flock for a Thursday sermon, when all heard the far-off echo of cannons and saw a red glow in the southern sky. Parishioners ran out and grabbed their guns to head for the coast.[36] Closer by, the entire town of Norwich prepared for war, ready to follow the first wave of militia to New London or to defend their own town from destruction. Even small boys "besought their troubled mothers for leave to gird on the harness, and go where danger called." Help was on the way. But as one Norwich woman said many years later, "Too late for defence! Too late for vengeance!"[37]

The Battle of Groton Heights

WHILE Benedict Arnold burned New London, Lt. Col. Edmund Eyre and a strong force of British regulars landed on the east side of the bay and headed toward Groton Heights. Eyre had the Fortieth and Fifty-Fourth Regiments and the rest of the Yagers and artillery.[1] They met no resistance at the beach and cautiously marched up the low hills toward the fort. As they tramped north, they were shot at by William Ledyard's friend Joshua Baker and a few scouts who knew the area well. They did what they could to slow the enemy advance, but British sharpshooters forced them north to the forest. The landscape of cedar swamps and rocky hills did its own work, however: the Loyalist battalion of the Third New Jersey volunteers, which came in the second wave of boats and included the artillery, promptly got lost, "entangled among the ledges, copses, and ravines."[2]

In the backcountry to the north and east of Groton, Americans were still mustering for battle. Two men rode up to Capt. Hubbard Burrows at his farm and told him the alarm was real, and as he girded up to leave, his wife asked him, "When will you get back?" "Good-by. God knows!" he told her. The gigantic Amos Stanton, a captain in the Continental army, was home on furlough and ran to Fort Griswold, while John Starr, kicked out of Nova Scotia for supporting the Revolution, entered as a volunteer. Peter Richards, captain of the privateer *Hancock*, also came in as a volunteer, bringing with him every member of his crew. Capt. William Latham, who had fired the alarm cannon, brought his twelve-year-old son to help run ammunition from the magazine to the walls. His servant, Lambert, had taken the Latham family to a house deep in the woods and then ran back to the fort and joined his master.[3] Richard Winchester of Hartford, who had fought beside Benedict Arnold at Ridgefield, showed up as a volunteer. Two Native Americans showed up as well: Pequot Tom Wansuc and Mohegan Ben Uncas.[4]

William Ledyard had a difficult decision to make. Should they stay in the fort or, as Capt. Amos Stanton suggested, abandon the fort and attack the larger British force by skirmishing? If they left, the British warships could sail up the river, and Groton itself would certainly be lost. On the other hand, volunteers would continue gathering, and it was possible that they could build a sufficient force to give the redcoats real trouble. Supposedly 200 or 300 American militiamen were on their way. As they were considering, Stephen Hempstead arrived with the other soldiers who abandoned Fort Trumbull. They were received "with enthusiasm," considering their experience with cannons.[5]

Ledyard now had somewhere between 165 and 178 men, including many from his family, like his brother, Ebenezer; his nephews, Youngs Ledyard and Billy Seymour; and his servant Jordon Freeman. The extended Avery, Eldridge, Chester, and Perkins families showed up in force. Men brought their sons, like Lt. Parke Avery, accompanied by seventeen-year-old Thomas. But there were not enough experienced gunners for the twenty-two cannons and not enough prepared cartridges for them to use. Without those cartridges, a prolonged, step-by-step practice of dipping ladles into powder kegs and measuring each charge needed to take place. In a battle this was a job for only the most experienced gunners. With another 100 men and more ammunition for the cannons, Ledyard might have held out indefinitely. But instead he had to make do with children, untrained volunteers, and inexperienced militia. Nevertheless, he honorably but fatefully decided to hold the fort.

The British approached within a half mile and hunkered down in a forest to the south behind a rock ledge. Occasional shots from both sides sang through the air. Youngs Ledyard's half brother Andrew Billings arrived just as the gates shut and climbed into the fort on a rope thrown down to him, the last man to enter before the British surrounded them.[6] John Clark had crossed the harbor in a rowboat with a bag of musket cartridges and lugged them up the hill to the fort, but he reached the top just as the British came into view. They shot him just before he reached the gate.[7]

There was a long pause as a knot of British soldiers with a flag of truce advanced to within forty rods, where the Americans stopped them with a warning shot. Tension filled the air while the Americans hurriedly loaded guns and cannons and Ledyard called a council of war. They agreed to send three officers, who walked out to receive the standard terms: surrender the fort or face death by gun or bayonet. Another meeting was held. The garrison unanimously agreed that they

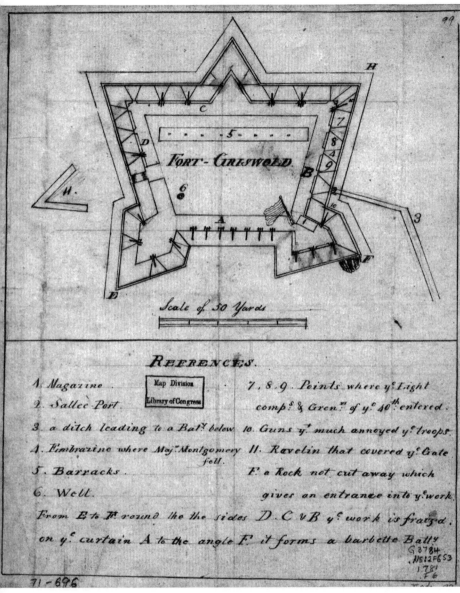

William Ledyard built the star-shaped Fort Griswold stone by stone, and he defended it to the death. Fort Griswold, 1781, Geography and Maps Division, Library of Congress.

couldn't hold out against such odds, but thinking reinforcements were on the way, they sent back a defiant no.[8]

By this time Arnold's soldiers on the other side of the river had brought cannons into Fort Trumbull in New London and began lobbing cannon shot across the Thames at Groton Heights. The cannonballs did not have enough force to reach the fort on the hill, though, and the Americans sent more effective volleys back across the harbor.[9] Lieutenant Colonel Eyre used this distraction to begin his assault. The British invaders split into two and probed for weak points. Eyre led the light infantry and grenadiers of the Fortieth and Fifty-Fourth Regiments against the northeast corner, and Maj. William Montgomery led the bulk of the force against the south and southwest flanks. As Eyre's force approached, a small group of defenders fired three-pound cannonballs at them from a small refuge three hundred yards from Fort Griswold. But after a few rounds, the defenders fled, some back to the larger fort and one to a nearby cornfield.[10]

Eyre took the small redoubt, marching his soldiers "in close order," pushed forward by their officers. The soldiers discharged their guns, but they were driven back by the spray of grapeshot from one of Ledyard's eighteen-pound cannons. Twenty redcoats fell, and the rest scattered. But now Montgomery's force raced up, and the general battle was joined with the fierce fire of grapeshot and musket fire, keeping off the attackers. For over a half hour's time the British tried again and failed, and a third time with the same result. Redcoats littered the rocky plateau, and the groans of the wounded filled the air, including the dying Eyre. Montgomery considered a prudent retreat. Taking shelter behind rocks, the British regulars sent occasional shots at the fort and suddenly noticed the flag on the southwest bastion down. Exultant, thinking that the Americans had surrendered, they charged a fourth time, not knowing that the flag's halyard had been cut by a stray bullet.[11]

The assault was fierce, as straining, sweaty men with powder-blacked hands grappled at the walls. Outnumbered six to one, the Americans dropped hot shot on the attackers in the ditch below, as enemy hands struggled to find purchase between the pickets. A colossal soldier named Samuel Edgecomb lifted huge eighteen-pound cannonballs and threw them into the press.[12] Then, like warriors of some earlier century, the defenders used long spears and sharp pikes to drive the British from the parapets. Captain Shapley and Jordon Freeman stabbed Major Montgomery as he clambered up, killing him.[13] Stephen Hempstead was stationed at gate firing a cannon when a musket ball grazed his skull above his right ear. His comrades tied a handkerchief to stop the gush of blood. A minute later a British soldier broke one of the log pickets, and Hempstead grabbed a pike. Another ball crashed into his arm, and he dropped the spear but picked it up and "cleared the breach" with the help of his comrades.[14]

A small boy named Daniel Williams ran with measures of powder from the magazine to the soldiers until a shot brought him down.[15] One of the crew of the *Hancock*, Christopher Latham, had been shot with a musket ball, which lodged in the bones of his forearm; he was knocked senseless. Andrew Baker fell dead, and his brother Joshua threw himself backward as a musket butt swung at his head and received a blow on his side that snapped all his ribs.[16] Parke Avery told his son Thomas to "do your duty!" and he replied "Never fear, father." A moment later he fell, and his father exclaimed, "'Tis a good cause" and kept fighting.[17]

The redcoats clambered up the southwest bastion and fought fiercely. Fewer than ten defenders had fallen, and fewer than twenty had been wounded, but William Ledyard gave the order to cease fire and surrender the fort. As the Americans threw down their weapons, the gate was forced and hundreds of British soldiers, mad with anger and pain, surged inside. Ledyard walked from the south side of the fort toward the onrush at the north gate, surrendering his sword to the enemy. Rufus Avery, stationed on the west side of the fort, ran to the south end near the barracks, watching his commander. He ducked enemy fire, and when he looked back, he saw Ledyard down.[18] The brave commander had been completely run through with a sword from his right side to his left.

Chaos broke out. Seeing Ledyard killed in the act of surrendering, his nephew Youngs and his companions charged the British and were cut down. Realizing that the whole garrison would be butchered, Capt. Amos Stanton yelled, "My God, must we die so!" and rushed the enemy with his musket, clubbing a huge swath of British soldiers off the west parapets before falling with many bullet and bayonet wounds. Rufus Hurlbut was stabbed through the chest. Stephen Hempstead was stabbed in the right hip above the joint, and Tom Wansuc was stabbed in the neck. Capt. Hubbard Burrows was shot through the head. Jordon Freeman, who had killed the British major with a pike, was slain, and John Holt, who had brought the powder and beef that morning, was killed. Already wounded, Billy Seymour was stabbed fourteen times with a bayonet.[19]

Whole families went down to death together: nine Averys, four Allens, and six Perkins.[20] Capt. Simeon Allyn and his brother and nephew were all killed. John Whittlesey was shot through the forehead, and his brother Stephen killed by a bayonet thrust, though both were punctured with multiple bayonet wounds apparently given after their deaths. Lambert Latham stood by his master's son, twelve-year-old William Latham, firing into the enemy ranks until he was slain, his body punctured thirty-three times with bayonets. Little William held up a hand to stop a bayonet; it sliced through his hand, and he fell. After seeing his two brothers killed in front of him, Charles Chester jumped onto the roof of the barracks, shooting one of the several redcoats who ran at him with bayonets. But by now the British had flooded the ground below, and an officer offered Chester protection if he surrendered.[21]

A few others escaped the slaughter. Upon being told by a redcoat that he would be killed, Rufus Avery "looked him very earnestly in the face and eyes, and asked for mercy."[22] John Deboll was wounded in the hand and then knocked down by a musket. Another soldier threatened to run him through while he begged for his life. Luckily, an officer stopped him, saying, "There, you damned rebel, I have saved your life." Wounded in the knee, Charles Eldredge begged for his life, buying it from a British soldier with a gold watch. Samuel Jaques killed a young British soldier in fierce hand-to-hand combat, leaped from the wall, and ran. Henry Mason jumped off the wall and somehow limped away despite a leg wound. Richard Winchester ran for the forest and escaped. But most who leaped off were caught and immediately run through with bayonets.[23]

Many of the wounded Americans had taken refuge in the ammunition magazine, and the British soldiers discharged their guns into them twice before an officer yelled, "Stop firing! You'll send us all to hell together!"[24] Perhaps this sobered up the attackers, because a drum called the British to order, and the slaughter stopped. Little William Latham, his father shot in the thigh and piled among the wounded, asked the British what they were going to do. "Let you run home to your mother, sonny, if you'll promise not to grow up a damned rebel," they answered.[25] They gathered the survivors on the parade ground at bayonet point. Eighty-three Americans were dead, and another thirty-six wounded, many mortally. The British lost only forty-eight men, but 135 suffered wounds, a quarter of the men who had attacked Groton Heights.[26]

Once everything was under control, the invaders began plundering both the dead and the wounded, leaving many literally naked on the field of battle, like the lifeless Capt. Samuel Allyn, robbed of his coat, sword, belt, knee, and shoe buckles. The surviving British officers buried the British dead in a ditch and left the Americans where they fell. They put their own considerable number of wounded in the shade and left the Americans in the sun on the west side of the barracks. Many of the wounded were in the process of dying, like Youngs Ledyard, gasping on the lap of Rufus Avery, asking for water. The guards told Avery and the others that they would all be put to death before nightfall. Avery suspected the water he was brought was poisoned, but the British soldiers were being only psychologically cruel.[27] A few of the officers were kinder, offering water and makeshift dressings for wounds.[28]

The invaders forced everyone down the hill toward town, putting those that could not walk into an ammunition cart, including Stephen Hempstead and Ebenezer Avery. As some of the British maneuvered it along the slope, they lost control and the cart careened over rocks and holes, finally crashing into a large apple tree stump.[29] The wounded men were gathered on the beach to be transported to the warships as prisoners, but Ebenezer Ledyard, himself wounded and his brother dead, convinced the British to parole them instead. Hempstead and the others were taken north along the water to the corner of Thames and Latham Streets and put onto the ground floor of the closest house, which happened to belong to one of the wounded, Ebenezer Avery, shot through the neck.

The New Jersey Loyalists who had gotten lost finally showed up and helped to burn the town and take prisoners back to the ships.[30] Rufus Avery and the other unwounded men were led to the harbor, where an officer told them, "Come, you rebels, go on board the boats." Avery "realized that I should have to leave my dear wife and my good neigh-

Stephen Hempstead was one of only a few who survived the Battle of Groton Heights, though he spent eleven harrowing months recovering from multiple wounds. George Dudley Seymour, Documentary Life of Nathan Hale, *University of Bridgeport Archives.*

bors and friends, and also my native land, and suffer with cold and hunger, as I was in the power of a cruel foe." But he put his faith in God and splashed into knee-deep water and tumbled into a rowboat. The British rowed the prisoners out to an armed sloop and shut them in the hot and smoky hold, stopping up the hatchway. Avery and the others could barely breathe and begged for mercy. They received some, being allowed to come onto the deck one or two at a time at bayonet point. But they did not get anything to eat for a full day, when they were given "a mess made of hogs' brains" that they "could hardly swallow."[31]

Meanwhile, the British forces proceeded northwest to the center of the small town of Groton and burned it to the ground, from the docks to the Heights. The houses of the Ledyards the Eldridges, and the Chesters were destroyed, along with the house and all the stores of Thomas Mumford, who was in Hartford meeting with Jonathan Trumbull at that very moment.[32] Some of the angrier soldiers also set fire to the Avery House, but luckily someone extinguished it before all the wounded men were burned alive. Once again Ebenezer Ledyard came to the rescue, making sure the house was under guard so that no one else would harass or kill the wounded.[33] Two burning towns now flanked the harbor, sending columns of black smoke into the late afternoon sky.

Uphill at the fort, the British spiked the cannons and took what musket ammunition they could carry. They set fuses and left trains of powder to the powder magazine, intending to blow up the entire fort, with all the American dead and a few wounded left inside it. Then they prepared hastily to board the ships themselves. The Avery House, full of American wounded, was one of the only left standing, and it began to receive gunfire from the departing soldiers on the decks of the warships, which had advanced up the harbor below the fort. The wounded were moved into a nearby barn.

Arnold did not order the warships to pursue the escaped American ships up the harbor toward his hometown of Norwich, perhaps fearing that the growing number of militia would make the British suffer heavily, as he had done himself at Ridgefield. Or worse, he could be captured. And if the Norwich militia captured him, he could probably not expect a quick and official hanging but something far worse. Luckily for him, Clinton's orders had not included Norwich; the troops had only two days provisions, and the ships carried few horses and no tents. So as afternoon lengthened on the New London side of the harbor, he moved his soldiers south away from the burning town. Zabdiel Rogers and the Norwich militia harassed them down to their boats, killing five and wounding twenty, including a German captain, who they took prisoner. A dozen of Rogers's soldiers were wounded and four were killed.[34] Other than the fatally wounded who lingered for hours or days before succumbing, they were the last to die.

The Battle of Groton Heights was the bloodiest battle of the entire war, with the highest percentage of soldiers participating killed. And almost all the Americans had been killed after the surrender. New London suffered the highest percentage of destruction of any American city. People would argue over the next century whether these shocking deeds were intentionally ordered or unplanned acts of rage on the part of the British regulars. Was Arnold himself watching from the hills responsible? In the way that all commanders are ultimately responsible, yes, and in one other way. He was responsible because he wanted that responsibility, wanted not just to be a political traitor but in military command of units that until recently had been his enemy. He asked for this command, and he asked to assault his homeland.

Between Arnold's attempted sale of West Point and his invasion of Connecticut, he wrote, "You have felt the torture in which we raised our arms against a Brother — God Incline the Guilty protractors of these unnatural dissentions, to resign their Ambition, and Cease from their Delusions, in Compassion to kindred blood."[35] The hypocrisy of this statement was never clearer than when he killed his fellow countrymen on September 6, 1781. And all of his contemporaries, British and American, knew it. A week afterward Arnold's former neighbor Jedediah Huntington said, "No instance of Conduct in the Enemy since the War has raised so general a resentment as that at N[ew] London. It is said that the Behaviour of Arnold is reprobated in N[ew] York."[36]

Any arguments we might make in calmer times should take into account the immediate reactions of these contemporaries, who felt the effects, who lived with the horror, and who properly assigned responsibility to the commander of the invading forces. Their anger did lead to exaggerations about Arnold's purposefully vengeful intentions, because that was a comforting idea to them. In reality, the situation was as more objective onlookers saw it: just another opportunity to prove his military skills to his new superiors.[37] Of course, the idea that he would be indifferent is much worse than anger or hatred. It can be more comforting to think someone hates you rather than you don't matter at all.

The smoke from the burning towns could now be seen as far away as Colchester and Lebanon, which Ledyard's messenger had reached that afternoon. Trumbull's son-in-law, the signer of the Declaration of Independence William Williams, jumped on his horse and rode twenty-three miles over rocky roads in only three hours. He arrived at the smoldering town of New London just as Arnold and the British were boarding their ships.[38] On the other side of the river Maj. Nathan Peters of Norwich was first to enter Fort Griswold. He found a trail of fire burning from the gate inside, halfway to the powder magazine. With his own hands he snuffed it out, five minutes before it would have "blown him and all those who immediately followed him into eternity."[39]

The widows followed him, trying to recognize their mutilated and mangled husbands. Fanny Ledyard, who fled from Long Island to avoid rape and served as a bridesmaid in her cousin's July wedding, crept up to the Avery barn where the wounded lay groaning in agony. On entering, she said she "walked ankle deep in blood." One of the "stiff, mangled, and wounded" men lying on the bare floor was Stephen Hempstead, bloodied beyond recognition, and she gave him a cup of hot chocolate.[40] Soon afterward, someone told her that her uncle was dead.

Remember New London

NATHANIEL SHAW returned the evening of September 6 to scenes of horror. Women stumbled around by candlelight, trying to identify their sons and husbands among the bodies piled under a huge elm tree, some so disfigured as to be unidentifiable. Widows were left without shelter or husband: Mary Allen, Lucy Whittlesey, Sarah Stedman, and many more. Anne Ledyard was left a widow with a ten-day-old son and four other small children, and all her husband's holdings destroyed.[1] Stephen Hempstead's wife searched for him in the barn, but he was so covered in gore that she did not recognize him and left to search among the dead, only finding out later that he was still alive, though barely.

All through the night and following day, Arnold's old acquaintance Dr. Philip Turner, along with Dr. Amos Prentiss and the father and son team Drs. Joshua and Avery Downers of Preston worked feverishly on the wounded. As they came in they encountered various injuries, dressing them as they moved closer to the fort, where they found the scene of tragedy at the Avery House. They treated Stephen Hempstead and saved his life, though he spent eleven months recovering.[2] They fixed Daniel Stanton's twenty bayonet slashes and bullet wound, Ebenezer Avery's neck wound, and a hole in sixteen-year-old Azel Woodworth's head. Parke Avery had been stabbed in the eye, exposing his brain, but the doctors somehow saved him. The wound in Edward Stanton's chest had exposed his heart "to the light," but he also lived.[3] And Dr. Turner amputated the leg of Billy Seymour, Colonel Ledyard's nephew, in an operation that saved his life.[4] But even these skilled doctors had their limits. John Starr, the Nova Scotian revolutionary, lived but had his right arm disabled for life. Joseph Moxley had been in the cart that rolled down the hill and died that night of a bayonet wound to the stomach.[5] In the morning the doctors finally had time to look at the dead; Dr. Prentiss saw William Ledyard and cried, "Oh my God, I cannot endure this!"[6]

When the British warships left the mouth of the harbor that morning, John Hempsted rowed across the harbor "to see the carnag which

Ebenezer Avery's house in Groton served as a hospital for the wounded; as long as he lived he would not let the bloodstains on the floorboards be cleaned. Courtesy of the author.

was Dredful to Behold." After he recrossed the Thames, he made his way to inspect the damage at Fort Nonsense, and his cousin William called to him from the nearby house. He wanted to offer John some of the gin they had hidden, which the British had not found. After a pull of the bottle together, they went to where John had hidden behind the wall near the fort and fired on the knot of British soldiers. He had hit at least two. "It was Evident as that there had been two hogs kild, by the blood and whare they draged them away through a feald of potatoes," he wrote, satisfied that he had at least accounted for some of the invaders.[7]

In the light of day Shaw and leaders from the surrounding settlements tried to sort out the damage, finding the two towns completely ruined. Zabdiel Rogers gave the bad news to another of Arnold's old business associates, Thomas Mumford, that "they have burnt your house and all your stores at Groton."[8] Fort Griswold suffered little other than spiked cannons, though the close call with the powder magazine gave everyone pause. The destruction of ammunition, wharfs, and the town itself left the harbor completely unprotected, though, making it possible for "any small party and one armed vessel to come and blow up the fort or make any other destruction."[9] The greatest problem was with "bereaved widows, fatherless children who had lost their all and let without the least sustenance, wandering in the streets."[10] When he arrived from Hartford, Thomas Mumford called it a "barbarous scene" and wrote that "the conduct of the enemy cannot be fully ascertained but from those that saw or felt the Bloody Tragedy, our wounded left behind are exercised with great pain the half of them are dangerously ill." His son-in-law, Peter Richards, lay among the dead.[11]

Governor Trumbull had returned to Hartford on August 25 and was alerted of the invasion at sunrise on September 7. He promptly ordered a troop of militia toward New London. On the eighth he received a full report of the tragedy and the same day received word that the French fleet had reached the Chesapeake.[12] Once he had the particulars, he wrote to his son, who was acting as secretary to George Washington, saying that "the sufferers are in amazing distress" but assured him "your Family, Friendly connections are well."[13] The governor included a letter to Washington, describing how "on the 6th inst. A Party under the command of that infamous Arnold made wanton destruction both of lives and property in New London and Groton." He gave the commander in chief a detailed account of the attack and of the property lost, and then added, "yet what is more to be regretted is the unhappy fate of that brave renowned officer Col. Ledyard and those brave men . . . who so gallantly fought and unhappily fell with him victims to British Cruelty."[14]

The rest of the Connecticut coastline was not out of danger yet. News of the burning reached Ezra Stiles in New Haven on September 7, and three days later he reported nervously, "Last Even[ing] the fleet seen off Killingworth. Alarm. Militia flocking into New Haven, & ordered in along the whole Sea Coast to Connect. From N. London to Stamfd." A day later he wrote that everyone feared that Yale's commencement "will be interrupted by the Enemy. . . . Arnold & his fleet returned in a scattering manner to Long Isld." By September 16 Stiles was still jumpy, receiving an "express" that on the fifteenth at sunset

Arnold's fleet was sailing east again, intending to strike "most probably New Haven or Newport." People in towns along the coast hid their goods and went to church to ease their apprehensions.[15]

Then on the seventeenth, at a quarter to two, the "Alarm Guns were fired," and the news that ships had anchored off West Haven reached Stiles. "I removed 8 Beds &c &c," he wrote hastily. But at daybreak, he realized only "3 or 4 small Vessels" had approached, landing a few small boats. These were driven away by the West Haven militia, and the next day 2,000 militia from the surrounding towns appeared.[16] Some newspapers, however, exaggerated this event, reporting that Benedict Arnold and his "banditti" attempted to land at New Haven.[17] The same day, September 17, a fleet was spotted off Stamford, and Captain Bulkley marched there with a brigade, telling Silas Deane's stepson, "the Burning Murdering poor Pittifull set of Dogs had weighed Anchor and made the best of their way to York." Bulkley's troop was kept in readiness to march to the seaside towns, but as he said, repeating news from a letter from the south, "I think Mr. Cornwallis will git the Thorough put taken out of his Eyes this heat. Should this be the case I think Mr. Arnold Burning expedition will be at an end."[18] Arnold was already in fact in British-controlled New York, but no one knew that and every random warship in the Sound became an occasion for terror.

In New York there were no victory celebrations. On September 9 one of the German mercenaries on Long Island said that Arnold "had to retreat with heavy losses and the wounded were now arriving here."[19] But the British officers were more worried about the news from the south that Bulkley had alluded to, hoping for a naval victory that would crush the French fleet, something they believed could end the rebellion. On the tenth the *Lively* came into Manhattan, and the people "imagined she came from Chesapeak [*sic*], and as an account of Events of the utmost importance is expected from thence, every one entertained the most sanguine hopes of success in that quarter." The same day they had news of Arnold, who had sheltered in Gardiner's Bay due to southern winds, and knew that he had been successful, though the Fifty-Fourth Regiment had "suffered much in Storming Fort Griswold."[20] On the twelfth Arnold arrived in Manhattan with his wounded soldiers, who were sent to the hospitals.[21]

With them came the news of the burning and massacre, though of course no one called it that among the British officers. They knew that they had done something appalling, though, and they worked hard to spin the event in the press. *Rivington's Royal Gazette* commended the British officers' "thirst for glory" at the "detestable nest of pirates" and declined to mention the dead, saying only that out of "250" [*sic*] defenders, 40 had been wounded and 70 taken prisoner.[22] General Clinton promptly blamed the victims, lamenting the "obstinacy" of the Griswold defenders; in fact, he thought the whole expedition "to annoy the enemy's coasts and endeavor to cause a diversion somewhere" had been a middling affair at best.[23] Clinton also exculpated Arnold, assuring "that he took every precaution in his power to prevent the destruction of the town, which is a misfortune that gives him much concern."[24] Arnold blamed the burning on a "change of wind" and reported that "eighty-five men were found dead in Fort Griswold, and sixty wounded, most of them mortally." Arnold's neat, professional handwriting was calm and clear and carefully neutral. He used the words "were found" as if his soldiers had just happened across the dead bodies, and he bragged that most of the officers on the "enemy" side were killed, including Colonel Ledyard.[25] He failed to mention, of course, that he knew Ledyard and had sailed with his brothers years earlier.

Meanwhile, the survivors were picking up the pieces. The New London newspaper, the *Connecticut Gazette*, astonishingly published an edition a few days later. Page 1 complained about the new taxes being levied, and then on page 3 the editor broke in, dating his comment September 10: "We had prepared our paper thus far for publication when at about daybreak on Thursday morning last twenty-four sail of the enemy's shipping appeared to the west." The editor went on to detail the attack, saying, "the neighborhood feels sensibly the loss of many deserving citizens, and tho' deceased can't but be highly indebted to them for their spirit and bravery in their exertions and manly opposition to the merciless enemies of our country in their last moments."[26] The *Norwich Packet* called Arnold a "parricide" and began the process of advertising lost property, including a "sorrel mare" taken on the road from New London. Of course, the owner was notified that he could have it back after "paying charges."[27] There were always people ready to take advantage of someone else's sorrow.

Much of the news focused on the wickedness of Arnold. The parishioners of New Scotland returned to Arnold's old teacher Reverend Cogswell with the news of New London in ashes and his former pupil, "abandoned of all good and to all evil."[28] But Ledyard's death also became a focal point for news about the attack, and almost everyone who recorded the event mentioned his bravery. Zabdiel Rogers told Trumbull in a hasty letter on the seventh that "Ledyard made a noble defence. Repuls'd the Enemy Two or Three times. But at last was oblidg'd to surrender the fort to superior force."[29] Ledyard's story quickly became exaggerated, with a final dialogue invented. A British officer supposedly asked, "Who commands here?" as he came in, and Ledyard replied, "I did, sir, but you do now." This was followed by the officer running him through with his own sword. This dialogue and the courteous way Ledyard surrendered in this account became great propaganda for the American press. The idea that he had died heroically regardless was not enough; he had to have died defending Griswold against the most dastardly, amoral villains. Since Arnold was not on this side of the river, then another officer would have to do. The butchery that had taken place was not enough, either, and it was heightened to an *intentional* butchery, ordered by Arnold or other officers.

The event in New London was soon transformed further into literature. One song used the popular Guy Fawkes Day tune, changing the lyrics about the sixteenth-century British terrorist attack into ones about the raid:

Don't you remember, the 6th of September,
When Arnold burnt the town,
He took the buildings one by one,
And burnt them to the ground,
And burnt them to the ground.

And here you see these crooked sticks,
For him to stand upon,
And when we take him down from them,
We'll burn him to the ground,
We'll burn him to the ground.

"Hark! my little bell goes chink! chink! chink!
Give me some money to buy me some drink.

We'll take him down and cut off his head,
And then we'll say the traitor is dead,
And burn him to the ground,
And burn him to the ground.

The remaining townspeople also tried to move the entire November holiday Guy Fawkes Day to September, reframing it in remembrance of the attack, and for several years the children of eastern Connecticut sang that song. Other towns throughout New England also hung effigies of Benedict Arnold instead of Guy Fawkes.[30] In Arnold's hometown of Norwich they sang a different song, supposedly composed by Oliver Arnold, Benedict's patriot cousin:

Born for a curse to virtue and mankind,
Earth's broadest realm ne'er knew so black a mind,
Night's sable veil your crimes can never hide,
Each one so great would glut historic tide.
Defunct, your cursed memory will live
In all the glare that infamy can give.
Curses of ages will attend your name,
Traitors alone will glory in your shame.

Almighty vengeance sternly waits to roll
Rivers of sulphur on your treacherous soul.
Nature looks shuddering back with conscious dread
On such a tarnished blot as she has made.
Let hell receive you riveted in chains,
Doomed to the hottest focus of its flames.[31]

In general, the people of Connecticut gave the event greater weight than the attacks on New Haven, Fairfield, and Danbury. Was it because Arnold commanded it? Because of the massacre at Groton Heights? Because of the quantity of property destroyed? Whatever the case, people talked about it in a way that they had not talked about the previous attacks.[32]

Jedediah Huntington urged revenge for the "barbarity of the enemy," saying, "I hope it will be in the power and will of the country to make the enemy feel the force of a just indignation."[33] And revenge was occasionally taken, though not on the people responsible. Two men who had served in the British Loyalist regiments were arrested in Philadelphia and found guilty of plotting to carry off the "secret journals of Congress" to the British in New York. They were questioned and revealed other names, but this did not help their case, and they were sentenced to death. When the first was hanged, the paper commented, "The enemy, who at this period seem equal to no exploits superior to robbing mails and stealing papers may thank the monster Benedict Arnold, their beloved friend, for the untimely death of this young man."[34] But there were no reprisals on random Loyalists or British prisoners, and no one stained their hands with the blood of Arnold's innocent children.

Some took more direct action. The day after the attack, a few privateers from New London who had escaped upriver promptly sailed out after the British ships. Unfortunately, this revenge plan went awry, and they were captured and clapped into irons in the infamous prison ship, *Jersey*.[35] The stalwart Benjamin Tallmadge was more successful. He snuck across the Sound with a picked squad of one hundred men, taking the garrison of another Long Island fort in the middle of the night, leaving several dead and wounded. "The recollection of Fort Griswold and Groton" was fresh, he said, and "occasioned a more severe treatment than they otherwise would have received." But he did not stoop so far, telling Governor Trumbull that "our treatment was very different from theirs." Tallmadge also did not lose one soldier on this raid.[36]

Depositions were given to assess responsibility for the New London disaster. One of the first things was to figure out what had been burned and what had been stolen and if any of it could be returned. The newspapers continued to list lost items, like a Bay horse, bedsheets, clothes, red silk handkerchiefs, and a new purple-and-white spotted gown "left in the hands of a young man who promised to bring it back."[37] Of course, there were many who lost things in the burning who did not have "friendship to the Independence of the United States." Shaw and the remaining town officials had to judge individually whether they should receive recompense.[38]

Eventually military responsibility was assessed in an official court-martial. A Hebron man testified that he saw a guard of militia soldiers stationed outside Daniel Latimer's house.[39] But Latimer was acquitted of wrongdoing, as were Zabdiel Rogers and several others. Only a few did not come out of the court-martial so well. Capt. John Morgan was suspended, Thomas Wheeler and John Williams were cashiered, and the infamous Joseph Harris, whose cowardice John Hempsted and Jonathan Brooks both witnessed, was judged "not suitably qualified for military service." It was less than he deserved, and his position as a "worthy member of society" may have saved him from the noose.[40]

The people of New London and Groton were understandably terrified, especially after a few privateers had successfully brought in even more prizes, and the citizens wrote to Governor Trumbull, asking for 150 men for Fort Griswold: "We observe further it is our opinion if the late worthy Col. Ledyard whom we sincerely lament had only fifty good men in the fort under his absolute command, he with them might have impressed and compelled into its defense two or three hundred seaman and others. . . . He was as a man without hands, and could get none into the fort only by persuasion." They also urged Trumbull to make stricter laws regarding behavior during attacks, to make it a crime to flee rather than muster for defense, one that was severely punished.[41]

Nathaniel Shaw's wife and house had survived, but little else in town had. Some of his best friends were dead, and his command was effectively over, with no ships or wharves or town from which to run his business or the war. There was one thing he could do: save the prisoners taken by Arnold. He knew the conditions Americans were subjected to in New York prisons, having supervised exchanges for years. And he was right; even after a few days the lack of food and water had made the new prisoners from New London and Groton desperate. Rufus Avery reported that some talked of breaking out. This talk got back to the British, who brought them onto deck one by one, their hands tied, dumped them over the side into rowboats, and took them to another ship to stand in the rain at bayonet point for two hours. Avery was sure they would all be shot. But after four more days without much to eat or drink, he was put on another ship until he was exchanged.[42]

Shaw and Ebenezer Ledyard were designated as "Flag Officers" "to negotiate the Liberation or Enlargement" of the prisoners taken by Arnold during the raid.[43] One can only imagine Ledyard's emotions during this endeavor. Shaw's private yacht, the *Queen of France*, had been one of the ships saved. Now under a flag of truce Shaw and Ledyard sailed it down the Devil's Belt to Whitestone, New York, to hand over prisoners from Norwich in exchange.[44] Everything was done in a polite and professional manner, and by September 20 many of those taken by Arnold had been returned. But possibly due to poor record keeping by the British, not everyone was released when Shaw made the trade. Walter Buddington spent almost a year on the *Jersey* prison ship and finally on his release had to walk home to Groton. On the way, a weakened and starving fellow prisoner died from eating an ordinary meal at a tavern.[45]

Those, like Avery, who did return to New London throughout the autumn had already suffered and remained "in a languid condition."[46] Ebenezer Ledyard spoke of their "shocking condition" as they returned, many naked and unconscious. When he returned, he also found that "some evil-disposed people" had robbed him and discovered that some of the Tories in town were gloating about the distress of his brother's widow and family. To have to come back from the prison ships to that was almost more than he could bear.[47] The prisoners were not just starving, though; they had already contracted disease in their short time in British prisons. Daniel Eldredge, whose brother had bought his life with a gold watch, was nearly dead of starvation and illness when they brought him back on December 3. His family gave him a bowl of "cider and suppawn" to drink, but the meal was apparently too much for a body on the edge of ruin, and he died.[48] Many others were taken to the Shaw Mansion, where Lucretia Shaw took care of them. Unfortunately, she contracted whatever disease they had and joined the ranks of the seriously ill.

Along with recovering prisoners, Governor Trumbull and the state also had to take up the fate of the war widows, a bureaucratic process that took years. Anne Ledyard begged Governor Trumbull and the assembly to pay William's wages and debts for work done on the fortifications, around £520, saying that she "humbly prays this honorable assembly to take her case with that of her unfortunate children into your wise and equitable consideration." They gave her the money, using the sale of confiscated Loyalist lands, but it took several years.[49] They also granted money to other widows from the two towns, though that took even longer.[50]

The requisition of those funds may have taken so long because money was still needed for the ongoing war. Trumbull had to balance the needs of everyone, using very limited resources. Obviously, the people of New London and Groton felt they were in the greatest need of military support and improved fortifications. Shaw and Mumford prepared a report on what needed to be done, though they pointed out that "an engineer will be of more service than either of us."[51] Others around the state urged Trumbull "to be prepared at all points [on the Connecticut coast] to receive the villains."[52] The network of suppliers in Connecticut served them well, even at this late date, but getting all the flour, meat, and cooking essentials in a wartime economy was difficult. Trumbull did his best: requisitioning new fortifications, acquiring seven hundred French muskets, and trying to get the French fleet to guard the coast.[53]

But the French fleet was busy. Washington and Rochambeau's army was on the road between Philadelphia and Baltimore at the same time Arnold attacked New London, and the soldiers had that day received fantastic news:

> [The French Admiral] de Grasse had anchored in the Chesapeake Bay with 28 ships of the line, which had put 3000 troops ashore under the command of the Marquis de Saint-Simon. These had already joined forces with the Marquis de La Fayette, who was occupying a position designed to prevent Lord Cornwallis from retreating by land, while the French squadron blockaded him by sea. There was great joy throughout the camp.[54]

Many speculated that Cornwallis was trapped, and that probable victory was at hand. They were more right than they knew. Admiral de Grasse had in fact arrived off the Chesapeake on August 15, and in British New York City, General Clinton had already received the information and acted on it, sending his fleet from New York to attack the French. When they reached the Virginia capes, they were met on September 5 by de Grasse, who outgunned and outmaneuvered them. By the next day it was clear that the French had gotten the best of the action, and after a few days the British fleet slunk back north. The defeated British admiral could have probably used the ships under Arnold in Long Island Sound.[55]

During the previous month the British had fortified the York peninsula in Virginia, while the Marquis de Lafayette watched and waited, skirmishing occasionally. Cornwallis seemed unconcerned about Lafayette's movements, since his own troops far outnumbered the Frenchman's. All that had changed when Admiral de Grasse arrived, reinforced Lafayette, and surrounded the peninsula. Washington and Rochambeau rode south from Mount Vernon on September 14. They joined Lafayette and by the eighteenth of September Washington and Rochambeau came on board the flagship of de Grasse. Along with his troops and fleet, de Grasse brought a gift of 12,000 francs from the Spanish admiral, Don Solano, without which the Americans would not have been able to pay for their supplies. The allied French and American forces gathered at Williamsburg and marched toward Yorktown on September 27.[56]

In New York City fears and rumors about the naval encounter proliferated. General Clinton sent an "alarming report" to England as early as September 7 about the situation in Virginia.[57] By the thirteenth British officer Frederick Mackenzie wrote shrewdly, "we certainly are now at the most critical period of the war," noting that all depended on the battle between the fleets, and on Cornwallis's "firmness." Two days later he repeated the concerns of "all ranks of people" and said, "Should our fleet be defeated the loss of the whole army under Lord Cornwallis is much to be dreaded, the consequence of which would be that we could no longer attempt to prosecute the war against the Rebels, and must necessarily admit their claim of Independence." When the fleet returned on September 20, defeated, everyone knew that Cornwallis and the British in Virginia were doomed.[58] The attack on Connecticut now seemed like a grave tactical error.[59]

In contrast, the news of the French fleet's victory off the capes sent Americans into raptures. Thomas Mumford prophetically "hope[d] soon to hear of the capture of Cornwallis and his army at Virginia, as the British fleet has returned to New York with loss. They give up that army."[60] By September 30 Washington and Rochambeau had finally been informed of Arnold's deadly expedition to New London. But "this diversion tended in no way to impede our operations."[61] Through a series of small battles and maneuvers they pushed Cornwallis farther and farther back into the barricades and defenses. The increasingly desperate British army apparently attempted germ warfare by spreading smallpox, throwing the bodies of dead animals and slaves into the wells. Trenches were dug, and big cannons rolled up into makeshift batteries. On the afternoon of October 8, Washington and his men opened fire. By the tenth the noise was deafening, and the British retorts became fewer and fewer.[62]

By October 14 British dead were piling up, and that evening Washington put Lafayette in charge of taking two large redoubts to the east of Cornwallis's main defenses. The young Alexander Hamilton led one of the assaults with four hundred light infantry that included five companies from Connecticut.[63] As the men left the lines, they heard Lafayette sternly whisper, "Remember New London." They took the redoubts at bayonet point, but as the British soldiers pled for mercy, the Americans did not retaliate for Arnold's actions but spared every soldier who surrendered.[64]

In New York the British were in chaos. Frederick Mackenzie gamed out an attack on New Jersey and spent his time worrying about refitting the fleet for a second attack on the French. But as early as October 1 he wrote, "It appears very doubtful that the Navy will after all attempt, or undertake any thing towards the relief of Lord Cornwallis." He put the blame on the ship captains who squabbled among themselves and wasted time.[65] The *Continental Journal* reported on this failure in happy astonishment two weeks later: "Sir Henry Clinton remains quiet in New York notwithstanding the imminent danger hanging over the head of his colleague in wickedness Lord Cornwallis."[66]

With his characteristic ambition, Arnold himself was less idle. On October 17 the Americans in Norwich heard that "a number of light horse had joined the Traitor Arnold at White Stone" on Long Island and they feared another attack on Connecticut.[67] By October 22 the British had apparently changed the plan to send Arnold up the Hudson Valley with a "small Corps" and use a pincer movement from Canada to attempt again the physical separation of New England that had failed, in part due to Arnold's own exertions, years earlier.[68] At the same time, Clinton sent twenty-five warships and seven thousand troops as a last ditch effort to relieve Cornwallis. But they were already too late. Cornwallis had surrendered on October 19.

In the surrender terms Washington avoided the bloody retribution that some called for the Loyalists and deserters who had holed up with Cornwallis, saying that their fate was a civil matter to be decided at a later date.[69] Between that magnanimity and Alexander Hamilton's lack of retaliation for the massacre at Groton Heights, the Americans

Cornwallis Is Taken! *A Currier and Ives print shows Lieutenant Colonel Tilghman of Washington's staff announcing the surrender at Yorktown from the steps of the State House (Independence Hall) at midnight, October 23, 1781.* Prints and Photographs Division, Library of Congress.

could be sure of an honorable victory. Men such as Ebenezer Huntington, John Lamb, Jonathan Trumbull Jr., and many other soldiers who had worked for this day proudly watched the British soldiers respectfully passing through their blue-coated lines and throwing down their weapons. The surrendering British officers did not behave as well as the enlisted men, grumbling and grousing, humiliated by the scope of the defeat.[70]

News flew across the continent. One of Shaw's ship captains who had been at sea during Arnold's attack sent him a letter from Philadelphia commiserating for their losses, but cheerfully reporting that Cornwallis had surrendered.[71] Governor Trumbull wrote in his diary on October 26, "surrender of Ld Cornwallis & his Army — 9000 men, seamen included — quantity of Warlike Stores — one 40 gun ship — 1 frigate — about 100 Transports. Praised be the Lord of Hosts!" The next day he sent news around the state, and by October 31 multiple confirmations arrived, including one from his son Jonathan Jr. On November 6 Trumbull wrote to his friend Washington,

> My warmest and most sincere congratulations await your Excellency on an event so honorable and glorious to yourself, so interesting and happy to the United States . . . an event, which will hasten the wished-for happy period, when your Excellency may return to and securely possess the sweets of domestic felicity and glorious rest from the toils of war, surrounded by the universal applauses of a free, grateful, and happy people.

Washington thanked Trumbull profusely, and told him, "I most earnestly hope that this event may be productive of the happy consequences you mention."[72]

By November people in Connecticut were more confident but still jumpy about another attack. Samuel Huntington wrote to a colleague, "We have had a report that the enemy were preparing at N. York to make us a visit at Norwich, which gave us some trouble to be in readiness for their reception." But, he added, "The capture of Cornwallis may alter their plans."[73] And though the big news had overshadowed the terror at New London, rumors about Arnold still swirled. Governor Trumbull's grandson had just arrived at Yale and wrote his grandfather that a rumor was swirling around "that the infamous traitor Arnold is taken but it is not believed."[74] The *Courant* gleefully conflated the two subjects:

> All the late New York papers have at length confessed the surrender of Lord Cornwallis to be real. They have even condescended to insert the articles of capitulation verbatim from the Philadelphia gazette. The women are in tears, the soldiery in a panic, the merchants selling off their goods for much less than the first cut in Europe, the Tories are in the utmost consternation, and Benedict Arnold himself, it is said, trembles like an aspen leaf.[75]

In Virginia Rochambeau's forces dismantled the trenches around Portsmouth, built earlier that year by Arnold, and then tramped north. When they marched back through Connecticut, Trumbull issued a proclamation that no one should raise their prices, as merchants were expected to do when armies passed through. In fact, Rochambeau said that "the inhabitants obeyed this injunction so generously, that each mess were able to add, every evening, to the common allowance every kind of provision at a very low price."[76] This was generous, considering the perilous economic situation in Connecticut.

Used to acquiring considerable personal debt, Governor Trumbull brushed aside talk of statewide fiscal austerity, sent new troops to the coast, ordered a contribution for the "sufferers at New London and Groton," and gave a proclamation for Thanksgiving — that New England holiday of old, now given new meaning by the victory at Yorktown.[77] One of those sufferers was Nathaniel Shaw, who had lost "more than Twelve thousand Sterling."[78] But life had more to throw at him. After contracting a "putrid fever" from the prisoners she nursed at their home, his wife, Lucretia, died on December 11, 1781. All that terrible winter, with "Dear friends reduced to extream poverty & Distress," the broken Shaw tried to bring order to eastern Connecticut.[79]

Somehow he made it to the following spring, when he tried to relax in his favorite way, going on an early season duck hunting trip. On April 12, 1782, at four in the afternoon, he and four friends returned along the coast in a small boat. The wind was "blowing fresh," and, fearing an accident, Shaw went to the back of the boat "to secure the musquet[s], one of which had gone off in the Morning." As he was putting them in the cuddy, one accidentally fired "full Loaded with Goose Shott" into his right side, breaking three ribs, injuring his liver and lungs, and destroying "the Muscular parts." The shot actually passed through his body and wounded two others in the boat. The other hunters wrapped Shaw's "mangled body" in a tablecloth, but he bled only a little, "so seard with the blaze of the Explosion."[80]

They covered him with their coats and brought him to beach south of New London, near where Arnold and his soldiers had disembarked. Landing, they carried him in "excruciating pains" to the shell of a fisherman's house burned the previous autumn, and the following morning carried him carefully to his stone mansion, because he "wanted to Die at home." Shaw's brother, Thomas, sent for Dr. Philip Turner, but when he arrived he could do nothing. Shaw remained "perfectly resigned to the will of God" and had enough presence of mind to make a will, giving out his possessions and freeing all his slaves.[81] He died of his wound two days later on April 15, another bitter loss for the grieving people of New London.

The Fall of Silas Deane

WHILE Benedict Arnold betrayed and attacked his homeland throughout 1780 and 1781, Silas Deane had returned to Europe to try to regain his lost reputation, along with the financial files that Congress asked him to gather. After two years absence he again met with Benjamin Franklin, who had also been treated poorly by Congress. Lafayette had warned Franklin of "enemies in America," and he was not exaggerating.[1] Unlike the imperturbable Franklin, though, Deane could not recover so easily from the politics that threatened to sink their characters and careers. He had been accused of war profiteering, his wife had died, and his Connecticut commerce had long since dried up. Then he watched the French mood cool toward the financially defaulting Americans, and he became even more depressed.[2] As Pierre-Augustin Caron de Beaumarchais put it, "After [Deane's] departure I reflected that it was perhaps a grave political error to drive to desperation those who have rendered important service to the state."[3] The passion that had made Deane such a valuable patriot now became his greatest flaw, as he began to work himself into a manic fury.

He still had many friends in America who knew he had been abused, and he should have paid more attention to them and less to his political enemies. Titus Hosmer of Middletown wrote to Thomas Mumford with the good news that Spain was allying with France to help the war effort and mourned "our poor friend Deane" who primarily arranged this.

> My dear sir, this country is indebted to Mr. Deane for as great services as any public minister ever did for a country, he has saved his country, and he is paid with ingratitude, calumny, and insult. I say he hath saved his country because I think, had not France and Spain come to our aid and joined their forces in the war, we could not singly have resisted the power and perseverance of Great Britain.[4]

But Deane's friendship with Benedict Arnold had put him in a very bad place. Following the initial treason in the autumn of 1780, Massachusetts delegate Francis Dana was in Paris with John Adams and claimed that Deane justified Arnold's treason in conversation.[5] Pennsylvanian James Wilson warned Deane that "you will not be surprised to hear that your enemies and mine have endeavoured to throw a shade over the characters of those who had any acquaintance with him."[6] Another Pennsylvania friend wrote to Deane from America, saying that "the infamous behavior of Arnold has put a weapon into the hands of your enemies, which they make use of to this day, by giving you every now and then a slashing stroke in coupling his name and yours together in their publications, and always affecting to speak of you in the light of a condemned man."[7]

Though Deane clearly had many genuine friends, throughout the winter of 1781 Arnold's friendship hurt him and, perhaps more seriously, influenced his attitudes and opinions. During the time they spent together in Philadelphia, had Arnold infected Deane's mind with notions of America's inevitable defeat? Deane had been softened up by the political machinations of the Lee family and the cowardice of Congress and was therefore ripe for doubt and despair. Unfortunately, he had yet another dangerous friend, the double agent Edward Bancroft, who was now ostensibly working to gather intelligence for John Adams. What passed between Bancroft and Deane is uncertain, but at the least Deane became so melancholy that his talk became looser throughout that spring, and worse, he began to talk of defeat.[8]

Benjamin Franklin noticed the change in Deane's character, saying, "His conversation, since his return from America . . . [has] at length come to an open vindication of Arnold's conduct. . . . I imagine it will end in his going over to join his friend Arnold in England. I had an exceeding good opinion of him when he acted with me, and I believe he was then sincere and hearty in our cause. But he is changed, and his character ruined in his own country and in [France]."[9] When hearing of some of Deane's careless, bitter statements in France, his friend John Jay tried to counsel him "to hold yourself constantly in readiness to seize the first proper opportunity of convincing the world, that you merit the thanks, not the reproaches, of your country. . . . In this enlightened age, when the noise of passion and party shall have subsided, the voice of truth will be heard and attended to."[10] Jay may have had too rosy a view of politics, but his advice to a friend was helpful. Unfortunately, Deane did not take it and continued to talk loosely about America's inescapable failure.

Already moody and forlorn about his political exile, Silas Deane was hurt even more by his friendship with the traitorous Arnold. Benoit Louis Prevost, S. Deane, Popular Graphic Arts, Library of Congress.

Finally, perhaps inevitably, he moved from conversation to the written word. In May 1781 Deane began writing letters to close friends in America, the sad missives of an angry and broken man. They included worrying about future commerce with Europe and decreasing morals in America, wishing for peace, condemning Congress, doubting democracy, and wondering whether we were better off under Great Britain. Deane had been saying much the same in letters to friends and family since 1779, but throughout early 1781 he increased his imprecations and made stronger pleas.

He began quietly on May 10 in a letter to James Wilson, putting his opinions mildly: "A gentleman lately here from America assured me that it was considered by our countrymen as political heresy or treason to entertain a doubt that France would, under any circumstances whatever, give up our independency by withdrawing from its alliance with us." He said that he had "favorable ideas" about France but questioned their ability to keep their word.[11] Four days later he wrote that "I can see no prospect of our being so happy," probably mistaking his personal unhappiness for his country's.[12] In another letter he cited other Americans in Paris who had lost hope, including a supposed member of Congress, but admitted, "I consider the people of America to be still too violently agitated to listen to any thing which appears to contradict their favourite wish."[13]

On May 20 he wrote to his old protégé, Benjamin Tallmadge, beginning with hometown pride, "If ever a state was calculated for democracy, it must've been Connecticut." But he quickly moved to his main point about being caught between England and France, saying, "I view our situation as with Scylla on the one hand and Charybdis on the other, and our pilots drunk with the intoxicating ideas of independent sovereignty, madly pushing us into that vortex in which our peace, liberty, and safety will be swallowed up and lost forever."[14] Things went downhill from there. Written on the same day, a letter to Jesse Root is longer and more formulaic, copying much of the material from the others and excising any personal appeals. He gamed out future conflicts between Britain and France, as if he and someone else, perhaps Bancroft, had discussed the matter. On June 19 he apparently gave a number of enclosed letters to two ship captains, with the instructions that if the ship should be captured, "sink or destroy them."[15]

The worst part was that he knew he was making a mistake but couldn't help it, saying, "I take up my pen almost every day to write to some friend or other in America. I determine not to let any thing political fall from it, yet before I have finished one page I find myself in the full force of a current which I cannot escape or resist."[16] His depression and anger was causing him to see the worst results and the worst in people. He wrote that though his friends might think him a Tory, "I cannot help it. I have for some time since had the fate, though I shall never have the fame, of Cassandra." He then quoted the *Iliad*, "I could still prophecy, but the cold hand of despair is on me."[17] He also saw himself increasingly as the victim of injustice, writing, "I am kept out of my money in a cruel and unprecedented manner."[18] And his appeal to his friends is real and painful to hear: "Can any one blame me if I lay before the world the history of that injustice and ingratitude under which I have suffered, and of those vile intrigues and detestable cabals which have occasioned the most complicated misery and distress to my country? I am confident no disinterested or impartial man will censure me for doing myself justice."[19] Of course, if he had stuck to those concerns, he would have only annoyed people with his complaints. Unfortunately, his letters did not focus just on his own situation but rather on what he saw as the politically untenable position of his fellow Americans.

During all this, Deane had talked to Paul Wentworth, a Loyalist originally from New Hampshire, now working as an agent of the king. Reasserting his political position of American independence, Benjamin Franklin had refused even to meet with Wentworth unless money was left out of the discussion. Deane was slightly more pliable, though it is unclear whether it was because he trusted Wentworth as another American or simply because he needed a business deal that would help him pay for his time in France.[20] But King George III definitely tried to buy Deane's loyalty at some point that spring, approving the money for a bribe. This attempt was not unusual; almost everyone, including Franklin, had been approached at some point. They may also have misled him under the auspices of a possible business opportunity rather than a bribe.

It is much more likely that they simply decided to seize the letters. They knew his mind already from Bancroft, and the British secret service was adept at stealing mail.[21] On July 19 King George wrote, "I have received Lord North's boxes containing the intercepted letters from Mr. Deane for America." The king's use of "intercepted" seems to imply that they were not given freely, though his worry that they have "too much appearance of being concerted with this country" is more ambiguous.[22] On August 7 he wrote, "I think them too strong in our favour to bear the appearance of his spontaneous opinions."[23] This vague statement could mean that the letters were indeed written in concert with Bancroft or some other agent, or it could mean that Deane had simply taken too much the part of the English in his own angry rants, and the king was worried the letters looked faked.

Private letters criticizing the conduct of the war or the behavior of Congress were certainly not unusual. Even George Washington was not immune to despair, stating in 1780, "Unless a system very different from that which has long prevailed be immediately adopted throughout the States, our affairs must soon become desperate, beyond the possibility of recovery. . . . Indeed, I have almost ceased to hope."[24] The letters of Deane's old enemy Arthur Lee are full of conspiracy theories and personal malice. But he remained individual with his hatreds and never took his own problems to mean the ruin of the country.[25] Ebenezer Huntington, the much younger brother of Arnold's childhood acquaintance Jedediah, was two years behind Nathan Hale and Benjamin Tallmadge at Yale and wrote a number of despairing letters to his father. In them he complained that many hungry soldiers were ready to flee the army, sick of receiving letters from their wives, saying, "pray come home."[26] He went further than Deane with many statements, writing, "I despise my countrymen. I wish I could say I was not born in America, I once gloried in it but am now ashamed of it . . . my cowardly countrymen who flinch at the very time when their Exertions are wanted, and hold their Purse Strings as tho they would Damn the World, rather than part with a Dollar to their Army."[27] Huntington continued to be furious throughout his service in the Continental army, from Bunker Hill to beyond Yorktown.

Some would say that Huntington had earned the right to complain, especially in his private correspondence, and the same might be said for Deane. But after Arnold's actions, political dissent became more difficult. And Deane's private dissent was about to become public, because King George decided to publish the letters for all to see, sending them to New York to be printed in *Rivington's Gazette* in an attempt to sow discord. It does not appear that Deane was ever given money for this; all his actions and words before and afterward show a man not in the pay of the English king. The Continental Congress still owed him 300,000 livres, so the king would have had to offer him a hefty sum to outweigh the hopeful return of that money. Furthermore, there is no proprietary intelligence in the letters themselves, nor could Deane have actually given the British any useful information. He was not in the position to give up West Point, certainly, or even give intelligence on the negotiations with France. He had merely fallen into a very personal and politically suicidal despair.

Throughout the autumn Deane continued to write letters with the same conspiracy theories, including one to his brother Barnabas, which was not intercepted. Nor was a second one to Benjamin Tallmadge, or a third to Jonathan Trumbull on October 21.[28] These were his real opinions and, while not treasonous, were politically disastrous. The day before he wrote to Trumbull, October 20, his letters were published in *Rivington's Gazette* in New York. Cornwallis had surrendered on the nineteenth. The political firestorm of indignation and condemnation was immediate and total. By November 11 Deane's brother Barnabas wrote to a mutual friend, saying that Silas's name was now synonymous with Arnold's, and "he has now given his enemies just the opportunity they wanted to ruin him."[29] And Deane's letters continued to be stolen. One he wrote to Thomas Mumford was much too late to have been sent with the others but was now intercepted and read in front of Congress, including his woeful claim, "My faith is, I fear, even less than a grain of mustard seed."[30] This sort of defeatism might have seemed merely preposterous after Yorktown but instead was viewed by most as traitorous.

Benjamin Tallmadge received the copy of *Rivington's Gazette* in which Deane's letter to him appeared and lamented to Deane's brother Barnabas, "Rivington has hauled my name in among the rest."[31] He wrote back to his former mentor, "Comparing your former character and late conduct together, the epithet of *Traitor* is freely bestowed on you, and that you have sold your conscience, your political principles, and with them, like Arnold, would have been glad to have sold your country is but little doubt." Tallmadge then refuted all Deane's claims and worries, one by one, saying his own words "are the sentiments of one who is engaged in the profession in the defense of the liberties and independence of his country, firmly persuaded that a reunion with Great Britain would be the ruin of America, and that our political happiness, honor, and prosperity rests solely in the freedom, serenity, and independence of the states."[32] Tallmadge also held out hope that the letters were forged, but unfortunately Deane had already written him a second letter, railing against the French and urging the young man to resign: "Never, like *Arnold* betray your trust, but quit the service and declare without reserve your reasons for it."[33] Tallmadge never wrote to Deane again.

Meanwhile, Deane left France for Ghent in the Netherlands, remaining oblivious to the political firestorm in America or the responses his letters were generating, continuing to write other, more professional letters to Congress and other business associates. While in Ghent he wrote to Bancroft, furious that he was not writing him back, not knowing that the double agent had achieved his purpose.[34] A week later he finally heard the news of Arnold's burning expedition, writing again to Bancroft, "You know that I had many friends in New

London with whom I have been intimately connected from my child-hood. The thoughts of their being ruined affects me sensibly."[35] Of course, he still knew nothing about Yorktown. Then, in the middle of November he finally discovered that his letters had been published. He actually apologized to Bancroft for writing the letters, and he reported the content to him as if for the first time, "In the months of May and June last I wrote to several of my friends in America. . . . I expressed my sentiments and the reasons at large on which they were founded."[36] He didn't know that Bancroft had used him and turned to this false friend in a last tragic hope for understanding.

Deane had been terrible at choosing friends, and now even the legitimate ones were leaving him. Some, like John Jay, tried to maintain their correspondence with him that winter:

> I was your friend, and should still have been so, had you not advised America to desert that independence which they had pledged each other their lives, fortunes, and sacred honor to support. . . . I still indulge the idea that your head may have been more to blame than your heart, and that in some melancholy despondent hour the disorder of your nerves affected your opinions and your pen. God grant this may have proved to have been the case, and that I may yet have reason to resume my former opinion, that you were a valuable, a virtuous, and a patriotic man.[37]

Very few stood up for Deane's right to freely express his opinions. His brother Barnabas wrote to Deane's beloved stepson Samuel Webb that he despised Congress for not paying their debts: "I will not add on this Disagreeable Subject for I should be Branded as a Tory, Traitor & Every Other Odious Epithet Can Be Express'd, which is the Case where a man writes Only Truth & his Letters happen to be intercepted & Get into the hands of one of our Printers. . . . He is at Once without Further Enquiry held up as the Vilest Traitor & Villain on Earth, which is the Case with my Brother S[ilas] D[eane]."[38] Most kept their mouths shut, perhaps afraid that they would be swept up in the hunt for traitors. In a Philadelphia newspaper Deane was reported, "now in all respects, as he ever has been, the bosom friend of Arnold."[39]

Meanwhile, Benedict Arnold sailed for London on December 15, 1781, on the *Robuste* with the paroled Lord Cornwallis, fresh from his defeat at Yorktown, while Peggy and the children sailed on a less militarized ship. On January 22, 1782, they arrived in London, where Arnold attended court, spoke to King George, and at first began to enter the high London society. But many disliked his presence, including Edmund Burke, who spoke in the House of Commons against Arnold being granted another military command. The *General Advertiser and Morning Intelligencer* derided him as a "mean mercenary" and that he had as good a "chance of being hanged here as he does in America." Arnold apparently tried to visit the dead spy John Andre's mother and sister, but they refused to see him.[40] One probable reason he was not accepted was because of his low birth; the aristocratic system he hated as a young man now came back to haunt him. But the lower classes had little use for him either. A month after the New London attack, British prisoners in Fishkill, New York, planned to escape, but one informed their jailor of the plot. The escape was stopped, and the other prisoners labeled the man "Benedict Arnold The Traitor."[41]

Arnold also had to start over financially. His confiscated Mount Pleasant estate in Philadelphia was sold for £1547, and his New Haven property was auctioned off in a coffeehouse.[42] He tried to obtain money from the British for the loss of Mount Pleasant in particular and lied on the claim, putting the price far above its actual value. He continued to try to get more money until 1786. When he made the case to Parliament to continue the war, could he have been thinking of his properties rather than the British cause? In truth, he had no real attachment to the British point of view. Then, when the so-called War Ministry was voted out of power in March 1782, the new government effectively ignored him, ending his influence in British politics completely. The British military decided that it had no use for him either and refused to give him command in India, as they did for Cornwallis.[43]

In America, despite the victory at Yorktown and rumors of peace, the war of attrition continued throughout 1782. Benjamin Tallmadge continued his spy work and obtained intelligence on illicit Long Island commerce, capturing many British trading boats.[44] On his travels he met his future wife, a Long Island refugee named Mary Floyd, daughter of one of the signers of the Declaration of Independence. She was living in exile in Middletown, Connecticut, close to where Arnold's young sons and sister still lived.[45] But Tallmadge's work went on into 1783, when he was still involved in capturing enemy ships. On one occasion he teamed up with Capt. Amos Hubbel of Stratfield, Connecticut; they engaged a British vessel, boarded it with bayonets, and captured it, again without losing a single man.[46]

Washington retained his trust in Tallmadge, despite the troubling correspondence from both Arnold and Deane. Of course, Washington had already put Arnold's former friend Richard Varick in charge of collecting his papers associated with the war; unlike Deane, he had learned to let his political enemies disparage him without becoming publically angry. Of course, it was one thing to trust loyal subordinates and another entirely to trust the American public. Yet in June 1783 he wrote in a circular letter to the states, saying he put his faith in "the prevalence of that pacific and friendly disposition among the people of the United States, which will induce them to forget their local prejudices and policies, to make those mutual concessions which are requisite to the general prosperity, and, in some instances, to sacrifice their individual advantages to the interest of the community."[47] Though in some ways it was a plea for a stronger central government, it was also a plea for social unity and trust.

It was an important appeal, because just a few months later, peace was declared, British forces began packing their bags, and the thirteen former colonies were left with the responsibility they had so long desired. Bells rang throughout the continent, and when Washington's general orders announcing the peace to the army were read, as Tallmadge put it, "the hardiest soldiers were unable to restrain the copious flood of tears."[48] Following Washington's example, others tried to rise to the moment. Despite dealing with accusations of disloyalty, corruption, and war profiteering from his political enemies, Governor Trumbull nevertheless echoed Washington's appeal to trust. In his retirement speech to the assembly in October 1783, he argued that men should not fear their fellow citizens of the new United States, especially in regard to legislative decision making:

> Who, my fellow citizens, are the men we have to fear? Not strangers who have no connection with our welfare: — no, they are men of our own choice, from among ourselves; a choice (if we are faithful to ourselves) dictated by the most perfect freedom of election. . . . They are our brethren — acting for themselves as well as for us —

and sharers with us in all the general burthens and benefits. They are men, who from interest, affection, and every social tie, have the same attachment to our constitution and government as ourselves.

The federalist elements of his speech were derided by the Connecticut House of Representatives, full of small farmers and anti-tax merchants. But the speech was bigger than a plea for national union; it was a plea in favor of entrusting fellow citizens with power. He continued, "I exhort you to love one another: let each one study the good of his neighbor and of the community, as his own."[49]

Trusting the percentage of the population who had remained loyal to Britain was the most difficult task. Popular opinion ran high against them, especially those who had served in the British army. Tallmadge thought it "not a little amusing" to find the Tories of New York now begging for his protection against "the dreaded rage of their countrymen."[50] In 1783 a Loyalist returned to Wallkill, New York, to visit his parents and was shaved, tarred, feathered, hitched to a hog yoke, and sent back to the city complete with a placard on which someone drew a picture of Benedict Arnold, the devil's imps, and a Tory driving off a cow.[51] Local committees voted on various violent resolutions, as "the spirit of persecution and violence against the unhappy loyalists does not appear to abate in any degree, since the cessation of hostilities. They are not suffered to go into the country even to take a last farewell of their relations." Trumbull and other politicians wanted to stop these localized atrocities but did not know how. A danger of democracy was rearing its ugly head: mob rule. As one former Loyalist put it that September, "The people have been taught a dangerous truth, that all power is derived from them."[52]

It was up to a few brave leaders to stop the spread of mob violence, as some had done throughout the war. After all, the Virginia government under Thomas Jefferson had not hanged a single man for treason in the entire seven years, despite a variety of insurrections and Arnold's deadly attack.[53] Now Connecticut took an even bigger step in 1784. Despite being attacked and partially burned with the help of local Tories only a few years earlier, New Haven voted to allow their return, and many actually encouraged the Loyalists of New York to settle there. Even more surprisingly, Gen. Samuel Parsons sent an invitation for them to come to the shattered town of New London.[54]

Many others throughout the country followed suit, slowly influencing the attitude of the public and probably stopping the spilling of even more blood. Moreover, the tyranny that many Loyalists and neutral observers feared did not happen. When an American officer suggested that Washington become a military dictator for the good of the country, Washington gave him a written flogging, and his Connecticut secretaries Jonathan Trumbull Jr. and David Humphreys signed the reprimand as insurance of its authenticity.[55]

As the British prepared to leave Manhattan and Long Island, Washington sent Benjamin Tallmadge ahead to protect their spies from retaliation. Tallmadge found that the Tories who could not afford to leave on the British ships were in a state of shock, and Washington described them as "dejected," "crying," and "almost speechless."[56] Finally, on November 25, 1783, a small contingent of eight hundred American soldiers marched into New York City for the first time in seven years, where Benjamin Tallmadge and other patriots experienced "the joy of meeting friends, who would been long separated by the cruel rigors of war."[57] Washington established himself at Fraunces Tavern on Pearl Street, cleaned up the mess left by the British and established order in the city and on Long Island.

Then, at noon on December 4, 1783, Washington walked downstairs into the tavern to meet Tallmadge, Henry Knox, and the other remaining officers. They drank wine together, and Washington said, "With a heart full of love and gratitude, I now take leave of you. I most devoutly wished that your latter days may be as prosperous and happy as your former ones have been glorious and honorable." Each officer took their general in chief's hand in parting, and the burly General Knox embraced his friend, sobbing. He was not the only one. As Tallmadge put it, "tears of deep sensibility filled every eye — and the heart seemed so full, that it was ready to burst from its wonted abode. Not a word was uttered to break the solemn silence that prevailed, or to interrupt the tenderness of the interesting scene." Then Washington went outside, passing through a group of light infantry on parade and walking silently through the crowds to a waiting barge. As the boat crossed the Hudson River, Washington "waved his hat, and bid us a silent adieu."[58]

Washington rode to Annapolis, Maryland, where Congress had temporarily located. On December 20 he announced his intentions in a letter to Thomas Mifflin, the president of Congress and one of Washington's critics.[59] Mifflin and Congress decided that on the twenty-second they would throw him a dinner party, and he could resign at noon the following day. Hundreds of people showed up at the dinner, and all the women present lined up to dance with Washington. The following day he put on his dress uniform and walked into the Maryland State House, finding only twenty representatives of Congress present. All kept their hats on as a symbol of antimonarchist feeling. The galleries were opened, the people of the town packed the hall, and Thomas Mifflin rose and asked him for his "communications." Washington bowed to the congressmen, who now removed their hats. As he lifted his speech, he had to grasp it with both trembling hands as he spoke, saying hoarsely, "Having finished the work assigned me, I retire from the great theater of action; and bidding an affectionate farewell to this august body under whose orders I have so long acted, I here offer my commission and take my leave of all the employments of public life." He handed his military commission and the speech to Mifflin, sweeping away all the expectations of dictatorship in one moment. Then among the admiring weeping of the assembled crowd, he walked outside, mounted his horse, and rode off to home.[60]

Before settling in Connecticut permanently, Tallmadge returned to Brookhaven, Long Island, to his father, whom he had not seen during the war. They roasted an entire ox on the public green in celebration, and the victorious cavalry officer and spy was appointed master of ceremonies for the occasion. He wrote years later,

> When the ox was well roasted, the noble animal in his spirit was removed to a proper place, and after a blessing from the God of battles had been evoked by my honored father, I began to carve, dissect, and distribute to the multitude around me. The aged and the young, the male and the female, rejoiced to receive a portion, which, from the novelty of the scene, and being in commemoration of so great an event, obtained a peculiar zest. All was harmony and joy, for all seemed to be of one mind.[61]

It was a celebration, and a feeling, that neither Benedict Arnold nor Silas Deane would ever have.

But the cease-fire that spring meant that Deane could at least travel from Ghent to a place where he spoke the language. Since Congress

According to painter Benjamin West, King George said of Washington's planned resignation, "If he does that, he will be the greatest man in the world." John Trumbull, General George Washington Resigning His Commission. *Courtesy of Architect of the Capitol.*

had exiled him from America, Deane sailed across the North Sea to London during 1783. In the past year he had realized his political errors somewhat and fervently denied taking money from the British.[62] It was a reasonable claim; he was quite poor now. He took a small flat at 135 Fleet Street, three miles away from the community of wealthy American exiles in the Portman Square area, including Benedict Arnold. Nevertheless, Arnold must have heard that he was arriving, because he promptly knocked on his old friend's door and tried to rekindle their camaraderie.

Deane was in his chamber with several other American businessmen when Arnold appeared, unannounced. According to Deane, "a remembrance of past personal civilities and of hospitality would not permit me to shut the door in his face." Embarrassed, Deane exchanged a few pleasantries, and Arnold invited him to dine at his house, "in company with gentlemen of rank and character." Deane refused but continued to receive invitation cards from Arnold to dine. Then, Arnold showed up again, "in the same unceremonious manner as before," obviously eager to renew their former bond. On the stairs outside his rooms, Deane told him that "his visits were disagreeable to me, and could be of no service to him; that I could not return them, except that I might call with mr. Sebor some evening to pay our respects to Mrs. Arnold, from whom I had received so many civilities in Philadelphia." He did so, stopping by to see Peggy, and then, according to him, never saw Arnold again.[63]

Nevertheless, rumors of their renewed friendship spread. Adams linked Arnold and Deane again in his letters.[64] And Franklin mentioned Deane's friendship with Arnold to John Jay.[65] So in 1784 Jay finally severed all contact with his former friend, telling him that "I love my country and my honor better than my friends, and even my family, and am ready to part with them all whenever it would be improper to retain them." He told Deane that "every American who gives his hand to that man [Arnold], in my opinion, pollutes it."[66] Deane wrote back, saddened, "whatever imprudences I have been guilty of in my letters or conversation, I am neither the enemy of my country nor the intimate of General Arnold."[67] He also wrote to Franklin and others denying his connection. But he was not believed. He had of course been a friend of Arnold before the treason, and his despairing letters had sealed the fact for most. These last visits in London had only made things worse. In fact, Deane's and Arnold's names would continue to be linked for decades. As late as 1815, John Adams, while speaking of America's foreign policy, wrote that if he had sent thousands of men to their death in a foreign war, the rest of the country would be "cursing John Adams as a traitor to his country, and a bribed slave to Great Britain — a Deane, an Arnold, a devil!"[68]

Deane retained a few friends in America, but they could do nothing to bring him back from exile. Jeremiah Wadsworth visited him in London after reporting on his commissary work for Rochambeau in Paris. But otherwise, Deane's contacts remained by letter, mostly to his brothers and his stepson Samuel Webb.[69] To them he could continue complaining of the injustice of his situation, though now he admitted some responsibility for his own fall, saying, "how greatly have I been to blame in credulously relying and reposing my fortune and fame on the

gratitude and justice of men, whose interest it has been to ruin me."[70]
But despite his complete rejection by America, he never decided to
throw in his lot with England, as Arnold did. All he wanted was to go
home.

As time passed, he acknowledged "that I was misinformed and misled in some, and even in many things, and that I was imprudent to
write or speak at all on the subject, yet as a free citizen I had a free
right to do both."[71] This appeal to free speech was technically correct,
but as many have found out over the centuries, such arguments did
not matter in the minds of most. Like the Loyalists who were twenty
years out of step, Deane simply had the wrong opinion at the wrong
time. His error was equating the venomous politics of Congress with
the prospects of his country, while Arnold's error was equating Congress's political infidelity with his own military betrayal. The American
peoples' error was equating Deane's political infidelity with Arnold's
military betrayal. They were all common enough errors, but seldom did
they result in such tragic consequences, for these two men and for the
emerging nation.

In July 1784 Arnold applied for a job at the fabled East India Company. The director, George Johnstone, asked for a written account of
the betrayal, and Arnold sent a letter, saying, "I declared that my only
object was to obtain a redress of grievances; and at the same time I dis-
claimed any idea of independence or a separation from Great Britain.
These, Sir, were invariably my sentiments during every period of the
war." He went on to state that he switched sides only when assured by
Clinton that Britain would no longer tax America. This was a lie. In the
correspondence with Clinton there is no mention of this, and of course
Arnold's signed oath of loyalty to the American cause was based on the
creation of "free, independent, and sovereign states." Johnstone wrote
back with an unusually perceptive analysis of Arnold's fate: "Under
an unsuccessful insurrection all actors are rebels. Crowned with success they become immortal patriots. A fortunate plot holds you up as
a savior of nations; a premature discovery brings you to the scaffold or
brands your fame with dark and doubtful suspicions."[72] Arnold's application was denied.

The following year Arnold left Peggy in a small house in London's
Portman Square district and sailed to New Brunswick, Canada. Many

Loyalist refugees already resided there, such as Martha Lyon of Fairfield. Like most other refugees, she had been forced to relocate to Canada with only a few possessions. Arnold, on the other hand, still had over £6000 of treason money, and this may be one reason he was resented by many of the other residents.[73] Others did not like that he took so long to join the British, and some did not approve of his dishonorable conduct, regardless of the side he finally chose. Across the border American newspapers reported that Arnold arrived at Saint John, Nova Scotia, in a brig packed full with £30,000 of goods. Apparently, an "elementary contention arose," and "the accumulated rewards of treason and murder were quick deposited in the bowels of the ocean."[74] A few years later they reported that he was hated in New Brunswick and had been hung in effigy in Saint John in the noon marketplace.[75] Whether these rumors were accurate or not, they showed a need for the people of America to believe that others felt the same way about this traitor that they did, and in some cases they were no doubt right.

But Arnold lived a generally peaceful life on Campobello Island, on the border of Canada and Maine, down the road from an American patriot named John Allen. In fact, Colonel Allen did not do anything aggressive about the traitor down the street and even sold him rum from his general store.[76] Through middlemen Arnold actually traded with many New England merchants, who either remained blissfully unaware they were doing business with the traitor or decided that profit was more important than patriotism.[77] After all, his movements were still occasionally reported in American papers. In 1786 supposedly some inhabitants of Saint John offered to "deliver him up to the Americans for ten dollars," but Arnold "escaped" to Halifax.[78] Two years later his store in Saint John was reported to have been burned.[79] Gossip followed that he had set fire to it to receive the insurance money.[80] Later he was rumored to have offered his services to the Belgian army.[81] As always happens in the press, the reports were sometimes close to the reality of his situation and sometimes very far from it.

In 1787 Peggy and their sons sailed from London and joined him, followed by Hannah and his elder sons, who had hidden away in Connecticut. Hannah's feeling about Arnold's treason and its fallout for her own life remains a mystery, as does her fate after 1787, when she disappears from records entirely. But for a few years Arnold and Peggy lived well, with feather beds, mahogany furniture, and a nice easy chair for nights in front of the fire. He was sued and taken to court often, but that was no different from any other merchant of the day.[82]

Trapped in London, Silas Deane continued to occasionally try to clear his name, but by now knew his appeals fell on deaf ears:

> I do not blame my Countrymen for their suspicions of Me, on this subject, they know that I am a Man greatly injured, that I have in effect been ungratefully proscribed, and driven from my Country, and they know that I am not devoid of Passion, & resentment, and the Conclusion which they draw, from thence is natural, and though in the present instance unjust, it would be To no purpose, to attempt To convince them of it at present.[83]

After nearly a decade in exile he sent a congratulatory letter to George Washington on his election to the presidency of the new nation. In it he pled for the recompense of his money owed by Congress and a return from exile: "Though reduced to the extreme of poverty, & To an infirm & precarious state of health, by what I have suffered, I shall regard the past as of little consideration, if I can now obtain what I have so long since requested."[84] Four days later he wrote to William Samuel Johnson, one of the architects of the nation's new Constitution, asking to be brought "before the Tribunal of Country for a fair, & full examination."[85] At this point he just wanted a trial, a chance to let his voice be heard.

He also wanted desperately to come home. In September 1789 he decided to return from exile to Connecticut, either to force the issue of a trial or because he thought that the new government under Washington would do nothing to stop him. But while the ship he had boarded was being repaired off the English coast, he became mysteriously and rapidly ill, possibly from poison. Perhaps the deceitful Edward Bancroft felt threatened that Deane would testify in front of Congress, and his own treason would come under scrutiny.[86] Regardless of who did it, the illness was too sudden and violent to be natural. Vomiting and writhing in pain, Deane died in only four hours and was taken on shore and buried in an unmarked grave in Saint George's churchyard in Kent. He was only fifty-one years old.

His former friend Benedict Arnold lived on. In 1790 a few Americans conversed with him on board the *Echo*, a British warship. A newspaper commented on the event acerbically: "We would have the gentlemen, in some of his American excursions, to visit his countrymen at New London — where his presence may remind them of his friendship some years past — and be treated with due respect."[87]

* * *
Epilogue

IN MARCH 1794 the infamous French political impresario, Charles Maurice de Talleyrand-Perigord, was kicked out of England after fleeing Paris during the height of the Terror. He decided to travel to the new United States and left London only to meet a storm in the English Channel. Forced to dock at Falmouth, he put up at an inn. When he told the innkeeper he was headed for America, he was informed that an American general was also there riding out the storm. They were introduced, although the man at first declined to tell him his name. Talleyrand asked him about America, but as he put it, "from the first, it seemed to me that my inquiries annoyed him." The nameless general dropped the conversation several times, seemingly uninterested in the subject. After struggling to keep the dialogue going, Talleyrand asked for letters of introduction to the man's American friends.

> "No," he replied, and after a few moments of silence, noticing my surprise, he added, "I am perhaps the only American who cannot give you letters for his own country.... All the relations I had there are now broken.... I must never return to the States."

Of course the man was Benedict Arnold. Talleyrand confessed to feel "much pity for him," even though he acknowledged some will blame him for it. "I witnessed his agony," Talleyrand stated, and left it at that.[1]

We want to believe Talleyrand's story: that Arnold was in solitary agony in a Falmouth inn on a stormy night. It may even be true. But was that agony guilt? Regret? Was it the anguish of a man without a home? After all, Arnold had been not only a military leader but also a bookseller and a family man. He could have genuinely been tortured by his previous actions, or he could have merely been lonely. Or, like Lafayette hoping that Arnold would "blow his brains out," Talleyrand might have been projecting emotions that should have been there but were not.[2]

Whether or not Arnold had regrets, it is doubtful he saw himself as a villain: few do. Two years earlier Arnold had participated in a duel against James Maitland, the Earl of Lauderdale on July 1, 1792, and forced the lord to apologize for aspersion of character.[3] And later in 1794, in a letter about selling sugar, Arnold wrote of finding someone he can trust, who won't "squander his money." He was looking for a "good steady English cooper" and stated, "if you can by any means engage one for me that can be depended on." He repeated that he wanted a "good man."[4] These issues of dependability and goodness are insisted on, and Arnold saw no inconsistency in them.

Back in 1790 Washington had moved into the old Penn Mansion on Market Street in Philadelphia, the same house where Benedict Arnold lived with Silas Deane in 1778. It had been reconceived as the new executive mansion of the United States. That first year of Washington's presidency, both he and Thomas Jefferson repeated rumors that Arnold was in Detroit, planning an attack on either Louisiana, the Spanish settlements on the Mississippi, or the western American territories, "to surround these United States."[5] It was only a rumor, but it must have reminded Washington of his betrayal a decade earlier. Now, in 1794, he had the first real test of his presidency, a violent tax revolt in western Pennsylvania. Some leaders of this "Whiskey Rebellion" called for armed resistance to the new United States, attacked tax collectors, took up a flag of secession, and even mulled using guillotines.

Washington had a big decision to make. When Shay's Rebellion in Massachusetts broke out in 1786, he wrote to Henry Lee on the subject of this sort of treasonous action: "Know precisely what the insurgents aim at. If they have real grievances, redress them, if possible; or acknowledge the justice of them, and your inability to do it at the moment. If they have not, employ the force of government against them at once. If this is inadequate, all will be convinced that the superstructure is bad and wants support."[6] Now, as president, he was faced with taking his own advice. In September he called 13,000 soldiers into the field, commanded by Alexander Hamilton. At this show of force, the Pennsylvania uprising promptly dried up and 150 prisoners, the ringleaders, were taken into custody. A total of 24 men were indicted for treason, 10 of whom were captured. Only 2 men were convicted and sentenced to hang for treason. But despite knowing the sting of betrayal better than most, Washington decided to use the presidential pardon power for the first time and let them go.[7] It was a singular moment in American history, one that could have easily gone a different direction with another man in charge. Would he have done so if they had conspired with a foreign power and gone as far as burning American cities? Would he have ordered their kidnapping and execution, as he did for Arnold? That we will never know.

We do know that Washington set a precedent: a few years later President John Adams pardoned the dissident John Fries after another tax rebellion. Of course, these men and their policies were not perfect: far from it. A few years later Washington quietly approved John Adams's disastrous Alien and Sedition Acts during the Quasi-War with France, curtailing free speech and allowing easier imprisonment of foreigners — one of the worst government overreaches in American history.[8] It was a difficult process, building and maintaining a civil society without descending into the extremes of violent anarchy or guillotine madness. There were messy, gray areas. But it began with trust, with tolerance, with the "we" that Washington invoked when he was betrayed, the same "we" that ends the Declaration of Independence and begins the Constitution.[9]

"We" required individuals to represent the whole, to serve the society in which they lived. The man who had faithfully represented his state for fifty years, Jonathan Trumbull, had died in 1785, after two years of "literary philosophic retirement," reading his books and avoiding his creditors.[10] His friend George Washington commended "a long and well spent life in the service of his country" and placed Trumbull "among the 1st of patriots."[11] Two of his sons continued his legacy, with Jonathan Jr. becoming the second Speaker of the U.S. House of Representatives, then a senator, then governor of Connecticut. The other became "the painter of the Revolution," putting onto canvas the people and events that embodied the struggle to build a new country.

Others served as well. Arnold's old friend Richard Varick became the mayor of New York City, Ezra Stiles continued as the president of Yale College until his death, and former president of Congress Samuel Huntington replaced Trumbull as governor. His brother Ebenezer Huntington served in the militia and American armies for the next three decades without wish of fame or fortune, and Gen. Jedediah Huntington worked as the customs collector at New London, helping rebuild the ruined town. Jerusha and Daniel Lathrop had replaced Arnold as their surrogate son with a nephew, Daniel Lathrop Coit, and he took over the business when his uncle died, becoming one of the richest men in Norwich.[12] Their other nephew, Jeremiah Wadsworth, helped ratify the Constitution and then served in the U.S. House of Representatives.

After becoming a successful businessman in Litchfield, Benjamin Tallmadge also served eight terms as a representative to Congress and even served in the northern division of the army during the War of 1812. When the Marquis de Lafayette returned to New Haven in 1824, they met again after forty years, embraced and wept, remembering "the trying scenes through which they had passed the ardency of youth, and that they were severally blessed by the grateful feelings of their countrymen, and the most distinguished notice of our government." [13] As spying became more acceptable in American culture, Tallmadge and his friend Nathan Hale would also receive the accolades they deserved for that dangerous and thankless work. In fact, Hale's reputation grew every year, until he reached the status of national martyr, with his last words echoing as an ode to the love of country.

Hale's old sergeant Stephen Hempstead recovered from his bayonet wounds and eventually settled in Missouri, following many other survivors into the new western territories. By May 1792 Connecticut had finally compiled the lists of all the people who lost property during the various raids, especially Arnold's attack on New London, granting five hundred thousand acres in Ohio to be divided among them. By then, of course, many could not claim the lands, including Anne Ledyard, who died along with her youngest son in 1789. [14] Others stayed to rebuild, like Ebenezer Avery, whose house had served as the hospital for the wounded. He went on to father a large family, to marry four wives, three of whom were named Elizabeth, and to work at his large ten-room house as a tailor. Until his death he never allowed the bloodstains on the living room floorboards to be cleaned. [15]

Though not a national hero like Hale, William Ledyard became a local legend, and his memory was kept in annual celebrations on Groton Heights. Ninety-nine years later Connecticut senator Lafayette Foster addressed the crowd, "I say confidently as a son of Connecticut, I say proudly, there is no spot in any country on this green earth more consecrated by patriotic blood than this." [16] By contrast, speakers barely mentioned Arnold's name at these anniversaries, in order to honor the victims and not the parricide. On one of these occasions a New Londoner said, "Is it worthwhile to add another curse to his memory? The

"John Letter who died Sep 6th 1781 in Fort Griswold by traitor arnold's mudring Corps." This is one of many graves in southeastern Connecticut that remain as legacies of Arnold's brutal attack on his homeland. Courtesy of the author.

world has cursed him, not once, but in succession. . . . The memory of the wicked shall rot."[17]

The political situation in the new country changed swiftly. As many as eighty thousand Loyalists may have emigrated by 1783, and more did so during the next few years.[18] But thousands of others immigrated into the nation, including many of the German mercenaries who fought on the side of the British. And once it became clear that neither anarchy nor dictatorship resulted from the Revolution, many Loyalists or their children returned. Even the fanatical Tory reverend Samuel Peters, whom Arnold had confronted in New Haven, returned from exile and settled in New York. One of his nephews became a justice on the Connecticut Supreme Court, and another became its governor.[19]

The nation also divided almost immediately into new political factions that had little to do with the war itself, with people like Thomas Jefferson and Eleazar Oswald on one side and John Adams and Benjamin Tallmadge on the other. But these were political divisions, not violent ones. When the pro-Adams *Connecticut Courant* compared Jefferson to Arnold in the contentious 1800 election, even the most vehement partisans could see that the author of the Declaration of Independence was not as terrible as Arnold, no matter how destructive they thought his presidential policies might be.[20] Arnold became an exception, a bad example, an aberration.[21] John Adams wrote on this phenomenon just after the initial treason:

> When we consider that an officer of his high Rank, long services and brilliant Reputation, was not able to carry over with a single officer nor soldier, nor even his own Valet, nor his Wife nor his Child, — When We consider the Universal Execration in which his Treason was held by the whole Army and the whole Continent — When We consider the Firmness and Dignity with which Andre was punished, We must conclude the American Army and People stand Strong, as strong against the Arts and Bribes as the Arms and Valour of their Enemies.[22]

An act of villainy can bring a people together in agreement as surely as an act of heroism can. But defining boundaries is only the beginning of wisdom and creating a country, a home, a civil democratic society is a process, not an end.

No one knew that better than Connecticut wordsmith Noah Webster. On April 1, 1798, perhaps remembering his good times at Yale playing the fife while George Washington marched through town, he moved into Benedict Arnold's two-story New Haven home. The stocks no longer hung in the square outside, but the smuggler's vaults remained in the cellar.[23] Back in 1780 the young Webster had written two scathing responses to Arnold's post-treason "Letter to the Inhabitants of America" in the *Courant*.[24] Now he wrote his groundbreaking American dictionary in the very house used by that Yankee merchant who betrayed his country. He might have thought twice when he put pen to paper on the definition of "treason," echoing the Constitution and adding "the highest crime of a civil nature of which a man can be guilty." But it was his definition of "society" that remains unusually perceptive:

The union of a number of rational beings; or a number of persons united, either for a temporary or permanent purpose. Thus the inhabitants of a state or of a city constitute a society, having common interests; and hence it is called a community. In a more enlarged sense, the whole race or family of man is a society, and called human society. The true and natural foundation of society, are the wants and fears of individuals.[25]

Benedict Arnold's treason and terror gave the new American society some of its first conflicts between those wants and fears. It forced both the people and their government to weigh vengeance and forgiveness, security and freedom, and community and individual rights. And all those who tried to build rather than destroy, from Washington to Webster, created in the houses of the past the more perfect language of the future.

✳ ✳ ✳
A *Note on* Sources

There are dozens of biographies and treatments of Benedict Arnold, and the secondary sources on the American Revolution are numberless. But in many cases I have made sure to use letters, memoirs, and diaries to get to the root of problems, to understand the words and reactions of key players, and to mark the differences in this narrative from previous ones. Many of the primary sources for the war have, of course, been published, and I have used those when available, in particular *Connecticut's Naval Office, Documentary Life of Nathan Hale, American Archives, Public Records of the State of Connecticut, Historical Collection, A Hero and a Spy: The Revolutionary War Correspondence of Benedict Arnold*, and various published papers, diaries, and journals. The primary sources on the New London raid and Battle of Groton Heights are more limited, though a series of books containing primary source memoirs on the subject was republished and then added to throughout the nineteenth century, collected here in *Battle of Groton Heights*. Some interest in the subject has again surfaced in the form of articles and academic essays, though with the "rehabilitation" of Arnold by many scholars, it is not a popular theme and is often brushed over in biographies that otherwise contain valuable information on Arnold's life. Walter Powell's short book, *Murder or Mayhem*, from the year 2000, is a balanced source for the New London raid that is very useful in sorting through the conflicting accounts and in pointing the way toward certain sources.

ABBREVIATIONS

CHS	Connecticut Historical Society
CSLA	Connecticut State Library Archives
DP	Deane Papers
GWPLC	George Washington Papers at the Library of Congress
JTP	Jonathan Trumbull Papers (CHS)
JOTP	Joseph Trumbull Papers (CHS)
NHM	New Haven Museum
NLCHS	New London County Historical Society
NSRWP	Nathaniel Shaw Revolutionary War Papers (NLCHS)
NYHS	New York Historical Society
SDP	Silas Deane Papers (CHS)
TP	Trumbull Papers (CSLA)

✳ ✳ ✳
Notes

PREFACE

1 George Washington to Lt. Col. John Laurens, October 13, 1780, in *The Glorious Struggle: George Washington's Revolutionary War Letters*, ed. Edward Lengel (Washington DC: Smithsonian, 2008), 214.

2 Joseph Plumb Martin, *Private Yankee Doodle*, ed. George Scheer (1830; repr., Boston: Little, Brown, 1962), 204–5.

3 I mean a document other than the self-serving political "letter" published at the time in *Royal Gazette* and other newspapers. *Rivington's Royal Gazette* (New York), no. 421, October 11, 1780.

4 Benedict Arnold's obituary, *Gazette of the United States*, August 27, 1801. The obituary was reprinted throughout the country, except when only one line was given; in that case they just called him "notorious throughout the world" rather than giving a description of his deeds. Those that included a more detailed obituary also cited his "total want of moral principle" along with the admission of his early heroism.

5 L. H. Munson, "Benedict Arnold," *Connecticut Magazine* 12, no. 1 (March–April 1901): 49–58.

6 For example, see John Spears, "Benedict Arnold as Naval Patriot," *Harpers Monthly Magazine* 106, no. 632 (January 1903): 277–81.

7 Marian O'Keefe, quoted in Michael Knight, "Native Norwich Is Ignoring Benedict Arnold: 'Afraid of Reaction,'" *New York Times*, March 5, 1976; O'Keefe, interview with the author, Bridgeport, CT, January 24, 2013.

8 John Adams to Nathanael Greene, May 9, 1777, Philadelphia, in *John Adams: Revolutionary Writings, 1775–1783*, ed. Gordon Wood (New York: Library of America, 2011), 141.

9 Ellsworth Grant, "Benedict Arnold," *Hartford Courant*, June 28, 1976.

10 R. W. Apple Jr., "Benedict Arnold, Hero," *New York Times Magazine*, Best of the Millennium Edition, 1999.

11 Marquis de Lafayette, quoted in Charlemagne Tower, *The Marquis de La Fayette in the American Revolution* (New York: Da Capo, 1970), 2:166.

12 Henry Dearborn, quoted in Lloyd Brown and Howard Peckham, eds., *Revolutionary War Journals of Henry Dearborn, 1775–1783* (Chicago: Caxton Club, 1939), 218.

13 For example, James Kirby Martin, author of a laudatory book called *Benedict Arnold, Revolutionary Hero*, said recently, "I think he is a general in reha-

bilitation or, I guess, an American who is being rehabilitated. I think we are learning that the Revolution isn't the simplistic contest between good and evil that we were perhaps taught when we were schoolchildren, that indeed it was far more complex than that, and not all the good people were on one side and the bad people on the other side." Virginia Groark, "Beloved Hero and Despised Traitor," *New York Times*, April 21, 2002. Martin's claim is based in a truism, that we too often simplify history, especially when we use terms like "good" and "evil." But his conclusion that Arnold is a misunderstood hero is suspect, to say the least.

14 For example, a Norwich theater manager recently stated, "I am not going to pass judgment on whether this man is a traitor or not." See Adam Benson, "New Musical, Events, Bringing Benedict Arnold 'Out of Hiding,'" *Norwich Bulletin*, June 16, 2013. This article was picked up nationally by the Associated Press and other news agencies.

15 As a good recent argument for the Revolutionary War as a civil war, see Thomas B. Allen, *Tories: Fighting for the King in America's First Civil War* (New York: Harper, 2010). I would contend that Allen's point is valid only from the perspective of the Loyalists themselves, and while the Revolutionary War had aspects similar to a civil war, was not one from the American or even the British perspective. Rather, a considerable portion of the population, perhaps 15 percent, actively supported the invading British forces, while 40 percent actively opposed them, with the remaining percentage neutral or undecided. On their own without the British army, navy, and supplies, the Loyalists could never and would never have created a civil war.

16 Charles Jarvis, "An American's Experience in the British Army," *Connecticut Magazine* 11, no. 2 (1907): 191–215, and no. 3 (1907): 477–90. This is a remarkable document in its honesty and detail.

17 "Evidence in the Claim of Saml. Ketchum, Jan. 24, 1787," in Alexander Fraser, *United Empire Loyalists* (Toronto: L.K. Cameron, 1905), 231.

18 Joseph Bettys is a good example of this sort. After playing both sides and taking part in a number of ruthless arsons and murders, he was caught and executed as a traitor in 1782.

19 Washington Irving, *Life of Washington*, vol. 14 of *Works of Washington Irving* (n.p.: Jenson Society, 1907), 198.

20 James Wilson wrote the rough draft of this article and in his papers was very careful to separate treason from political disagreements, felonies, or "piracy" and clearly denoted treason as belonging to two species of actions, even though English law used much broader definitions. The founders' intentions may have been to narrow the definitions to prevent government overreach, but it is interesting that they stopped narrowing at the point describing Arnold's exact crimes; it was clearly on their minds. See James Wilson, *The*

Works of the Honourable James Wilson, vol. 3 (Philadelphia: Lorenzo, 1804). Also see James Madison's explanation in the forty-third letter of *The Federalist Papers*. Alexander Hamilton, James Madison, and John Jay, *The Federalist Papers* (Toronto: Bantam Books, 1982), 217–25.

21 Brian Carso, *"Whom Can We Trust Now?" The Meaning of Treason in the United States, from the Revolution through the Civil War* (Lanham, MD: Lexington Books, 2006), 22–23, 113–14. Such legal categories may be academic: Timothy McVeigh was not prosecuted for "domestic terrorism," either—he was convicted on fifteen counts of murder and conspiracy.

22 It's interesting to note that Chief Justice Marshall was part of the futile resistance at the destruction of Richmond, Virginia, by Arnold's troops.

23 For the mention of Lincoln, see *Harper's Weekly*, October 6, 1863, 626; for Davis, see *Harper's Weekly*, November 19, 1864, 738. Mentions of Arnold spiked during the Civil War with "Judas Iscariot, Benedict Arnold, and Jefferson Davis" lumped together in Northern papers. See *Hartford Daily Courant*, January 10, 1863. On the opposite side, though many compared Lincoln to Arnold, the *Richmond Inquirer* mentioned Arnold in a positive light while talking about the lack of Yankee commanders: "If we except Benedict Arnold, there never was a Northern man who was fitted to command." Reprinted in the *New York Times*, May 10, 1861.

24 Thomas Jefferson to William Carmichael and William Short, April 24, 1792, in *The Writings of Thomas Jefferson*, ed. H. A. Washington, vol. 3 (Philadelphia: Lippincott, 1871), 353.

25 Charles Royster, "The Nature of Treason: Revolutionary Virtue and American Reactions to Benedict Arnold," *William and Mary Quarterly*, 3rd ser., 36, no. 2 (1979): 186 et al.

26 Lori J. Ducharme and Gary Alan Fine, "The Construction of Nonpersonhood and Demonization: Commemorating the Traitorous Reputation of Benedict Arnold," *Social Forces* 73, no. 4 (1995): 1311–12, 1327, 1328.

27 "Benedict Arnold's New Haven Home," *New Haven Register*, June 1, 1902.

28 Carso, *"Whom Can We Trust Now?,"* 19.

29 "Terrorism 2002–2005," U.S. Department of Justice, accessed April 10, 2013, http://www.fbi.gov/stats-services/publications/terrorism-2002-2005.

30 Bruce Hoffman, *Inside Terrorism* (New York: Columbia University, 1998), 32.

31 See Noah Webster's *Dictionary* (1828): "HOMEBRED, a. Native; natural; as homebred lusts. 1. Domestic; originating at home; not foreign; as 'homebred evil' from Spenser's *Faerie Queene*." See Samuel Johnson's 1755 *Dictionary of the English Language*, which also quotes "homebred evil" from Spenser.

32 See Webster, *Dictionary* (1828), s.v. "parricide." The fourth definition reads, "One who invades or destroys any to whom he owes particular reverence, as his country or patron." Jefferson used the term quite often, as in Thomas

Jefferson to George Washington, January 10, 1781, in *Memoir, Correspondence, and Miscellanies from the Papers of Thomas Jefferson*, ed. Thomas Jefferson Randolph, vol. 1 (Charlottesville: Carr, 1829), 200. See also various other sources, such as the *Norwich Packet*, September 13, 1781, 3: "Led by that parricide of his country Benedict Arnold." The term is nearly identical to "homegrown terrorist," though it can also refer to a political tyrant.

ON THE EDGE OF SPRING

1 John Bissell, *Hartford Times*, February 18, 1899, Bolton Historical Society, www.boltoncthistory.org. The article repeats a weather report given by Bolton town clerk John Bissell in 1741.

2 D. Hamilton Hurd, *History of New London County Connecticut* (Philadelphia: Lewis, 1882), 21.

3 Ernest Rogers, *Connecticut's Naval Office at New London during the War of the American Revolution* (New London, CT: New London County Historical Society, 1933), 4. This book contains an edited collection from Nathaniel Shaw Jr., Mercantile Letter Book, December 25, 1765, to July 23, 1783, New London, CT, photostat copy, 387 fsh 27, CSLA. I have checked the letter book at the CSLA but have used Rogers's version in most cases for ease of reference.

4 Bond for Hezekiah Huntington for £2000, MS73846, CHS.

5 *Vital Records of Norwich, 1659–1848* (Norwich: Society of Colonial Wars in the State of Connecticut, 1913), 1: 124, 153.

6 Iain Murray, *Jonathan Edwards: A New Biography* (Edinburgh, Scotland: Banner of Truth, 1987), 169; Wilson H. Kimnach, ed., *The Sermons of Jonathan Edwards: A Reader* (New Haven, CT: Yale University Press, 1999), 49–65 et al.

7 Ezra Stiles, quoted in Louis Leonard Tucker, *Connecticut's Seminary of Sedition: Yale College* (Chester, CT: Pequot, 1974), 32.

8 Richard Buel, *Dear Liberty: Connecticut's Mobilization for the Revolutionary War* (Middletown, CT: Wesleyan University Press, 1980), 4–5. Compared to many other states, Connecticut's slave and servant population was quite small, though both were certainly present.

9 Benjamin Tinkham Marshall, ed., *A Modern History of New London County* (New York: Lewis, 1922), 1:189.

10 Buel, *Dear Liberty*, 7–10.

11 Lydia Sigourney, *Letters of Life* (New York: Appleton, 1866), 6.

12 Oliver Arnold, deed of sale, NLCHS.

13 "Ground Plan of the Norwich Town Church, 1756–1761," in Mary Perkins, *Old Houses of the Antient Town of Norwich* (Norwich, CT: Bulletin, 1895), 353.

14 Frances Caulkins, *History of Norwich* (Hartford, CT: Case, Lockwood, 1866), 276; O. Arnold, deed of sale, NLCHS.

15 William Harris, *The Battle of Groton Heights: A Collection of Narratives, Official Reports, Records, Etc. of the Storming of Fort Griswold, the Massacre of Its Garrison, and the Burning of New London by British Troops under the Command of Brig. Gen. Benedict Arnold, on the Sixth of Sept., 1781*, ed. Charles Allyn, rev. ed. (New London, CT: Allyn, 1882), 216–17.

16 Ellen Larned, *History of Windham County, Connecticut* (Worcester, MA: Hamilton, 1874), 1:411.

17 Hannah Arnold's letters, *Historical Magazine* 4, no. 1 (1860): 418. Arnold's music and practice verses still exist.

18 Hannah Arnold to Benedict Arnold, August 30, 1753, in *Magazine of History*, 3:258.

19 H. Arnold to B. Arnold, April 12, 1754, in Caulkins, *History of Norwich*, 410.

20 H. Arnold to B. Arnold, August 9, 1754, Pierpont Morgan Library, New York City.

21 Benedict Arnold Sr., warrant for arrest, November 4, 1754, Huntington Digital Library, San Marino, CA.

22 Caulkins, *History of Norwich*, 327–28; *New London Summary*, July 11, 1760.

23 There are a number of descriptions of Arnold scattered around diaries and letters; all agree on gray or black eyes, stocky build, and black hair. The best likeness of him is a painting done as a miniature for his second wife, when he was around forty, in his new British uniform. But this is owned by Arnold's descendants, and as of yet it is kept under lock and key. One exception is at the Saratoga National Historical Park, where there is a postcard with this image available for sale. It shows a handsome man with thin lips, large eyes, and receding powdered hair, starting to put on a little midlife weight.

24 Sigourney, *Letters of Life*, 14. Much of Arnold's early life often noted in biographies is based on early secondary sources that seem to have created a rich back story out of nothing, years later. I have tried to eliminate this suspect anecdotal evidence as much as possible, even though such stories might have served my purpose in presenting Arnold's home life. But Sigourney was hearing this story directly from Jerusha Lathrop, and considering Arnold's physical bravery, it seems reasonable.

25 Glenn Weaver, *Jonathan Trumbull: Connecticut's Merchant Magistrate* (Hartford: Connecticut Historical Society, 1956), 11–21.

26 Robert Armstrong, *Historic Lebanon* (Lebanon, CT: First Congregational Church, 1950), 7.

27 Weaver, *Jonathan Trumbull*, 4.

28 David Morris Roth, *Connecticut's War Governor: Jonathan Trumbull* (Hartford: American Revolution Bicentennial Commission of Connecticut, 1974)

7–9; Isaac Stuart, *Life of Jonathan Trumbull, Sen.* (Boston: Crocker and Brewster, 1859), 28–29.

29 J. H. Trumbull and C. J. Hoadly, eds., *Public Records of the Colony of Connecticut, 1636–1776* (Hartford, CT: 1850–90), 8:175, 212, 242, 245–46, 343–54; 9:134, 380, 428, 445, 467, 538–39, 566–67; 10:219–20; 11:412, 460, 559.

30 Harold Selesky, *War and Society in Colonial Connecticut* (New Haven, CT: Yale University Press, 1990), 77, 85.

31 Weaver, *Jonathan Trumbull*, 72–90. See also various letters at CHS and CSLA.

32 John Ledyard to Jonathan Trumbull, July 17, 1761, et al., folder 3, box 2, JTP, CHS.

33 Cass Ledyard Shaw, *The Ledyard Family in America* (West Kenebunk, ME: Phoenix, 1993), 9–10. This is a real stretch, though with his knowledge of drugs it made sense to people at the time. It was probably only a coincidence, or at the most someone who actually stood to gain from their deaths was responsible.

34 William Ledyard to Jonathan Trumbull, October 30, 1761, folder 3, box 2, JTP, CHS.

35 Joseph Trumbull to John Ledyard, September 12, 1761, et al., folder 3, box 2, JTP, CHS.

36 Robert Livingston of New York, quoted in Selesky, *War and Society*, 65–66. See also Buel, *Dear Liberty*, 4.

37 *New York Mercury*, May 28, 1759, published an ad looking for the deserter Benedict Arnold, eighteen years of age, by trade a weaver, with "dark complexion, light eyes, black hair." The physical description and age fit exactly, though he was not a weaver.

38 *Rolls of Connecticut Men in the French and Indian War I*, vol. 9 of *Collections of the Connecticut Historical Society* (Hartford: Connecticut Historical Society, 1903); and *Rolls of Connecticut Men in the French and Indian War II*, vol. 10 of *Collections of the Connecticut Historical Society* (Hartford: Connecticut Historical Society, 1905).

39 Roth, *Connecticut's War Governor*, 17–24.

40 Selesky, *War and Society*, 216–19.

41 Benedict Arnold Sr., warrant for arrest, May 26, 1760, Historical Society of Pennsylvania.

42 *New London Summary*, August 8, 1760.

43 Daniel Lathrop, mortgage, Miscellaneous Papers, Historical Society of Pennsylvania, in Willard Sterne Randall, *Benedict Arnold: Patriot and Traitor* (New York: Morrow, 1990), 35.

44 Sigourney, *Letters of Life*, 16.

45 Ibid., 13–14.

1 Photograph of broadside advertisement originally in Toledo Museum, MSS 106, folder L, Papers of Benedict Arnold, 1761–94, Whitney Library, NHM.

2 Sign, Whitney Library, NHM. Though many historians might wish the sign has a deeper meaning, it was more likely a bad translation, something like "everything in one," an ad for the store that has everything.

3 "Voyage of the Phoenix," June–July 1765, with Samuel Mansfield, oversize item 5, MSS 106, Papers of Benedict Arnold, 1761–94, Whitney Library, NHM.

4 *Connecticut Journal*, December 1, 1769, and September 27, 1771.

5 Buel, *Dear Liberty*, 11.

6 "A Discourse Occasionally Made on Burning the Effigie of the ST — P M-N, in New London, in the Colony of Connecticut, 1765," C561, CHS, 7–11.

7 Oscar Zeichner, *Connecticut's Years of Controversy* (Williamsburg, VA: Institute of Early American History and Culture, 1949), 51, 53–54; Royal Hinman, ed., *A Historical Collection from Records, Files, Etc. of the Part Sustained by Connecticut during the War of the Revolution* (Hartford, CT: Gleason, 1842), 56–57.

8 Eliphalet Dyer to William Samuel Johnson, December 8, 1765, William Samuel Johnson Papers, CHS.

9 David Humphreys, *The Life and Heroic Exploits of Israel Putnam, Major-General in the Revolutionary War* (Hartford, CT: Andrus and Son, 1847), 68.

10 Nathaniel Shaw to Joseph and William Packwood, January 20, 1766, in Rogers, *Connecticut's Naval Office*, 171.

11 Rogers, *Connecticut's Naval Office*, 7. No paintings of Shaw exist, but he apparently bore a strong resemblance to his brother, Thomas, and his mother, Temperance, both of whom sat for paintings in the 1790s.

12 Mercantile Letter Book, in Rogers, *Connecticut's Naval Office*, multiple pages.

13 George Clark, *Silas Deane: A Connecticut Leader in the American Revolution* (New York: Knickerbocker, 1913), 3.

14 Silas Deane to David Webb, April 2, 1765, et al., folder 1, box 1, SDP, CHS; Advertisement, January 8, 1765, *Connecticut Courant*, 1.

15 Silas Deane to Hannah Arnold, January 24, 1776, folder 25, box 1, SDP, CHS.

16 Jonathan Trumbull to William Samuel Johnson, June 23, 1767, in Roth, *Connecticut's War Governor*, 27. Original in the William Samuel Johnson Papers, Columbia University Libraries.

17 Clark, *Silas Deane*, 17; *Connecticut Courant and Weekly Intelligencer*, July 19, 1774, and August 9, 1774, et al.; Silas Deane, minutes of meeting, February 20, 1770, folder 2, box 1, SDP, CHS.

18 James Case, "David Wooster, First Mason of Connecticut," paper read at the

annual convocation of Virginia College, Societas Rosicruciana in Civitatibus Foederatis, typescript 7, MSS 7966, CHS.

19 Memorial to the Honorable General Assembly of the Colony of Connecticut, March 2, 1775, Whitney Library, NHM.

20 Papers of Benedict Arnold, 1761–94, MSS 108, Sherman Family Papers, Whitney Library, NHM.

21 Ibid.

22 Benedict Arnold to John Remsen, March 26, 1768, in Malcolm Decker, *Benedict Arnold: Son of the Havens* (Tarrytown, NY: Abbatt, 1932), 31–32. Original in Massachusetts Historical Society Collections.

23 Arnold to Remsen, April 21, 1768, in Decker, *Benedict Arnold*, 31–32. Original at Maryland Historical Society, MS 2018.

24 *Connecticut Journal*, April 18, 1782. Arnold's house may have been number 82 on "Pump Street." See "Journal of Lieutenant John Charles Philip Von Krafft of the Regiment Von Bose, 1776–1784," in *Collections of the New York Historical Society* (New York: New York Historical Society, 1868–), 15:170.

25 Benedict Arnold to Margaret Mansfield Arnold, January 21, 1774, in *Magazine of History* 3:259.

26 Benedict Arnold to B. Douglas, June 9, 1770, *A Hero and a Spy: The Revolutionary War Correspondence of Benedict Arnold*, ed. Russell Lea (Westminster, MA: Heritage Books, 2006), 5–6.

27 "History of Newspaper Publishing in Connecticut," Connecticut Newspaper Project, Connecticut State Library, November 1996, www.cslib.org.

28 Tucker, *Connecticut's Seminary of Sedition*, 30; Larned, *History of Windham County*, 544.

29 Tucker, *Connecticut's Seminary of Sedition*, 12; Henry Johnston, *Yale and Her Honor-Roll in the American Revolution* (New York: Putnam, 1888).

30 Brooks Mather Kelley, *Yale: A History* (New Haven, CT: Yale University Press, 1974), 40, 60.

31 Robert Cray, "The Revolutionary Spy as Hero: Nathan Hale in the Public Memory," *Connecticut History* 38, no. 2 (1999): 87; "Lieutenant Elisha Bostwick's Narrative," in *Documentary Life of Nathan Hale*, ed. George Dudley Seymour (New Haven, CT: Tuttle, Morehouse, and Taylor, 1941), 324–25. Hale's minister and teacher was Joseph Huntington, brother of the future president of Congress. It was a small world.

32 Benjamin Tallmadge, *Memoir of Col. Benjamin Tallmadge* (New York: Holman, 1858), 5–6.

33 Benjamin Tallmadge to Nathan Hale, [1772?], folder 1, Correspondence, Nathan Hale Collection, CHS.

34 *Connecticut Journal and New Haven Post Boy*, September 10, 1773.

35 Tucker, *Connecticut's Seminary of Sedition*, 15 et al.

36 In reality, it was far more than that — see Ireland, for example.

37 Zeichner, *Connecticut's Years of Controversy*, 85–86.

38 Nathaniel Shaw to Peter Vandevoort, October 22, 1773, in Rogers, *Connecticut's Naval Office*, 251.

39 Benedict Arnold to Peggy Arnold, January 21, 1774, in Decker, *Benedict Arnold*, 40–41. This letter is in private hands and recently went for auction online, allowing me a direct look at the manuscript.

40 Buel, *Dear Liberty*, 26–27.

41 Frances Caulkins, *History of New London, Connecticut* (New London, CT: Utley, 1895), 503.

42 Silas Deane, *Connecticut Courant*, quoted in Samuel B. Webb, *Correspondence and Journals of Samuel B. Webb*, ed. Worthington Chauncey Ford, 3 vols. (New York: Arno, 1969), 1:31.

43 Diary entry, August 15, 1774, *The Adams Papers, Diary of John Adams*, ed. L. H. Butterfield (Cambridge, MA: Bellknap Press of Harvard University, 1961), 2:98; Deane to Trumbull, August 16, 1774, DP, in *New York Historical Society*, 1:3–4; Silas Deane to Elizabeth Deane, August 29, 1774, DP, in *New York Historical Society*, 1:5–8.

44 Memorial of delegates of New London and Windham counties, re. militia law, September 8, 1774, folder 2, box 1, Jedediah Huntington Papers, 1758–1814, CHS.

45 Reverend Samuel Peters to [?], 1774, *American Archives: A Documentary History of the North American Colonies; Of the Causes and Accomplishment of the American Revolution*, ed. Peter Force, 4th series (Washington DC, 1837–53), 1:716–17.

46 Hezekiah Huntington et al., testimony, December 6, 1774, Windham, in Force, *American Archives*, 1:717–18; Hinman, *Historical Collection*, 19.

47 Samuel Peters, *General History of Connecticut* (1781; repr., New York: Appleton, 1877), 268–69. Take this account with a grain of salt; Peters's book is full of self-serving rhetoric, exaggerations, distortions, and mistakes.

48 *Connecticut Journal*, March 1, 1775.

49 *Holt's Journal*, February 16, 1775, in *Diary of the American Revolution from Newspapers and Original Documents*, ed. Frank Moore (1858; repr., New York, Arno, 1969), 1:18.

50 Force, *American Archives*, 1:1038–75, 1202, 1210, 1215, 1236–38, 1258–60, 1270.

51 Jonathan Trumbull, speech, part 1, box 20, TP, CSLA, 101a–c.

52 Shaw to Trumbull, April 25, 1775, in Rogers, *Connecticut's Naval Office*, 26.

53 Shaw to Vandevoort, April 8, 1775, ibid., 269.

54 Buel, *Dear Liberty*, 35–36. Though widely reported, the Putnam anecdote is probably a classical reference rather than a genuine occurrence. But if taken metaphorically, it is certainly accurate.

55 Johnston, *Yale and Her Honor-Roll*, 8–9.

56 William Phipps Blake, *A Brief Account of the Life and Patriotic Services of Jonathan Mix of New Haven* (New Haven, CT: Tuttle, Morehouse, and Taylor, 1886), 2–6; Memorial to the Honorable General Assembly of the Colony of Connecticut, March 2, 1775, Whitney Library, NHM.

57 Trumbull and Hoadly, *Public Records of the Colony*, 14:308–9, 327–28.

58 The Connecticut Historical Society Collections include hundreds of letters between all these men (and others). Benedict Arnold was one of these interconnected merchants, and we can guess that most of his letters to these men were burned later. Those that do survive point to a much more extensive correspondence with Deane, Shaw, and Mumford, at least, and probably Wooster, Lamb, Varick, Oswald, and others.

RESIST EVEN UNTO BLOOD

1 Hinman, *Historical Collection*, 29–31, 280; Details of these confusing and inconsistent financial shenanigans can be found in the Revolutionary War Series 1, 1775, CSLA, reel 3, 3:20a, 21a, 26b, 53, 633a, et al.

2 Ethan Allen to Abraham Yates, May 11, 1775, in *Proceedings of the Vermont Historical Society, October 8, 1872* (Montpelier: Vermont Historical Society, 1872), 109–10; Arnold to Committee of Safety, May 11, 1775, in Lea, *Hero and a Spy*, 27–28.

3 Jonathan Trumbull to Eliphalet Dyer, Roger Sherman, and Silas Deane, May 15, 1775, folder 10, box 3, Correspondence, 1785, JTP, CHS.

4 Benedict Arnold, regimental memorandum book, in *The Pennsylvania Magazine of History and Biography* (Philadelphia: Historical Society of Pennsylvania, 1884), 363–76; Memorial to the Honorable General Assembly of the Colony of Connecticut, March 2, 1775, Whitney Library, NHM.

5 Benedict Arnold to Connecticut General Assembly, May 19, 1775, folder 10, box 3, Correspondence, 1785, JTP, CHS.

6 Benedict Arnold to John Stephens, May 21, 1775, folder B, box 11, American Revolution Collection, CHS.

7 Arnold, regimental memorandum book, in *Pennsylvania Magazine*, 363–76.

8 *Connecticut Journal*, August 9, 1775.

9 Isaac Arnold, *Life of Benedict Arnold: His Patriotism and His Treason* (Chicago: Jansen, McClurg, 1905), 47.

10 Hinman, *Historical Collection*, 238.

11 Silas Deane to Elizabeth Deane, August 29, 1774, DP, in *New York Historical*

Society, 1:15. See also folders 8 and 9, box 1, SDP, CHS, for more examples of Deane's excitement that summer.

12 S. Deane to E. Deane, July 1, 1775, DP, in *New York Historical Society*, 1:66.

13 Ibid., July 20, 1775, 1:74–75.

14 John Adams, "Notes of Debate in Continental Congress," diary entry, September 23, 1775, Adams Family Papers, Massachusetts Historical Society, www.masshist.org.

15 S. Deane to E. Deane, June 18, 1775, DP, in *New York Historical Society*, 1:61.

16 S. Deane to E. Deane, June 16, 1775, DP, ibid., 1:58–59. The letters to his wife before and after this are full of the merits of George Washington.

17 Buel, *Dear Liberty*, 36–37.

18 Rogers, *Connecticut's Naval Office*, 75.

19 Caulkins, *History of New London*, 515.

20 Records of artillery or Independent Company of New London with articles of formation, 1762, kept until 1777, NLCHS.

21 Benjamin Tallmadge to Nathan Hale, July 4, 1775, in Seymour, *Documentary Life*, 37–39. Original letter at Historical Society of Pennsylvania.

22 Caulkins, *History of New London*, 515.

23 "Hale's Army Diary," in Seymour, *Documentary Life*, 211.

24 Rogers, *Connecticut's Naval Office*, 85–86. This information comes from Shaw's account books, kept in the Shaw Collection at Yale University.

25 Cray, "Revolutionary Spy," 87; "Hale's Army Diary," in Seymour, *Documentary Life*, 183–84, 253, et al.

26 Gilbert Saltonstall to Nathan Hale, December 18, 1775, folder 2, Correspondence, Nathan Hale Collection, CHS.

27 "Hale's Army Diary," in Seymour, *Documentary Life*, 180.

28 Stuart, *Life of Jonathan Trumbull*, 180–81.

29 Washington to Jonathan Trumbull Jr., January 1784, in "Jonathan Trumbull, Governor of Connecticut," in *Records and Papers of the New London County Historical Society*, pt. 5 (New London: New London County Historical Society, 1904), 2:443.

30 "Jonathan Trumbull, Governor of Connecticut," in *Records and Papers*, 444. "Brother Jonathan" was used much as the term "G.I. Joe" would be used in the twentieth century. See Dudley S. Gould, *Life and Times of Brother Jonathan* (Middletown, CT: Southfarm, 2001).

31 Ambrose Serle, *The American Journal of Ambrose Serle, 1776–1778*, ed. Edward Tatum (New York: New York Times, 1969), 215–16.

32 DP, in *New York Historical Society*, 4:76.

33 Joseph Trumbull to George Washington, December 13, 1776, and Washington to Trumbull, December 16, 1776, both in *The Papers of George Washing-*

ton, Revolutionary War Series, ed. Philander Chase, Dorothy Twohig, and W. W. Abbott (Charlottesville: University Press of Virginia, 1988), 5:328–29, 360–61.

34 Hundreds of letters still exist today, probably only a fraction of those received by Joseph Trumbull during his two years in this position.

35 George Washington to the President of Congress, June 28, 1776, in *The Writings of George Washington from Original Manuscript Sources, 1745–1799*, ed. John C. Fitzpatrick (Washington, DC: U.S. Government Printing Office, 1933–44), 5:192.

36 *Connecticut Courant*, June 13, 1780.

37 Hoadly, *Public Records of the State of Connecticut* (Hartford: Case, Lockwood, and Brainard, 1894), 1:139, 242, 377, 425; 14:415–16; 15:14–15, 119, 135, 314, 413.

38 Ibid., 11:40, 173, 190, 258; 14:418; 15:17–18, 127, 317–18, 323.

39 Benedict Arnold to Richard Varick, July 26, 1776, MS 101153, Benedict Arnold, CHS.

40 "Rolls and Lists of Connecticut Men in the Revolution, 1775–1783," *Connecticut Historical Society Collections*, vol. 8 (Hartford: Connecticut Historical Society Museum, 1901), multiple pages; Roth, *Connecticut's War Governor*, 52–53.

41 "Hale's Army Diary," in Seymour, *Documentary Life*, 177.

42 Gideon Saltonstall to Nathan Hale, December 4, 1775, folder 2, Correspondence, Nathan Hale Collection, CHS.

43 Washington to Joseph Reed, November 28, 1775, in Fitzpatrick, *Writings of George Washington*, 4:137–38.

44 Returns of December 30, 1775, and January 8, 1776, in Force, *American Archives*, 4:491–92, 631.

45 Deane to Thomas Mumford, October 3, 1775, folder 21, box 1, SDP, CHS.

46 Rogers, *Connecticut's Naval Office*, 54–55.

47 Shaw to John Mackibbins, July 12, 1775, in Rogers, *Connecticut's Naval Office*, 275.

48 Shaw to Samuel Solly Wintworth, January 16, 1776, ibid., 278.

49 Shaw to Washington, July 22, 1776, ibid., 285; Shaw to William Constant, January 16, 1776, ibid., 279.

50 Shaw to Joseph Trumbull, January 8, 1776, Correspondence, January 1776, JOTP, CHS.

51 William Ledyard to Samuel Gray, May 30, 1778, MS 67562, William Ledyard Letters, 1778, 1780, CHS.

52 Ebenezer Ledyard and William Ledyard to Joseph Trumbull, September 25, 1775, Correspondence, July 1775, JOTP, CHS.

53 Ledyard and Ledyard to Trumbull, July 31, 1775, ibid.

54 Ledyard and Ledyard to Trumbull, June 8, 1775, ibid.

55 Silas Deane to Hannah Arnold, January 24, 1776, folder 25, box 1, SDP, CHS.

56 Hannah Arnold to Jeremiah Wadsworth, October 4, 1777, folder 6, box 3, Jeremiah Wadsworth Papers, CHS.

57 Fitzpatrick, *Writings of George Washington*, 3:436–38, 472, 510.

58 John Joseph Henry, *Account of Arnold's Campaign against Quebec* (Albany, NY: Munsell, 1877), multiple pages. This work provides confirmation of the facts as well.

59 Ebenezer to Andrew Huntington, January 21, 1776, in *Letters Written by Ebenezer Huntington during the American Revolution*, ed. Charles Heartman (New York: Heartman, 1915).

60 Isaac Leake, *The Life of John Lamb* (Albany, NY: Munsell, 1857), 121–31.

61 Benedict Arnold to David Wooster, December 31, 1775, MS 101153, Benedict Arnold, JTP, CHS.

62 Later Lamb almost fought a duel with a partisan of Horatio Gates to defend Arnold's honor. See Leake, *Life of John Lamb*, 261.

63 Benedict Arnold to Silas Deane, March 30, 1776, in Force, *American Archives*, 5:549.

64 Silas Deane to Philip Schuyler, August 10, 1775, in Benson Lossing, *Life and Times of Philip Schuyler* (New York: Sheldon, 1872), 385.

65 Naval Committee of Congress to Silas Deane, November 17, 1775, DP, in *New York Historical Society*, 1:90–91; Secret Committee to Deane, March 1, 2, 3, ibid., 1:116–17, 119, 123; Silas Deane to Elizabeth Deane, March 2–3, 1776, ibid., 1:119–23.

66 The sum of 6 million livre is worth about $12 million today, although the actual impact of that kind of money at the time was much greater, perhaps ten times that amount. Deane himself may have paid this and been partially paid back — the whole exchange is quite a muddle and has never been satisfactorily explained.

67 Harlow Giles Unger, *Lafayette* (New York: Wiley, 2003), 8–22.

68 Agreement between the Marquis de La Fayette and Silas Deane, December 7, in Force, *American Archives*, 3:1090.

69 Multiple letters in Rogers, *Connecticut's Naval Office*, 34–44.

70 Nathaniel Shaw to Andrew Huntington, October 17, 1776, folder 7, MS 77743, series 1, Andrew Huntington Papers, CHS.

71 Joshua Hempstead, *Diary of Joshua Hempstead* (New London, CT: New London County Historical Society, 1901), 665.

72 Building and objects, NLCHS.

73 Samuel Huntington, congressional decree, April 2, 1776, 1907.07.21, NSRWP, NLCHS.

74 Blake, *Jonathan Mix*, 22–26.

75 Vote of New London on Articles of Confederation, December 29, 1777, in Caulkins, *History of New London County*, 504.

76 Nathaniel Shaw to Jonathan Trumbull, September 25, 1778, et al., folder 3, box 4, JTP, CHS.

77 Ledyard to Shaw, May 13, 1776, 1907.07.25, NSRWP, NLCHS; Ledyard to Shaw, May 14, 1776, 1907.07.26, NSRWP, NLCHS.

78 Hinman, *Historical Collection*, 365–66. Many of the important sites and homes described in this book still exist and can be visited, including Fort Griswold, the Shaw Mansion, the Hempstead Houses, the Nathan Hale School House, the Jonathan Trumbull House, the War Office, the Lathrop Mansion, the Samuel Huntington House, the Silas Deane House, the Avery House, and many more. Others, like Benjamin Tallmadge's home, remain intact and in private hands.

79 "Commission from the Colony of Connecticut," July 10, 1776, in Trumbull and Hoadly, *Public Records of the Colony*, 15:474; see also "Commission from the State of Connecticut," October 21, 1778, TP, CSLA.

80 Samuel Huntington to Nathaniel Shaw, May 4, 1776, in Rogers, *Connecticut's Naval Office*, 20.

81 John Hancock to Nathaniel Shaw, October 30, 1776, box 10, American Revolution Collection, CHS.

82 Shaw to Hancock, July 31, 1776, in Rogers, *Connecticut's Naval Office*, 286.

83 Shaw to Washington, August 1, 1776, series 4, GWPLC.

84 Washington to Shaw, August 7, 1776, in Rogers, *Connecticut's Naval Office*, 91.

85 Hinman, *Historical Collection*, 328–29.

86 Shaw to Trumbull, August 7, 1776, in Rogers, *Connecticut's Naval Office*, 286.

87 Ebenezer and William Ledyard to Joseph Trumbull, August 10, 1775, Correspondence, July 1775, JOTP, CHS.

88 Jedediah Elderkin, report to Jonathan Trumbull, Governor, November 1775, in Hinman, *Historical Collection*, 198; Ebenezer and William Ledyard to Joseph Trumbull, July 31, 1775, Correspondence, July 1775, JOTP, CHS.

89 Hinman, *Historical Collection*, 534 et al.

90 Hale to Tallmadge, copy from letter owned by Rev. D. Sprague, Albany, NY, folder 2, Correspondence, Nathan Hale Collection, CHS. See the Benjamin Tallmadge Collection at Princeton University for examples of Tallmadge's own rhymes.

91 Tallmadge, *Memoir*, 7.

92 "Nathan Hale's Receipt Book," in Seymour, *Documentary Life*, 248–78.

93 Tallmadge, *Memoir*, 9–10.

94 Israel Putnam, quoted in Benson Bobrick, *Angel in the Whirlwind: The Tri-*

umph of the American Revolution (New York: Simon and Schuster, 2011), 199.

95 For evidence of the panic caused by the situation, see Hoadly, *Public Records of the State*, 1:120, 123, 127, 162–63, 207–8, 591, et al.

1 George Washington to William Heath, September 1, 1776, in Fitzpatrick, *Writings of George Washington*, 6:1–2.

2 "General Hull's Account of the Last Hours and Last Words of Hale," in Seymour, *Documentary Life*, 307–10.

3 Stephen Hempstead, "The Capture and Execution of Capt. Hale, in 1776," *Long Island Star*, April 5, 1827, in Seymour, *Documentary Life*, 311–13.

4 Ibid., 307–13; Frederick Mackenzie, *Diary of Frederick Mackenzie*, vol. 2 (1930; repr., New York: Arno, 1968), 62.

5 "Diary of Enoch Hale" and *Kentish Gazette* (Canterbury, England), 1776, N 6–9, both in Seymour, *Documentary Life*, 301–2.

6 Tallmadge, *Memoir*, 29. He claims he started the New York spy ring in 1778 in his memoir, but he certainly started spying before then, in autumn 1777 at the latest.

7 Ibid., 7–8, 17–20.

8 Continental Congress, "Order Recognizing Merit of Benjamin Tallmadge," December 6, 1780, series 4, 1741–99, GWPLC.

9 Tallmadge, *Memoir*, 26–27.

10 Code book, images 22, 23, 24, 25, 26, series 3b; and multiple letters, series 4, GWPLC. The Connecticut Historical Society, Princeton University Library, and the Litchfield Historical Society are some of the other places that contain a nice selection of this correspondence, though many of the letters were probably destroyed for secrecy's sake.

11 Washington to Tallmadge, November 20, 1778, series 3b, GWPLC.

12 Putnam to Tryon, n.d., in Hinman, *Historical Collection*, 113.

13 William Benton, *Whig-Loyalism: An Aspect of Political Ideology in the American Revolutionary Era* (Rutherford, NJ: Associated University Press, 1969), 14–18.

14 Alanson Welton, "The First Political Disturbances in Connecticut: The Tory Agitation," *Connecticut Magazine* 12, no. 1 (1908): 117–18.

15 Quoted in George Greene, *Life of Nathanael Greene*, ed. Jared Sparks, Library of American Biography (New Orleans: Mygatt, 1852), 10:380.

16 Hoadly, *Public Records of the State*, 2:279.

17 "The Narrative of Joel Stone of Connecticut, 1776–1778," in *Loyalist Narratives from Upper Canada*, ed. James Talman (Toronto: Champlain Society, 1946), 323–29.

18 Samuel Huntington to Jabez Huntington, June 5, 1778, in *Letters Written*, 71.

19 Jonathan Trumbull, "Blank Warrant for Arrest of Person Concerned in 'Treasonable Practices,'" October 18, 1779, 973.3 D77fw, CSLA; Simeon Newell account for services detecting traitorous conspiracies, May 26, 1780, reel 151, Revolutionary War Series 1, 1763–89, CSLA, 31:140; Simeon Newell to Jonathan Trumbull, November 22, 1779, in Louis Middlebrook, *History of Maritime Connecticut during the American Revolution* (Salem, MA: Essex Institute, 1925), 1:206–7; Jesse Root to Samuel Huntington, December 24, 1791, folder H, box 11, American Revolution Series, CHS.

20 Trumbull to Silas Deane, August 31, 1775, 920 T771d, CSLA.

21 Hinman, *Historical Collection*, 89, 291.

22 Moore, *Diary of the American Revolution*, 1:398.

23 Simeon Newell to Jonathan Trumbull, November 22, 1779, and May 26, 1780, in Middlebrook, *Maritime Connecticut*, 1:206–7, 211.

24 Tucker, *Connecticut's Seminary of Sedition*, 21.

25 Nathan Hale to Enoch Hale, May 30, 1776, copy from letter owned by Rev. D. Sprague, Albany, NY, folder 2, Nathan Hale Collection, Correspondence, CHS.

26 Rosanna Sizer, quoted in *The Narrative of Jonathan Rathburn* (repr., New York: Abbatt, 1911), 57.

27 Carl Van Doren, *Secret History of the American Revolution* (New York: Viking, 1941), 3–6. Van Doren's narrative comes primarily from Beverley Robison to Sir Henry Clinton, November 13, 1780, Clinton Papers, William L. Clements Library, University of Michigan.

28 Ezra Stiles, *The Literary Diary of Ezra Stiles*, vol. 2, 1776–81 (New York: Charles Scribner's Sons, 1901), 366.

29 Williams Silliman to Gold Selleck Silliman, May 27, 1776, in Joy Day Buel and Richard Buel, *The Way of Duty: A Woman and Her Family in Revolutionary America* (New York: Norton, 1984), 111. Original in Silliman Family Papers, Yale University.

30 Buel and Buel, *Way of Duty*, 145–65.

31 John Bakeless, *Turncoats, Traitors and Heroes* (Philadelphia: Lippincott, 1959), 98–99.

32 Caulkins, *History of New London*, 522–23.

33 Frederic Mather, *The Refugees of 1776 from Long Island to Connecticut* (Albany, NY: Lyon, 1913), 187, 590, et al.

34 Leake, *Life of John Lamb*, 152.

35 Francis, Lord Rawdon, to Francis, Tenth Earl of Huntingdon, August 5, 1776, *Great Britain Historical Manuscripts Commission, Report on the Manuscripts of the Late Reginald Rawdon Hastings*, ed. Francis Bickley (London: H. M. Stationery Office, 1934), 3:179–80.

36 Papers and Affidavits relating to the Plunderings, Burnings, and Ravages Committed by the British, 1775–1784," item 53, reel 66, p. 29, Papers of the Continental Congress, U.S. National Archives and Records Administration, in Sharon Block, *Rape and Sexual Power in Early America* (Williamsburg, VA: Omohundro Institute of Early American History and Culture, 2006), 81.

37 "Jean Baptiste Antoine de Verger Journal," in *American Campaigns of Rochambeau's Army*, trans. and ed. Howard C. Rice Jr. and Anne S. K. Brown (Princeton, NJ: Princeton University Press, 1972), 1:139. Verger's account of this sort of brutality is only one of many among the French journals of the period. Though it is popular to defend Tarleton these days, eyewitness accounts are probably more reliable than a general feeling by historians that he behaved as an "English gentleman" should. If we can look honestly at the unsavory actions of Revolutionaries toward Loyalists, surely we can admit that the behavior of British soldiers in a foreign war often sunk below societal standards.

38 William Ledyard to Jonathan Trumbull, March 24, 1781, Council of Safety Papers, no. 47, CHS.

39 Washington to Arnold, September 14, 1775, in *Connecticut Courant*, July 22, 1828.

40 *Bucks County*, December 14, 1776; *Pennsylvania Evening Post*, December 28, 1776, et al. See Block, *Rape and Sexual Power*.

41 Mather, *Refugees of 1776*, 199.

42 Ray Raphael, *A People's History of the American Revolution* (New York: New Press, 2001), 112–13.

43 Theodore Sizer, ed., *The Autobiography of Colonel John Trumbull* (New Haven, CT: Yale University Press, 1953), 21.

44 Charles Royster, *A Revolutionary People at War: The Continental Army and American Character, 1775–1783* (New York: Norton, 1979), 54–58; "Hale's Army Diary," in Seymour, *Documentary Life*, 192.

45 Herbert H. White, "British Prisoners of War in Hartford during the Revolution," *Papers of the New Haven Colony Historical Society* (New Haven, CT, 1914): 255–76; Roth, *Connecticut's War Governor*, 8:66–70.

46 Council of Safety Meeting, July 9, 1779, in Trumbull and Hoadly, *Records of the State of Connecticut*, 2:357; William Ledyard to Jonathan Trumbull, April 13, 1780, in Middlebrook, *Maritime Connecticut*, 1:162–64; Hinman, *Historical Collection*, 53.

47 White, "British Prisoners," 255–76. There was a break of two years from 1778 to 1779, in which they were put in Hartford jail. Congress entered into negotiations with the state to formally use Newgate for British prisoners of war, but the war ended before that happened.

48 J. Watson Webb, *Reminiscences of General Samuel Webb* (New York: Globe Stationery and Printing, 1882), 100–101.

49 Blake, *Jonathan Mix*, 53–55.

50 William Ledyard to Jonathan Trumbull, December 19, 1780, 974.6.t 76, TP, CSLA, 13:237. For more sick prisoners, see Hinman, *Historical Collection*, 128 et al.

51 Hiram Stone, "The Experiences of a Prisoner in the American Revolution," *Connecticut Magazine* 12, no. 2 (1908): 245–47.

52 Ledyard to Trumbull, December 19, 1780, CSLA.

53 *Connecticut Gazette* (New London), December 11, 1778. For more evidence of poorly treated American prisoners returned to Connecticut, see Hinman, *Historical Collection*, 128–29 et al.

54 Tallmadge, *Memoir*, 9.

55 Hoadly, *Public Records of the State*, 1:82; Benjamin Payne to Jonathan Trumbull, February 22, 1777, JTP, CSLA, 6:49a–49b.

56 Trumbull to William Tryon, April 23, 1778, in *Massachusetts Historical Society Collections*, 7th ser. (Boston: Massachusetts Historical Society Collections, 1888), 2:228–29.

57 Deane to Trumbull, May 23, 1777, DP, in *New York Historical Society*, 2:56–58; Deane to Barnabas Deane, September 3, 1777, DP, in *New York Historical Society*, 2:121–22.

58 Deane to Committee of Correspondence, August 16, 1776, DP, in *New York Historical Society*, 1:212.

59 Benjamin Tallmadge to Silas Deane, October 14, 1777, DP, in *New York Historical Society*, 4:120–21.

60 Franklin to President of Congress, March 31, 1778, DP, in *New York Historical Society*, 2:445; Franklin to Deane, December 4, 1776, in Barbara Oberg, ed., *The Papers of Benjamin Franklin* (New Haven, CT: Yale University Press, 1998), 23:26–27.

61 Arthur Lee to Richard Henry Lee, February 15, 1778, in Clark, *Silas Deane*, 118, 121.

62 For some of these complicated transactions see Deane to Delap, July 29, 30, 1776, DP, in *New York Historical Society*, 1:166–70.

63 Bancroft to Deane, January 31, 1777, et al., ibid., vol. 1.

64 Tallmadge, *Memoir*, 31.

65 Van Doren, *Secret History*, 380–81; Arnold to Tallmadge, October 25, 1780, series 4, GWPLC. A copy was sent to Silas Deane's brother as well.

66 Tallmadge to Jared Sparks, February 17, 1834, *Magazine of American History* 3 (1879): 754.

1 Arnold, *Life of Benedict Arnold*, 121–22.

2 George Washington to Benedict Arnold, December 14, 1776, series 4, GWPLC.

3 Benedict Arnold to Mrs. Knox, March 4, 1777, in Caulkins, *History of Norwich*, 414.

4 Leake, *Life of John Lamb*, 152–53.

5 Benedict Arnold to George Washington, January 13, 1777, series 4, GWPLC.

6 Arnold to Washington, February 7, 1777, series 4, GWPLC.

7 Arnold to Washington, March 26, 1777, ibid.

8 Washington in conversation, October 23, 1786, recorded by his private secretary, in Lea, *Hero and a Spy*, 578.

9 Washington to Richard Henry Lee, March 6, 1777, ibid., 219.

10 Washington to Arnold, March 3, April 2, 3, 1777; and Arnold to Washington, March 26, 1777, series 4, GWPLC.

11 Mary and Gold Selleck Silliman to Joseph and Rebecca Fish, April 23, 1777, in Buel and Buel, *Way of Duty*, 132. Original in Silliman Papers, Yale University.

12 Stiles, *Literary Diary*, 2:163.

13 G. S. Silliman to Jonathan Trumbull, April 29, 1777; Jesse Brown to Trumbull, April 30, 1777; James Wadsworth to Trumbull, May 1, 1777, et al., 974.6.t 76, TP, CSLA, vol. 6; *Connecticut Journal*, April 30, 1777, in Moore, *Diary of the American Revolution*, 1:423–26; Leake, *Life of John Lamb*, 158–62.

14 Jared Sparks, *The Life and Treason of Benedict Arnold* (Boston: Hilliard, Gray, 1835), 91; Hinman, *Historical Collection*, 139.

15 Silliman to Trumbull, April 29, 1777; Brown to Trumbull, April 30, 1777; James Wadsworth to Trumbull, May 1, 1777, et al., CSLA; *Connecticut Journal*, April 30, 1777, in Moore, *Diary of the American Revolution*, 1:423–26; Leake, *Life of John Lamb*, 158–62.

16 Stiles, *Literary Diary*, 2:163. Arnold's estimate was not shared by the British. For example, Howe's secretary Ambrose Serle's account claimed only "14 were killed & 53 wounded." As in many other cases, the British certainly deflated their losses, while the Americans may have inflated them. Serle, *American Journal*.

17 "Comus," *Pennsylvania Gazette*, May 14, 1777, in Moore, *Diary of the American Revolution*, 1:432.

18 Arnold to Trumbull, April 30, 1777, 974.6.t 76, TP, CSLA, 6:90.

19 Trumbull to Washington, May 4, 1777, et al., and Washington to Trumbull, May 23, 1777, et al., Trumbull Papers, in *Massachusetts Historical Society Collections*, 5th ser. (Boston: Massachusetts Historical Society Collections, 1888), 10:59–61, 65–67.

20 Samuel Parsons to George Washington, May 25, 1777, in Charles Hall, *Life and Letters of Samuel Holden Parsons, Major General in the Continental Army and Chief Judge of the Northwestern Territory* (Binghamton, NY: Otseningo, 1905), 97–98.

21 Jedediah Huntington to Nathaniel Shaw, June 24, 1777, 1907.07.77, NSRWP, NLCHS.

22 Arnold to Gates, in Irving, *Life of Washington*, 2:505. Original in the Gates Papers, NYHS.

23 Arnold, *Life of Benedict Arnold*, 141, 144.

24 Washington to Congress, July 10, 1777, series 3a, GWPLC.

25 Washington to Philip Schuyler, July 18, 1777, series 3b, GWPLC, http://memory.loc.gov.

26 Sparks, *Writings of Washington*, 4:147–48.

27 Continental Army, Major General Benedict Arnold's Division, orderly book, September 20, 1777–October 4, 1777, photostat copy (Hartford, CT: Connecticut State Library, 1931).

28 Arnold to Lamb, September 5, 1777, in Leake, *Life of John Lamb*, 171.

29 Proclamation of Benedict Arnold on the Mohawk River, August 20, 1777, in Arnold, *Life of Benedict Arnold*, 156. Original in the Gates Papers, NYHS.

30 Livingston to Schuyler, September 23, 1777, in Arnold, *Life of Benedict Arnold*, 169. Original in Schuyler Papers, NYHS.

31 Arnold, *Life of Benedict Arnold*, 170–73. Quote from British soldier Roger Lamb.

32 Arnold to Gates, September 22, 1777, in Lea, *Hero and a Spy*, 269–71.

33 Richard Varick to General Schuyler, September 22, 1777, ibid., 269.

34 Livingston to Schuyler, September 23, 1777, in Arnold, *Life of Benedict Arnold*, 180. Original in Schuyler Papers, NYHS.

35 Senator Foster to Isaac Arnold, in Arnold, *Life of Benedict Arnold*, 204. Foster's father, whose house was "fifty yards" from Arnold's in Norwich, was present at the battle.

36 "Treaty of Alliance with France," *List of Treaties between the United States and Foreign Nations*, A Century of Lawmaking for a New Nation: U.S. Congressional Documents and Debates, 1774–1875, Library of Congress, http://memory.loc.gov, 6–10. The British knew Saratoga was a disaster for them too. See Serle, *American Journal*, 262.

37 Dr. James Brown to Jonathan Potts, December 24, 1777, in *New England and Historical Genealogical Register* 18 (1864): 34; Decker, *Benedict Arnold*, 274, 284.

38 Washington to Trumbull, February 6, 1778, in *Massachusetts Historical Society Collections*, 10:110–11.

39 Fitzpatrick, *Writings of George Washington*, 11:35, 417, 442, 453.

40 Washington to Trumbull, March 31, 1778, in *Massachusetts Historical Society Collections*, 10:111–13.

41 Stuart, *Life of Jonathan Trumbull*, 366–70. That spring the commissariat was reorganized under Connecticut's own Jeremiah Wadsworth, and the troubles of Valley Forge were not repeated for a while. During the entire war tiny Connecticut was second after the much more populous Massachusetts in supplying men to the Continental army (31,936) and first in supplying food.

42 Ezra Stiles to Jonathan Trumbull, January 29, 1778, folder 3, box 4, Jonathan Trumbull Sr. Papers, 1637–1787, CHS; Jonathan Trumbull to Ezra Stiles, March 15, 1778, folder 3, box 4, Jonathan Trumbull Sr. Papers, 1637–1787, CHS.

43 Tucker, *Connecticut's Seminary of Sedition*, 35–36.

44 Arnold to Betsey Deblois, April 8, 26, 1778, in Lea, *Hero and a Spy*, 294–95.

45 *Connecticut Journal*, May 6, 1778.

46 Washington to Arnold, January 20, 1778, et al., series 4, GWPLC; Washington to Arnold, May 7, 1778, in Fitzpatrick, *Writings of George Washington*, 11:359–60.

47 Brown and Peckham, *Revolutionary War Journals*, 121.

48 "Benedict Arnold's Oath of Allegiance, 05/30/1778," RG 93, Numbered Record Books, 1894–1913, Online Public Access, National Archives, http://research.archives.gov.

49 Washington to Arnold, June 19, 1778, series 4, GWPLC.

50 Joseph Trumbull to James Bates, February 23, 1778, and Eliphalet Dyer to Joseph Trumbull, July 8, 1778, box 4, JOTP, CHS; Jonathan Trumbull to Jonathan Trumbull Jr., July 6, 1778, and Jonathan Trumbull to General Horatio Gates, August 18, 1778, box 4, JTP, CHS.

51 Washington to Israel Putnam, March 16, 1778, in Fitzpatrick, *Writings of George Washington*, 11:95; see also Washington's General Orders of August 24, ibid., 12:353.

52 Middlebrook, *Maritime Connecticut*, 1:14–15.

53 William Ledyard to Thomas Mumford, May 29, 1778, Thomas Mumford Collection, CHS.

54 Jonathan Trumbull to Jeremiah Wadsworth, March 29, 1779, folder 10, box 5, Jeremiah Wadsworth Papers, CHS.

55 Stiles, *Literary Diary*, 2:327.

56 Caulkins, *History of New London*, 530; Hinman, *Historical Collection*, 607.

57 Stiles, *Literary Diary*, 2:351–57.

58 Thomas Painter, *Autobiography of Thomas Painter* (n.p.: printed for private circulation, 1910), 50–53.

59 "Elizur Goodrich's Narrative," in Johnston, *Yale and Her Honor-Roll*, 107.

60 Napthali Daggett, quoted in Tucker, *Connecticut's Seminary of Sedition*, 62–63.

61 Blake, *Jonathan Mix*, 41–43.

62 Stiles, *Literary Diary*, 2:351–57.

63 Blake, *Jonathan Mix*, 46–47. Mix's account of the running battle that day is absolutely gripping from beginning to end.

64 Ibid., 48.

65 *New York Journal*, July 19, 1779, in Moore, *Diary of the American Revolution*, 2:180–84.

66 Tucker, *Connecticut's Seminary of Sedition*, 62–63.

67 Stiles, *Literary Diary*, 2:351–57; John Burgis Kirby, "The British Invasion of New Haven," July 1979, New Haven, map; Ezra Stiles, "British Invasion of New Haven July 5th, 1779," map, both in Whitney Library, NHM. It is possible, though unlikely, that Arnold's house was spared because he had already opened a dialogue with the British. It was more likely simple luck.

68 *New London Gazette*, August 4, 1779, in Moore, *Diary of the American Revolution*, 2:185–88.

69 *Rivington's Gazette*, July 14, 1779, in Moore, *Diary of the American Revolution*, 2:190–91.

70 The Americans were engaged in propaganda as well, especially in the newspapers. But financial documents, memoirs, and other firsthand accounts confirm serious damage and abuse. This should be no surprise; soldiers fighting abroad in nearly every time and every place have behaved in this manner, and the British armies of the eighteenth century were no exception.

71 Tallmadge, *Memoir*, 30. Some British leaders apparently followed the strategy called "shrecklichkiet" by the German mercenaries. Leaders such as Adm. Samuel Graves and Gen. John Burgoyne favored the sacking and burning of New England towns, a harbinger of total war that became popular in central Europe. Officers who had served in Scotland and Ireland sometimes used this strategy as well. Even the rabidly pro-British Ambrose Serle writes that he was "mortified with the Accounts and Plunder, &c, committed on the poor Inhabitants by the Army and Navy. . . . It is a misfortune, we ever had such a dirty, cowardly Set of contemptible miscreants." *American Journal*, 246.

72 Buel, *Dear Liberty*, 194–95.

73 Tallmadge, *Memoir*, 32–33.

74 *Rivington's Gazette*, July 10, 1779, in Moore, *Diary of the American Revolution*, 2:192.

75 Thomas Belden et al. to Jonathan Trumbull, July 10, 1779, 974.6.t 76, TP, CSLA, 10:6b.

1 *Pennsylvania Packet*, July 14, 1778.

2 Van Doren, *Secret History*, 171.

3 *Connecticut Gazette*, June 27, 1777; Deane to Charles Dumas, October 1, 1777, DP, in *New York Historical Society*, 2:164. Deane trusts Arnold completely in February 1779, sending confidential information to General Schuyler by him. Deane to Schuyler, February 2, 1779, DP, in *New York Historical Society*, 3:342–45.

4 In addition to the letters mentioned before and after, Deane had written to Arnold recommending a French officer to the American service two years earlier. Deane to Arnold, November 12, 1777, box 5, SDP, CHS. As noted before, there were probably many more letters from Arnold to Deane and others, but most were no doubt burned after his treason. Considering the number that remain to Washington (who was unafraid and meticulous in keeping his correspondence), we can posit an even greater number to closer friends.

5 "Hale's Army Diary," in Seymour, *Documentary Life*, 196.

6 Gerard to President of Congress, January 5, 1779, DP, in *New York Historical Society*, 3:246–47 et al.

7 Beaumarchais to Congress, March 23, 1778, in Antoinette Shewmake, *For the Good of Mankind: Pierre-Augustin Caron de Beaumarchais Political Correspondence* (Lanham, MD: University Press of America, 1987), 290–96.

8 Coy Hilton James, *Silas Deane: Patriot or Traitor* (East Lansing: Michigan State University Press, 1975), 68–86.

9 Silas Deane to Jonathan Trumbull, February 1779, 974.6.t 76, TP, CSLA, 9:41.

10 Grace Growden Galloway, "Diary," in Raymond Werner, ed., *Pennsylvania Magazine of History and Biography* 55, no. 1 (1931): 48.

11 *Pennsylvania Packet*, February 27, 1779, et al.

12 Arnold to Shaw, June 8, 1777, 1907.07.143, NSRWP, NLCHS; Arnold to Shaw, July 10, 1777, 1907.07.144, NSRWP, NLCHS; Arnold to Shaw, March 20, 1778, 1907.07.145, NSRWP, NLCHS.

13 Arnold, *Life of Benedict Arnold*, 227.

14 Numerous contemporary sources commented on this event. See G. D. Scull, ed., *Journals of Captain John Montresor*, in *New York Historical Society*, 14:492 et al. Even British propagandist Ambrose Serle derided the money spent on this event as "folly." *American Journal*, 293–94. Note that there are disputes as to whether Peggy attended this festival; however, disputers have to explain away a contemporary report by Andre himself (which they do by claiming he wrote it before the event) and base her lack of presence simply on her family's word rather than any evidence.

15 Arnold to Peggy Shippen, September 25, 1778, in Lea, *Hero and a Spy*, 305–6.

16 Arnold to Shippen, February 8, 1779, ibid., 316–17.

17 Van Doren, *Secret History*, 187–88; John Watson, *Annals of Philadelphia* (Philadelphia: Edwin Stuart, 1899), 3:448–49.

18 Hannah Arnold to Peggy Arnold, September 10, 1780, series 4, GWPLC.

19 Washington to Arnold, multiple letters, 1778–79, series 4, GWPLC. This seems to be the period of heaviest correspondence between the two men, with dozens of letters passing back and forth. Captured in these letters is the entire process of Washington trying to talk Arnold off a ledge and constantly extending a hand, like a father to a prodigal son.

20 Arnold to Washington, May 5, 1779, series 4, GWPLC.

21 William Duane, ed., *Extracts from the Diary of Christopher Marshall Kept in Philadelphia and Lancaster during the American Revolution, 1774–1781* (Albany, NY: Munsell, 1877), 211.

22 Beverley Robinson to Major General Arnold, [May 1779?], in Lea, *Hero and a Spy*, 331–33. This letter is suspect and may have been written later.

23 Van Doren, *Secret History*, 196, 200–201, 207–8. The numerous letters that provide this evidence can be found in the Clinton Papers, William L. Clements Library, University of Michigan. Van Doren's book contains the most exhaustive treatment of this complicated series of communications, much too complicated for similar treatment here.

24 James, *Silas Deane*, 85.

25 "Records of the Trial of Benedict Arnold," in Arnold, *Life of Benedict Arnold*, 252. Isaac Arnold did not have the benefit of the secret records that later came out, and so he defends Peggy Arnold wrongly and puts the blame of Arnold's treason on the reprimand and disgrace after the trial. But as we know now, Arnold had begun his treasonous correspondence before 1780.

26 Washington's General Orders for April 6, 1780, in Fitzpatrick, *Writings of George Washington*, 16:225.

27 Arnold to Deane, March 22, 1780, DP, in *New York Historical Society*, 4:116.

28 Arnold to Andre, July 15, 1780, in Lea, *Hero and a Spy*, 401–2.

29 Van Doren, *Secret History*, 263.

30 Ibid., 265, 267–68.

31 Benedict Arnold, petition, 1780, reel 138, Revolutionary War Series 1, CSLA, 18:c2.

32 Edward Boynton, *History of West Point* (New York: Van Nostrand, 1871).

33 Joshua Elderkin to Nathaniel Shaw, August 26, 1779, et al., 1907.07.74, NSRWP, NLCHS.

34 Washington to Shaw, July 10, 1780, 1907.07.03, NSRWP, NLCHS; Washington to Shaw, July 19, 1780, 1907.07.02, NSRWP, NLCHS; Washington

to Shaw, July 31, 1780, 1907.07.04, NSRWP, NLCHS; Washington to Shaw, July 31, 1780, 1907.07.06, NSRWP, NLCHS.

35 Shaw to Washington, August 9, 1780, series 4, GWPLC.

36 For example, Tallmadge and Washington met at the Robinson House at West Point in the autumn of 1779. Washington to Tallmadge, October 9, 1779, series 3b, GWPLC.

37 Titus Hosmer to Thomas Mumford, June 6, 1780, Thomas Mumford Collection, CHS.

38 Lamb to Arnold, August 12, 1780, in Leake, *Life of John Lamb*, 248.

39 Lamb to Arnold, August 18, 1780, in Lea, *Hero and a Spy*, 422–23.

40 Sir Henry Clinton to Lord George Germain, New York, October 11, 1780, in "The Treason of Benedict Arnold, as Presented in Letters of Sir Henry Clinton to Lord George Germain," *Pennsylvania Magazine of History and Biography* 222, no. 4 (1898): 410–13. The amount of £20,000 is well over a million dollars in modern currency, offered in an age with far fewer millionaires.

41 Van Doren, *Secret History*, 292–93.

42 Arnold to Shaw, August 10, 1780, 1907.07.147, NSRWP, NLCHS. Arnold actually wrote to Shaw only a few days before his treason was discovered. Arnold to Shaw, September 19, 1780, series 4, GWPLC.

43 Tallmadge to Arnold, September 12, 1780, series 4 GWPLC; Arnold to Tallmadge, September 13, 1780, series 4, GWPLC.

44 Benedict Arnold, "Directions for Mrs. Arnold on Her Way to Wt. Point," n.d., in *Pennsylvania Magazine of History and Biography*, (Philadelphia: Historical Society of Pennsylvania, 1901), 25: 44–45.

45 Henry Phelps Johnston, "Colonel Varick and Arnold's Treason," *Magazine of American History* 8, no. 11 (1882): 718.

46 Richard Varick, *The Varick Court of Inquiry to Investigate the Implication of Colonel Richard Varick in the Arnold Treason*, ed. Albert Bushnell (New York: Hart, 1907), 134–85.

47 Van Doren, *Secret History*, 317, 413.

48 Washington to Arnold, September 14, 1780, in Fitzpatrick, *Writings of George Washington*, 20:48.

49 *Norwich Packet*, October 3, 1780, 3.

50 George Matthew Dutcher, *George Washington and Connecticut in War and Peace*, vol. 8 of *Committee on Historical Collections* (New Haven, CT: Yale University Press, 1933), 5; "Conference at Hartford," *The Papers of Alexander Hamilton*, ed. Harold Syrett (New York: Columbian University Press, 1961), 2:437–38.

51 Rochambeau, *Memoirs of the Marshal Count de Rochambeau Relative to the War of Independence of the United States* (1838; repr., New York: Arno, 1971), 18.

52 Van Doren, *Secret History*, 335–39.

53 Lieutenant Colonel Jameson to Benedict Arnold, September 23, 1780, in *The Writings of George Washington*, pt. 2, *Correspondence and Miscellaneous Papers Relating to the American Revolution*, ed. Jared Sparks (Boston: Andrews, 1840), 7:530.

54 Tallmadge, *Memoir*, 35–36. The commander, Jameson, made a lame excuse to Washington several days later about this foolish, if not treasonous, behavior. See also Joshua King regarding Major Andre, 1817, copy, box 10, American Revolution Collection, CHS, 10T (4) et al.

55 Varick, *Court of Inquiry*, 98–193. For the opposite point of view, see Joshua Hett Smith, *Narrative of the Death of Major Andre* (New York: Arno, 1969).

56 Varick, *Court of Inquiry*, 179–80.

57 George Washington to Samuel Huntington, September 26, 1780, in Edward Lengel, *The Glorious Struggle: George Washington's Revolutionary War Letters* (Washington, DC: Smithsonian, 2008), 210.

58 Hamilton to Washington, September 25, 1780, in Syrett, *Papers of Alexander Hamilton*, 2:438.

59 Arnold to Washington, September 25, 1780, ibid., 2:439.

60 For example, see Alexander Hamilton to Elizabeth Schuyler, September 25, 1780, ibid., 2:442.

61 Leake, *Life of John Lamb*, 263.

62 Varick, *Court of Inquiry*, 192–93.

63 Washington to Col. Nathaniel Wade, September 25, 1780, in Lengel, *Glorious Struggle*, 209.

64 Fitzpatrick, *Writings of George Washington*, 20:95.

65 Irving, *Life of Washington*, 4:149–50.

66 Hamilton to Clinton, September 30, 1780, in *The Papers of Alexander Hamilton*, digital ed., ed. Harold C. Syrett (Charlottesville: University of Virginia Press, Rotunda, 2011).

67 "Proceedings against John L. Andre as a Spy, by Continental Army Board of General Officers," September 29, 1780, series 4 GWPLC.

68 Tallmadge to Samuel Webb, September 30, 1780, in Webb, *Correspondence and Journals*, 2:293–97.

69 Tallmadge to Jeremiah Wadsworth, October 4, 1780, in Charles Swain Hall, *Benjamin Tallmadge: Revolutionary Soldier and American Businessman* (New York: Columbia University Press, 1943), 63. Original in Tallmadge Papers, Litchfield Historical Society.

70 This letter is mentioned in *Pennsylvania Packet*, October 10, 1780. See Moore, *Diary of the American Revolution*, 2:332.

71 Varick, *Court of Inquiry*, 167–86; Smith, *Narrative of the Death*, 289–90.

72 Oswald to Lamb, December 11, 1780, in Leake, *Life of John Lamb*, 266–67.

73 Leake, *Life of John Lamb*, 262.

THE SCANDAL OF THE AGE

1 Samuel Huntington to Jonathan Trumbull, October 1780, 974.6.t 76, TP, CSLA, 13:49.

2 Stiles, *Literary Diary*, 2:473–74.

3 Lafayette to Chevalier de La Luzerne, September 25, 1780, in Tower, *Marquis de La Fayette*, 2:164.

4 Royster, "Nature of Treason," 191 et al.

5 Jesse Root to Trumbull, September 30, 1780, 974.6.t 76, TP, CSLA, 13:46.

6 Benjamin Tallmadge to Samuel B. Webb, September 30, 1780, in Webb, *Correspondence and Journals*, 2:293.

7 Samuel Adams to Betsy Adams, October 10, 1780, Philadelphia, in *The Writings of Samuel Adams*, vol. 4, *1778–1802* (New York: Octagon Books, 1968), 209–10.

8 *Connecticut Journal* (New Haven), October 5, 1780.

9 Franklin to Lafayette, May 14, 1781, in *The Works of Benjamin Franklin*, ed. John Bigelow, (New York: Putnam's Sons, 1888), 7:235.

10 Martin, *Private Yankee Doodle*, 204–5.

11 Henry Biddle, ed., *Extracts from the Journal of Elizabeth Drinker* (Philadelphia: Lippincott, 1889), 129.

12 *Pennsylvania Packet*, January 16, 1781, in Moore, *Diary of the American Revolution*, 2:337–38; Peter Shaw, *American Patriots and the Rituals of the Revolution* (Cambridge, MA: Harvard University Press, 1981), 217.

13 *Boston Independent Chronicle*, December 8, 1780, in Moore, *Diary of the American Revolution*, 2:333–35.

14 James Searle to Benjamin Franklin, November 20, 1780, in Oberg, *Papers of Benjamin Franklin*, 34:34–35; Franklin to Searle, November 30, 1780, in Bigelow, *Works of Benjamin Franklin*, 7:162–63.

15 Trumbull to Washington, December 15, 1780, 974.6.t 76, TP, CSLA, 13:227a.

16 For example, see David Rowland, "Continental Thanksgiving," December 7, 1780, David Sherman Rowland Letterbooks: Sermons of Secular Interest, 1757–83, MS79809, CHS. Rowland gives a great account of the event and claims that God had "baffled the counsels of our enemies, yea, turned them into foolishness."

17 *Pennsylvania Packet*, October 7, 1780, is one of many examples.

18 *New Jersey Gazette*, November 1, 1780, in Moore, *Diary of the American Revolution*, 2:333.

19 *Connecticut Gazette* (New London), October 17, 1780.

20 "Address to the Vile Traitor," *Pennsylvania Packet*, October 24, 1780, TP, CSLA, 23:165a.

21 Even the name "Arnold" became an anathema for some. Two years later the governor and the assembly agreed to grant Jonathan Arnold of Hartford the surname of Steuben, at Baron von Steuben's request, to protect him from abuse. *Connecticut Courant and Weekly Intelligencer*, February 11, 1783.

22 *Fall of Lucifer, an Elegiac Poem of the Infamous Defection of the Late General Arnold* (Hartford, CT: Hudson and Goodwin, 1781), CHS. Original publication on January 1, 1781.

23 Alexander Hamilton to John Laurens, October 11, 1780, in *The American Revolution, Writings from the War of Independence*, ed. John Rhodehamel (New York: Library of America, 2001), 596–99.

24 Benedict Arnold to the Inhabitants of America, October 7, 1780, New York, in Rhodehamel, *American Revolution*, 592–95. See also *London Chronicle*, November 14, 1780, et al. Isaac Arnold claimed to have seen a copy of this document furnished by Arnold's grandson, in Benedict Arnold's own hand, so it is possible he wrote the entire thing himself.

25 Benedict Arnold to Lord Germain, October 7 1780, New York, in Rhodehamel, *American Revolution*, 596–99.

26 Van Doren, *Secret History*, 411, from Benedict Arnold to Sir Henry Clinton, January 23, 1781, in Clinton Papers, William L. Clements Library, University of Michigan.

27 Washington to Joseph Reed, November 20, 1780, in Fitzpatrick, *Writings of George Washington*, 20:370.

28 *Connecticut Gazette* (New London), October 6, 1780.

29 John Adams to Benjamin Franklin, December 6, 1780, in Oberg, *Papers of Benjamin Franklin*, 34:126.

30 Washington to Elias Dayton, April 11, 1781, in Fitzpatrick, *Writings of George Washington*, 21:446–47.

31 Jan Ingenhousz to Franklin, December 5, 1780, in Oberg, *Papers of Benjamin Franklin*, 34:124.

32 Stiles, *Literary Diary*, 2:474, 473.

33 Edmund Pendleton to James Madison, October 17, 1780, in *The Letters and Papers of Edmund Pendleton, 1734–1803*, ed. David John Mays (Charlottesville: University Press of Virginia, 1967), 1:317.

34 Andrew Elliot to William Eden, October 4–5, 1780, in Royster, "Nature of Treason," 187.

35 Roger Lamb, *An Original and Authentic Journal of Occurences during the Late American War* (1809; repr., New York: Arno, 1968), 313.

36 William Stone, ed. and trans., *Letters of Brunswick and Hessian Officers during the American Revolution* (Albany, NY: Munsell's Sons, 1891), 53.

37 John Mackey to Gold Selleck Silliman, November 22, 1780, 974.6.t 76, TP, CSLA, 13:165ab.

38 Sir Henry Clinton to Lord George Germain, New York, October 12, 1780, in "Treason of Benedict Arnold," 421.

39 William Willcox, ed., *The American Rebellion: Sir Henry Clinton's Narrative of His Campaigns, 1775–1782, with an Appendix of Original Documents* (New Haven, CT: Yale University Press, 1954), 216–17.

40 Clinton to Germain, October 11, 1780, in "Treason of Benedict Arnold," 414.

41 Clinton to Germain, October 30, 1780, New York, ibid., 422.

42 Sizer, *Autobiography*, 65.

43 Van Doren, *Secret History*, 383–84; Hannah Arnold to Benedict Arnold, September 4, 1780, Philadelphia, MS Am 1446, Benedict Arnold Papers, 1765–1886, Houghton Library, Harvard University.

44 Permission request from Samuel Birch, forward by Silliman, refusal by Williams, November 1780, 974.6.t 76, TP, CSLA, 13:284.

45 Charles Collard Adams, *Middletown Upper Houses: A History of the North Society of Middletown, Ct. from 1650 to 1800 with Genealogical and Biographical Chapters on Early Families* (New York: Grafton, 1908), 629.

46 *Norwich Packet*, November 28, 1780.

47 *Pennsylvania Packet*, November 14 and 18, 1780.

48 *Connecticut Journal* (New Haven), October 19, 1780.

49 George Washington to Benjamin Tallmadge, October 17, 1780, series 3b, GWPLC.

50 Tallmadge to Washington, October 11, 1780; Samuel Culper Jr. (Townsend) to John Bolton (Tallmadge), October 14, 1780, both in series 4, GWPLC.

51 Though it is widely believed Arnold found no American spies, the situation is murky. For example, Elizabeth Drinker of Philadelphia reported that a number of American spies were captured, using information taken from Arnold. She was a Loyalist, however, so she might have been the victim of wishful thinking.

52 Tallmadge, *Memoir*, 39–42.

53 Washington to Henry Lee, October 20, 1780, in Fitzpatrick, *Writings of George Washington*, 20:223–24.

54 George F. Scheer, "The Sergeant Major's Strange Mission," *American Heritage* 8, no. 6 (1957), www.americanheritage.com. See also Van Doren, *Secret History*, 382–90.

A PARRICIDE IN OLD VIRGINIA

1 Clinton to Arnold, December 14, 1780, in Michael Kranish, *Flight from Monticello: Thomas Jefferson at War* (Oxford: Oxford University Press, 2010), 164; John Graves Simcoe, *Simcoe's Military Journal: A History of the Opera-*

tions of a Partisan Corps, Called the Queen's Rangers, Commanded by Lieu-tenant Colonel J. G. Simcoe, during the War of the American Revolution (New York: Bartlett and Welford, 1844), 158–59 et al.

2 Kranish, *Flight from Monticello*, 162–63, 166–72; Thomas Jefferson to the County Lieutenants of Hampshire and Berkeley, *The Papers of Thomas Jefferson*, ed. Julian P. Boyd (Princeton, NJ: Princeton University Press, 1951), 4:229–30.

3 "Benedict Arnold to the Commanding Officer on Shore," January 2, 1781, *Connecticut Courant and Weekly Intelligencer*, February 13, 1781.

4 Johann von Ewald, *Diary of the American War: A Hessian Journal*, ed. Joseph Tustin (New Haven, CT: Yale University Press, 1979), 261; Thomas Jefferson to Benjamin Harrison, January 2, 1781, in Boyd, *Papers of Thomas Jefferson*, 4:381.

5 Kranish, *Flight from Monticello*, 180–83; Ewald, *Diary of the American War*, 261; Extracts from diary, January 9, 1781, in *The Works of Thomas Jefferson*, ed. Paul Leicester Ford, 12 vols. (New York: Putnam's Sons, 1904–5), 3:105–8.

6 Kranish, *Flight from Monticello*, 183–86. Harrison was father to the future president.

7 Ibid., 187–89; Simcoe; *Military Journal*, 160–61.

8 Kranish, *Flight from Monticello*, 190–92; Jefferson to Charles Lee, May 15, 1826, in Ford, *Works of Thomas Jefferson*, 12:277–81; Jefferson to John Nicholas, November 10, 1819, in *Writings of Thomas Jefferson*, ed. H. A. Washington (Washington, DC: Taylor and Maury, 1954), 7:144.

9 Michael Kranish, "Jefferson on the Run," *American History* 45, no. 2 (2010): 26–27; Kranish, *Flight from Monticello*, 193.

10 Thomas Jefferson, "Narrative of Arnold's Raid," January 13, 1781, Richmond, in Rhodehamel, *American Revolution*, 656–58.

11 Kranish, *Flight from Monticello*, 195–96; Arnold to Clinton, January 21, 1781, in *Documents of the American Revolution*, ed. Kenneth Gordon-Davies (Dublin: Irish University Press, 1981), 21:40–43.

12 William Seth Stubblefield, pension application, Charles City, www.charlescity.org; Simcoe, *Military Journal*, 167.

13 Ewald, *Diary of the American War*, 269–71; Johann von Ewald, *Treatise on Partisan Warfare*, trans. Rober Selig and David Curtis Skaggs (New York: Greenwood, 1991), 128.

14 *New Jersey Gazette*, January 31, 1781, in Moore, *Diary of the American Revolution*, 2:368.

15 John Trumbull, *Reminiscences of His Own Times from 1756–1841* (New York: Wiley and Putnam, 1841), 359.

16 John Page to Theoderick Bland, January 21, 1781, in Kranish, *Flight from Monticello*, 203.

17 Mackenzie, *Diary of Frederick Mackenzie*, 466.

18 Ibid.; Kranish, *Flight from Monticello*, 212–14; Ewald, *Diary of the American War*, 250.

19 Kranish, *Flight from Monticello*, 207–9; Ewald, *Diary of the American War*, 286.

20 Thomas Jefferson to General Muhlenburg, January 21, 1781, in *Writings of Thomas Jefferson*, ed. Andrew Lipscomb and Albert Ellery Bergh (Washington, DC: Thomas Jefferson Memorial Association, 1903), 4:154–56.

21 Bakeless, *Turncoats, Traitors, and Heroes*, 317. From the McLane Papers, NYHS.

22 Thomas Jefferson to Thomas Nelson, January 16, 1781, in Boyd, *Papers of Thomas Jefferson*, 4:382.

23 Jefferson to Arnold, March 24, 1781, in Lipscomb and Bergh, *Writings of Thomas Jefferson*, 4:399–400.

24 Edmund Pendleton to William Preston, October 11, 1780, in Mays, *Edmund Pendleton*, 1:316.

25 Van Doren, *Secret History*, 411.

26 Kranish, *Flight from Monticello*, 219–23.

27 About 2,500 slaves did apparently make it to "freedom," primarily in Nova Scotia, though many did not last long there. A few also made it to London, and a few were "repatriated" to West Africa. But most of the slaves who fled to British lines were the "property" of Loyalists and were taken back to slavery in the Caribbean or elsewhere. Others were probably given as "compensation" to the Loyalists who had lost their slaves by fleeing America.

28 Rochambeau, *Memoirs*, 36; Dutcher, *George Washington*, 6–7.

29 Washington to Lafayette, February 20, 1781, in Fitzpatrick, *Writings of George Washington*, 21:255.

30 Kranish, *Flight from Monticello*, 229.

31 Ibid., 232–35.

32 George Washington to Lund Washington, April 30, 1781, series 4, GWPLC.

33 Kranish, *Flight from Monticello*, 239–43.

34 Arnold to Clinton, May 16, 1781, in Arnold, *Life of Benedict Arnold*, 344–47.

35 Kranish, *Flight from Monticello*, 244–51; James Johnstone, pension application, in *The Revolution Remembered: Eyewitness Accounts of the War for Independence*, ed. John Dann (Chicago: University of Chicago Press, 1980), 405–6.

36 Tower, *Marquis de La Fayette*, 2:339.

37 Washington to Lafayette, May 31, 1781, in Fitzpatrick, *Writings of George Washington*, 22:139.

38 Scheer, "Sergeant Major's Strange Mission"; Van Doren, *Secret History*, 382–90.

39 *New Jersey Journal*, August 1, 1781, in Moore, *Diary of the American Revolution*, 2:461.

40 Charles Thomson to John Jay, July 11, 1781, Thomson Papers, in *New York Historical Society*, 11:41–60.

41 Arnold to Clinton, May 16, 1781, in Arnold, *Life of Benedict Arnold*, 344–47.

42 Dutcher, *George Washington*, 8.

43 George Washington to Noah Webster, July 31, 1788, copy, NLCHS; Rochambeau, *Memoirs*, 44–47.

44 Kranish, *Flight from Monticello*, 257–64.

WILLIAM LEDYARD'S LAST SUMMER

1 Ebenezer Ledyard to William Williams, February 12, 1778, and William Ledyard to Connecticut General Assembly, December 15, 1780, in Harris, *Battle of Groton Heights*, 174, 276–77.

2 Account of the committee classing the town of Groton for raising their quota of Continental soldiers, March 10, 1781, 974.62 G91c, CSLA.

3 William Ledyard to Jonathan Trumbull, April 12, 1779, TP, CSLA; Ledyard to Jeremiah Wadsworth, March 16, 1779, folder 10, box 5, Jeremiah Wadsworth Papers, CHS.

4 Ledyard to Benadam Gallup, September 21, 1778, in Charles Stark, *Groton, Conn. 1705–1905* (Stonington, CT: Palmer, 1922), 252–53.

5 Shaw to the Marine Committee of the Eastern Department, March 14, 1779, in Rogers, *Connecticut's Naval Office*, 322.

6 Shaw to Trumbull, March 13, 1779, in Middlebrook, *Maritime Connecticut*, 2:319–20.

7 Ledyard to Jean B. Donatien de Vimeur, Comte de Rochambeau, June 2, 1781, et al., series 4, GWPLC.

8 Ledyard to Washington, October 28, 1780, series 4, GWPLC.

9 Caulkins, *History of Norwich*, 393; Hinman, *Historical Collection*, 129 et al.

10 Ledyard to Samuel Gray, May 2, 1780, MS 67562, William Ledyard Letters, 1778, 1780, CHS.

11 Ledyard to Connecticut General Assembly, February 1781, et al., vol. 10, reel 146, Revolutionary War Series 1, CSLA.

12 Ledyard to Philip Turner, December 20, 1780, Ashbel and Woodward Collection 1698–1862, CHS.

13 Ledyard to Turner, February 9, 1781, box 11F, American Revolution Collection, CHS.

14 Phillip Turner to the Connecticut General Assembly, Memorial application, May 1783, vol. 26, reel 146, Revolutionary War Series 1, CSLA.

15 "Records of Artillery or Independent Company of New London with Articles of Formation," 1762, kept until 1777, NLCHS.

16 Hempstead, *Diary of Joshua Hempstead*, 619; Shaw, *Ledyard Family in America*, 32 et al.

17 Ledyard to Shaw, January 1, 1781, in Rogers, *Connecticut's Naval Office*, 28.

18 Caulkins, *History of New London*, 504.

19 Dutcher, *George Washington*, 9.

20 Thankfully, the paralyzed Israel Putnam lived long enough to see his old friend Washington elected to the presidency and the new nation he fought for born.

21 Jeremiah Wadsworth to Jerusha Lathrop, April 8, 1793, folder 15, box 18, Family Correspondence, Jeremiah Wadsworth Papers, CHS.

22 Roth, *Connecticut's War Governor*, 46–47.

23 Washington to Trumbull, January 6, 1780, in *Massachusetts Historical Society Collections*, 10:152–53.

24 There are dozens of letters from Washington to Trumbull in the Massachusetts Historical Society Collections and the Connecticut Historical Society Collections, each requesting provisions from the governor.

25 Washington to Trumbull, June 10, 1780, in *Massachusetts Historical Society Collections*, 10:170–71; 1763–89, Revolutionary War Series 1, CSLA, 19:273.

26 Buel, *Dear Liberty*, 159–72, 239–72.

27 Jonathan Trumbull to Jeremiah Wadsworth, March 27, 1779, folder 10, box 5, Jeremiah Wadsworth Papers, CHS.

28 Trumbull, *Reminiscences*, 337.

29 Tallmadge to Thomas Mumford, June 24, 1781, MS 73093 I-W, Benjamin Tallmadge, CHS.

30 Francois Jean Marquis de Chastellux, *Travels in North America* (New York: White Gallaher and White, 1827), 96–97, 127.

31 Samuel Huntington to Jonathan Trumbull, January 3, 1780, in *Letters from Delegates of Congress*, ed. Paul Smith (Washington DC: Library of Congress, 1988), 14:314–15.

32 Tallmadge, *Memoir*, 43.

33 Washington to Comte de Barras, June 4, 1781, in Fitzpatrick, *Writings of George Washington*, 22:159.

34 Jean-Francois-Louis, comte de Clermont-Crevecoeur, journal entry, in Rice and Brown, *American Campaigns*, 1:28.

35 Tallmadge, *Memoir*, 44; Tallmadge to George Washington, June 25, 1781, 973.3 D73t, CSLA.

36 George Washington to Noah Webster, July 31, 1788, copy, NLCHS.

37 "Minutes of Occurrences Respecting the Siege and Capture of York in Virginia, Extracted from the Journal of Colonel Jonathan Trumbull, Secretary to the General, 1781," in *Proceedings of the Massachusetts Historical Society, 1875–1876* (Boston: Massachusetts Historical Society, 1876), 331.

38 Rochambeau, *Memoirs*, 44–47. After receiving a copy, Rochambeau showed Chastellux the letter. He threw it into the fire in front of him "and left him a prey to his own remorse"; though the letter might have had good results, it was a serious lapse of judgment.

39 "Minutes of Occurrences," in *Massachusetts Historical Society*, 332.

40 Clinton to Earl Cornwallis, August 27, 1781, in Willcox, *American Rebellion*, 562.

41 Mackenzie, *Diary of Frederick Mackenzie*, 540.

42 William Smith, *Historical Memoirs of William Smith, 1778–1783*, ed. William Henry Waldo Sabine (New York: Arno, 1971), 428–29.

43 William Ledyard to Jonathan Trumbull, February 27, 1781, 974.6.t 76, TP, CSLA, 14:101a.

44 Stuart, *Life of Jonathan Trumbull*, 549.

45 Caulkins, *History of New London*, 545.

46 Stuart, *Life of Jonathan Trumbull*, 540–41.

47 Shaw, *Ledyard Family in America*, 17–20.

48 Stuart, *Life of Jonathan Trumbull*, 549.

49 "Minutes of Occurrences," in *Massachusetts Historical Society*, 332. The French arrived on August 26.

50 This suggestion could have been from Arnold himself, but that is disputed. It could also have been a "test of loyalty" by Clinton, but considering his personality that seems unlikely.

51 Mackenzie, *Diary of Frederick Mackenzie*, 610–11.

52 William Ledyard to Jonathan Trumbull, September 4, 1781, 974.6.t 76, TP, CSLA, 15:95. It may be the last letter he ever wrote.

53 Statement of Charles Chittenden and Statement of David Gray, Gray Pension File, S/38/776, RG15A, National Archives.

54 Jonathan Trumbull to George Washington, September 15, 1781, in *Correspondence of the American Revolution: Being Letters of Eminent Men to George Washington, from the Time of His Taking Command of the Army to the End of His Presidency*, vol. 3, ed. Jared Sparks (Boston: Little, Brown, 1853), http://founders.archives.gov.

55 "Minutes of Occurrences," *Massachusetts Historical Society*, 332.

56 Lieutenant Colonel Austin to Trumbull, September 6, 1781, 974.6.t 76, TP, CSLA, 15:99a.

57 "Narrative of Rufus Avery," in Harris, *Battle of Groton Heights*, 29–30. I have used the personal narratives and other documents in Harris because it is the most comprehensive collection of documents on Arnold's attack. There are several other collections as well. The details of the attack can also be found in numerous contemporary letters from eyewitnesses, but most of them simply repeat the main events and outcomes of the battle. For example, see Zab-

diel Rogers to Jonathan Trumbull, September 7, 1781, copy, R633, NLCHS; Thomas Mumford to Jonathan Trumbull, September 9, 1781, TP, CSLA, 974.6.t 76. XV:105. They are useful, however, to check the later narratives for errors and exaggerations.

58 "Narrative of Rufus Avery," in Harris, *Battle of Groton Heights*, 30.

59 Avery Downer, "Narrative of the Battle of Groton Heights," in Harris, *Battle of Groton Heights*, 83–84.

60 Harris, *Battle of Groton Heights*, 290. When Harris is cited alone, it is his research and commentary that I am citing rather than the direct words of a survivor narrative.

61 "Narrative of John Hempsted," in Harris, *Battle of Groton Heights*, 61–62.

62 Harris, *Battle of Groton Heights*, 212–13 et al.; Stuart, *Life of Jonathan Trumbull*, 542.

63 Harris, *Battle of Groton Heights*, 214; Inhabitants of New London to Connecticut General Assembly, April 22, 1782, Revolutionary War Series 1, CSLA, 22:337b.

THE SIXTH OF SEPTEMBER

1 Caulkins, *History of New London*, 547.

2 "Narrative of John Hempsted," in Harris, *Battle of Groton Heights*, 62–63. The brave and hilarious Hempsted is quite simply a terrible speller, and his narrative is very difficult to understand. I have kept the misspellings in for the most part but have chosen the more understandable quotes when possible. He probably misspelled his own last name, for example, as he was part of the extended Hempstead family.

3 "Narrative of Jonathan Brooks," in Harris, *Battle of Groton Heights*, 74–75.

4 "Brigadier-General Arnold's Report to Sir Henry Clinton," in Harris, *Battle of Groton Heights*, 98–99; Benedict Arnold to Sir Henry Clinton, September 8, 1781, Public Record Office, Copies, 1776–84, CHS. The version in Harris will be used from here on, because the page numbers make it more useful.

5 "Narrative of Stephen Hempstead," in Harris, *Battle of Groton Heights*, 47–48, 230, 222. See also Hempstead to Trumbull, [October 30?], 1781, 974.6.t 76, TP, CSLA, 15:164.

6 "Narrative of Jonathan Brooks," in Harris, *Battle of Groton Heights*, 75–76.

7 "Narrative of John Hempsted," ibid., 67–68.

8 Ibid., 63–64.

9 "Narrative of Jonathan Brooks," ibid., 76–77.

10 "Narrative of John Hempsted," ibid., 64.

11 "Narrative of Jonathan Brooks," ibid., 78–79.

12 Lieutenant Colonel Upham to Governor Franklin, in Caulkins, *History of New London*, 551.

13 "Narrative of John Hempsted," in Harris, *Battle of Groton Heights*, 66–67. Note that the "Jersey Tories" were actually gathered from around the entire northeast.

14 Rogers, *Connecticut's Naval Office*, 24, 22.

15 "Narrative of John Hempsted," in Harris, *Battle of Groton Heights*, 68.

16 Caulkins, *History of New London*, 555.

17 Saltonstall to Trumbull, October 10, 1781, 974.6.t 76, TP, CSLA.

18 Rogers, *Connecticut's Naval Office*, 9.

19 "The Spirit of 76: An Historic Dinner." *Harper's*, September 1895, 7. Stephen Hempstead's brother David had been captured earlier in the war while privateering and at the time of the attack rotted as a prisoner on the *Jersey*.

20 *Connecticut Gazette* (New London), October 5, 1781.

21 Ibid., September 14, 1781.

22 Caulkins, *History of New London*, 555.

23 "An Unrecorded Bit of History: Benedict Arnold's Narrow Escape from Death at the Hands of a Woman," *New York Times*, January 19, 1879. There was a painting of this incident in the possession of Thomas Day of Bergen Point, New Jersey. It may be that Hinman later regretted not killing Arnold when she had the chance and fabricated the bit about the gun.

24 "Narrative of Jonathan Brooks," in Harris, *Battle of Groton Heights*, 80–81; Caulkins, *History of New London*, 569. See also Zabdiel Rogers to Jonathan Trumbull, September 7, 1781, copy, R633, NLCHS.

25 "Narrative of Jonathan Brooks," in Harris, *Battle of Groton Heights*, 81–82.

26 Though, to be fair, the goods would have been burned or taken by the British anyway.

27 "Narrative of John Hempsted," in Harris, *Battle of Groton Heights*, 67.

28 Caulkins, *History of New London*, 554. It is interesting that the same people who defend Arnold because he was a great commander for the Americans contradictorily say that he is not responsible for the New London burning because he did not have full command of the soldiers.

29 Lorenzo Sabine, *Biographical Sketches of Loyalists of the American Revolution* (Port Washington, NY: Kennikat, 1966), 1:449.

30 Caulkins, *History of New London*, 553.

31 Ibid., 547.

32 Ebenezer Ledyard to Trumbull, November 7, 1781, 974.6.t 76, TP, CSLA, 15:239.

33 "Narrative of John Hempsted," in Harris, *Battle of Groton Heights*, 68.

34 "Brigadier-General Arnold's Report," ibid., 100. A story comes down to us from various sources that Arnold, upon hearing that William Ledyard was commanding, said, "I know Ledyard well, he will not give up while a drop of

blood is in his veins." Though this quote is apparently from Ledyard's niece Alice, the original source is lost. The rest of the repeated story is full of mistakes, so I have left it out of the narrative.

35 His claim that he tried to stop the attack makes little sense from any military perspective and of course was not in Arnold's (short-term) self-interest. Many modern historians have been disposed to take his word, but considering how often he lied, I find that surprising. How would his soldiers on that side of the river burn Groton or retreat if the fort had not been taken? They would have been exposed to cannon and musket fire and taken even more losses than they already had, and of course Arnold would have taken the blame for those losses. And worse, he would have been excoriated by his new British friends for allowing an American "victory" by the fort's defenders. He was clearly lying to Clinton to save himself from any shame associated with the massacre or the British losses beforehand.

36 James Cogswell, diary entry for September 8, manuscript, 1781–91, CHS.

37 Sigourney, *Letters of Life*, 16–17. She gets this information directly from her father, who was present at the event.

THE BATTLE OF GROTON HEIGHTS

1 "Brigadier-General Arnold's Report," in Harris, *Battle of Groton Heights*, 98.

2 Caulkins, *History of New London*, 557.

3 Harris, *Battle of Groton Heights*, 227 et al. Lambert was unfortunately put on the roll of the honored dead as "Lambo," probably someone's racist assumption that his name rhymed with "Sambo."

4 Daniel Murphree, ed., *Native America: A State by State Historical Encyclopedia* (ABC-CLIO, 2012), 153.

5 "Narrative of Stephen Hempstead," in Harris, *Battle of Groton Heights*, 48. Walter Powell has a good breakdown of this decision. *Murder or Mayhem? Benedict Arnold's New London, Connecticut Raid, 1781* (Gettysburg, PA: Thomas, 2000), 44, 81.

6 Harris, *Battle of Groton Heights*, 221.

7 Ibid., 247.

8 "Narrative of Stephen Hempstead" and "Narrative of Rufus Avery," both in Harris, *Battle of Groton Heights*, 48–49, 31–32. Ledyard supposedly said, "We will not give up the fort, let the consequences be what they may" (32). But this is probably a posthumous addition.

9 "Narrative of Rufus Avery," in Harris, *Battle of Groton Heights*, 32.

10 Harris, *Battle of Groton Heights*, 172, 234, et al.

11 "Narrative of Thomas Hertell," ibid., 70–73 et al.

12 Harris, *Battle of Groton Heights*, 50.

13 "Narrative of George Middleton," ibid., 91.

14 "Narrative of Stephen Hempstead," ibid., 51.

15 His father had been paid a hogshead of cider by a member of the Saybrook militia to let Daniel act as his substitute.

16 Harris, *Battle of Groton Heights*, multiple pages.

17 Ibid., 50.

18 "Narrative of Rufus Avery," ibid., 35–37 et al.; William Latham to Samuel Mott, deposition, April 11, 1782, TP, CSLA. See also Zabdiel Rogers to Jonathan Trumbull, September 7, 1781, copy, R633, NLCHS. Ledyard's death is subject to many speculations. From the evidence of his shirt, held by the Connecticut Historical Society, we know that someone certainly ran him through with a sword, going through the right side of his body and out the left, possibly one of the officers (Object no. 1841.5.0, CHS). Regardless of the legend (see chapter 12), all accounts agree that he offered to surrender to someone, and that person killed him. For further analysis, see Powell, *Murder or Mayhem*, 60–69.

19 Shaw, *Ledyard Family in America*, 18; Harris, *Battle of Groton Heights*, multiple pages. For further evidence of the slaughter, see Daniel Eldridge to Samuel Mott, deposition, April 12, 1782, TP, CSLA.

20 Harris, *Battle of Groton Heights*, 22–23.

21 Ibid., multiple pages. The information on Lambert Latham comes from "The Colored Patriots of the American Revolution," 1855, in Harris, *Battle of Groton Heights*, 284–86. It is not clear if he took those wounds before he died, or if the British soldiers mutilated him afterward.

22 "Narrative of Rufus Avery," in Harris, *Battle of Groton Heights*, 37.

23 Harris, *Battle of Groton Heights*, multiple pages. Harris's information on the wounded comes either from relatives of the wounded or, more often, directly from the Connecticut Archives. For example, see Samuel Mott, Elisha Lathrop, and Robert Crory (Committee) to the Connecticut General Assembly, January 2, 1783, reel 147, Revolutionary War Series 1, 1784, CSLA, 27:76b–77a.

24 "Narrative of Rufus Avery," in Harris, *Battle of Groton Heights*, 38. Avery speculated that the floor had been too wet with blood to catch fire.

25 Harris, *Battle of Groton Heights*, 227.

26 Powell, *Murder or Mayhem*, 55. This count has changed somewhat over the years, but Powell's numbers are the most updated. It is possible that the British lost far more men than that, and many officers in New York suspected the numbers had been tampered with, possibly by Arnold. Rufus Avery claimed that the British commissary told him that 220 men were missing from the rolls.

27 "Narrative of Rufus Avery," in Harris, *Battle of Groton Heights*, 39.

28 Charles Allyn, notes, NLCHS.

29 "Narrative of Stephen Hempstead" and "Narrative of Rufus Avery," both in Harris, *Battle of Groton Heights*, 53–54, 39.

30 Benedict Arnold to Sir Henry Clinton, September 8, 1781, Public Record Office, Copies, 1776–84, CHS.

31 "Narrative of Rufus Avery," in Harris, *Battle of Groton Heights*, 40–42.

32 Zabdiel Rogers to Thomas Mumford, September 7, 1781, in *Letters from Zabdiel Rogers and Thomas Mumford*, (Brooklyn: privately printed, 1881), Hathi Trust Digital Library.

33 Harris, *Battle of Groton Heights*, 54.

34 *Connecticut Gazette*, September 7, 1781; Harris, *Battle of Groton Heights*, multiple pages.

35 Arnold to the Inhabitants of America, October 7, 1780, New York, in Rhodehamel, *American Revolution*, 592–95; *London Chronicle*, November 14, 1780.

36 Jedediah Huntington to Andrew Huntington, September 17, 1781, *Collections of the Connecticut Historical Society* (Hartford: Connecticut Historical Society, 1923), 20:451.

37 This idea has been used, oddly, to *defend* Arnold by some modern historians, while it seems to me to be the most damning attack on his character anyone could make.

38 Stuart, *Life of Jonathan Trumbull*, 542. Levi Wells of Colchester wrote about the smoke in a panicked letter to Trumbull the evening of the sixth.

39 Caulkins, *History of Norwich*, 252–53; "Narrative of John Hempsted," in Harris, *Battle of Groton Heights*, 69. Hempsted saw the trail of powder the following morning, along with the marks of the finger that stopped it.

40 Shaw, *Ledyard Family in America*, 18–19; "Narrative of Stephen Hempstead," in Harris, *Battle of Groton Heights*, 55.

REMEMBER NEW LONDON

1 Harris, *Battle of Groton Heights*, 134–36. See also reel 146, Revolutionary War Series, CSLA, 26:292–98.

2 Harris, *Battle of Groton Heights*, 55–56.

3 Ibid., 50, 250, 252, et al.; Zabdiel Rogers to Thomas Mumford, September 7, 1781, in *Letters from Zabdiel Rogers*, n.p.

4 Carolyn Smith and Helen Vergason, *September 6, 1781: North Groton's Story* (Ledyard, CT: Ledyard Historical Society, 2000), 36. This leg was buried in the garden and found years later, causing speculation about a murder — until they remembered Seymour's operation.

5 Harris, *Battle of Groton Heights*, 219–20, 227.

6 "Narrative of Avery Downer," in Harris, *Battle of Groton Heights*, 83–84.

7 "Narrative of John Hempsted," ibid., 68–69.

8 Zabdiel Rogers to Thomas Mumford, September 7, 1781, in *Letters from Zabdiel Rogers*, n.p.

9 Sam Mott (Preston) to Jonathan Trumbull, September 12, 1781, 974.6.t 76, TP, CSLA, 15:113.

10 John Tyler to Trumbull, September 10, 1781, ibid., 15:110.

11 Mumford to Trumbull, September 9, 1781, ibid., 15:105.

12 Trumbull to Washington, September 15, 1781, in Sparks, *Correspondence*, 3:404–5.

13 Jonathan Trumbull to Jonathan Trumbull Jr., September 13, 1781, 974.6.t 76, TP, CSLA, 15:120. Trumbull mentions the enclosed letter to Washington.

14 Jonathan Trumbull to Washington, September 13, 1781, 974.6.t 76, TP, CSLA, 15:121a.

15 Stiles, *Literary Diary*, 2:553, 556.

16 Ibid., 2:557.

17 *Norwich Packet*, September 20, 1781, 3.

18 Captain Bulkley to Samuel B. Webb, September 17, 1781, in Webb, *Correspondence and Journals*, 2:364.

19 "Journal," in *New York Historical Society*, 15:149. See the note in the previous chapter about British losses possibly approaching 220.

20 Mackenzie, *Diary of Frederick Mackenzie*, 620.

21 The rest of his soldiers remained in Whitestone until the following day.

22 "Rivington's Royal Gazette," in Harris, *Battle of Groton Heights*, 94–97.

23 Willcox, *American Rebellion*, 331.

24 "Sir Henry Clinton's General Orders," in Harris, *Battle of Groton Heights*, 111.

25 "Brigadier-General Arnold's Report," ibid., 103; Benedict Arnold to Sir Henry Clinton, September 8, 1781, Public Record Office, Copies, 1776–84, CHS.

26 *Connecticut Gazette* (New London), September 7, 1781.

27 *Norwich Packet*, September 13, 1781, 3.

28 James Cogswell, diary entry for September 8, manuscript, 1781–91, CHS.

29 Zabdiel Rogers to Jonathan Trumbull, September 7, 1781, copy, R633, NLCHS.

30 For example, on November 5, 1785, the citizens of Portsmouth, New Hampshire, burned Benedict Arnold's effigy. *New Hampshire Gazette*, November 11, 1785.

31 Harris, *Battle of Groton Heights*, 284.

32 For example, see Mr. Wanton to his sister Mary (Saltonstall's wife), September 14, 1781, 974.6.t 76, TP, CSLA.

33 Jedediah Huntington to Andrew Huntington, September 17, 1781, in *Huntington Papers: Correspondence of the Brothers Joshua and Jedediah Huntington, during the Period of the American Revolution* (Hartford: Connecticut Historical Society, 1923), 45.

34 *Freeman's Journal* (Philadelphia), November 14, 1781.

35 Christopher Vail, *Journal*, transcription, www.americanrevolution.org, n.p. Original manuscript in Library of Congress collections.

36 Tallmadge to Trumbull, October 5, 1781, 974.6.t 76, TP, CSLA, 15:174.

37 *Connecticut Gazette* (New London), September 14, 1781.

38 Shaw et al. to Trumbull, November 7, 1781, 974.6.t 76, TP, CSLA.

39 Russell Smith, depositions certified by Moses Warren, Justice of the Peace, MsJ.Sm641, NLCHS.

40 "Court Martial," in Harris, *Battle of Groton Heights*, 113–17. Though charges were brought almost immediately, the court-martial did not take place until August 20, 1782.

41 Inhabitants of New London to Connecticut General Assembly, April 22, 1782, Revolutionary War Series 1, CSLA, 22:337b.

42 "Narrative of Rufus Avery," in Harris, *Battle of Groton Heights*, 42–43.

43 Copy of Flag of Truce document, in Rogers, *Connecticut's Naval Office*, 29.

44 Rogers, *Connecticut's Naval Office*, 30–34. Several letters and orders for this operation exist and are kept in the Shaw Collections at Yale and New London County Historical Society. For example, see "Permission to Sloop *Queen of France* to Return to New London," September 14, 1781, m1907.07.47, NLCHS.

45 Harris, *Battle of Groton Heights*, 290.

46 *Norwich Packet*, September 20, 1781, 3.

47 Ebenezer Ledyard to Trumbull, November 7, 1781, 974.6.t 76, TP, CSLA, 15:239.

48 Harris, *Battle of Groton Heights*, 243.

49 Anne Ledyard to Governor Trumbull and the General Assembly, May 2, 1782, Revolutionary War Series 1, CSLA, 22:378–80.

50 Grants, 1763–89, reel 146, Revolutionary War Series 1, CSLA, 26:292–98.

51 Mumford to Trumbull, September 28, 1781, 974.6.t 76, TP, CSLA, 15:158a.

52 Jabez Bowen to Trumbull, September 14, 1781, ibid., 15:124a.

53 Richards to Trumbull, October 10, 1781, ibid.

54 Jean-Francois-Louis, journal entry, in Rice and Brown, *American Campaigns*, 1:50.

55 "Minutes of Occurrences," *Massachusetts Historical Society*, 332.

56 Rochambeau, *Memoirs*, 60–61; Jerome Greene, *The Guns of Independence: The Siege of Yorktown, 1781* (New York: Beatie, 2005), 70, 88.

57 Clinton to Germain, September 7, 1781, in Willcox, *American Rebellion*, 564.

58 Mackenzie, *Diary of Frederick Mackenzie*, 630, 633, 653.

59 Though not a popular strategic opinion today, the notion that the sacrifice at Groton Heights led directly or indirectly to victory at Yorktown was certainly part of common military lore in the eighteenth and nineteenth centuries. One hundred years later Gen. William Tecumseh Sherman attended the centennial of Groton Heights and said that "the battle of Groton Heights gave us Yorktown." *Celebration of the One Hundred and Tenth Anniversary of the Battle of Groton Heights* (New London, CT: Morning Telegraph, 21). I am not sure that is quite accurate, but the ships Arnold took would have certainly been useful in the battle of the Chesapeake.

60 Mumford to Trumbull, September 28, 1781, 974.6.t 76, TP, CSLA, 15:158a.

61 Rochambeau, *Memoirs*, 67.

62 J. Greene, *Guns of Independence*, 111, 190–234.

63 Ibid., 240–47.

64 Nathaniel Shaw Perkins, "Lafayette's Visit to New London," in Rogers, *Connecticut's Naval Office*, 136; Charles Henry Browning, "Lafayette's Visit to the United States, 1824–1825," *American Historical Register*, April 1895, 1377; Harold Syrett, ed., *The Papers of Alexander Hamilton* (New York: Columbia University Press, 1979), 26:31.

65 Mackenzie, *Diary of Frederick Mackenzie*, 653.

66 *Continental Journal* (Boston), October 18, 1781.

67 Leffingwell to Trumbull, October 17, 1781, 974.6.t 76, TP, CSLA, 15:200.

68 Mackenzie, *Diary of Frederick Mackenzie*, 673.

69 William Fowler, *American Crisis: George Washington and the Dangerous Two Years after Yorktown, 1781–1783* (New York: Walker, 2011), 7.

70 J. Greene, *Guns of Independence*, 311.

71 Alex Foster to Shaw, October 22, 1781, 1907.07.197, NSRWP, NLCHS.

72 Stuart, *Life of Jonathan Trumbull*, 554–56.

73 Samuel Huntington to Connecticut delegate, November 8, 1781, in George Dreher, *Samuel Huntington, President of Congress "Longer Than Expected," 1779–1781* (n.p.: Longshanks Books, 1995), 183.

74 Jabez Huntington to Jonathan Trumbull, November 7, 1781, 974.6.t 76, TP, CSLA.

75 *Connecticut Courant and Weekly Intelligencer*, November 20, 1781.

76 Rochambeau, *Memoirs*, 94–95.

77 Stiles, *Literary Diary*, 2:571. Stiles received these proclamations on December 9.

78 Nathaniel Shaw to John De Neufville, April 10, 1782, in Rogers, *Connecticut's Naval Office*, 329.

79 Shaw to Josiah Waters, April 25, 1782, ibid., 329–31; Rogers, *Connecticut's Naval Office*, 9.

80 Ibid.

81 Ibid.

THE FALL OF SILAS DEANE

1 Franklin to Lafayette, May 14, 1781, in Bigelow, *Works of Benjamin Franklin*, 7:235.

2 Virtually every letter from Deane to Barnabas Deane, April 20, 1780, DP, in *New York Historical Society*, vol. 4, to the end of his life shows varying degrees of depression.

3 Beaumarchais to Vergennes, December 2, 1780, DP, in *New York Historical Society*, 4:267. Beaumarchais had his own reason to be bitter; Congress never paid him back for his loans.

4 Titus Hosmer to Thomas Mumford, August 10, 1779, Thomas Mumford Collection, CHS.

5 Francis Dana to John Adams, January 1, 1781, DP, in *New York Historical Society*, 4:274.

6 James Wilson to Deane, January 1, 1781, ibid., 4:270.

7 Robert Morris to Deane, June 7, 1781, DP, ibid., 4:400.

8 In *Secret History* Van Doren posits that Deane was working with the British here, but again, the evidence is opaque — missives among the British themselves that could mean several things. For the opposite point of view, see Joel Richard Paul, *Unlikely Allies: How a Merchant, a Playwright, and a Spy Saved the American Revolution* (New York: Riverhead, 2009).

9 Benjamin Franklin to Robert Livingston, Passy, March 4, 1782, in Benjamin Franklin, *Essays, Articles, Bagatelles, and Letters, Poor Richard's Almanack, Autobiography* (New York: Library of America, 1987), 1045.

10 John Jay to Deane, March 28, 1781, DP, in *New York Historical Society*, 4:293–96.

11 Deane to James Wilson, May 10, 1781, ibid., 4:311.

12 Deane to Samuel Parsons, May 14, 1781, ibid., 4:326.

13 Deane to Simeon Deane, May 16, 1781, ibid., 4:338.

14 Deane to Tallmadge, May 20, 1781, ibid., 4:388–89.

15 Deane to Jesse Root, May 20, 1781, ibid., 4:349–60; Deane to Jonathan Nesbitt, June 19, 1781; and Deane to Joshua Johnson, June 19, 1781, ibid, 4:442. He also told John Jay in a letter of June 25 that he had not sent his letter yet, so perhaps he had sent none. But if he had sent letters with the captains as written, then Deane's account of what happened next is almost certainly true.

16 Deane to Simeon Deane, May 16, 1781, ibid., 4:345.

17 Deane to William Duer, June 14, 1781, ibid., 4:429.

18 Deane to Jeremiah Wadsworth, June 13, 1781; Deane to Samuel Parsons, May 14, 1781, ibid., 4:424.

19 Deane to Simeon Deane, May 16, 1781, ibid., 4:346–47.

20 Van Doren, *Secret History*, 61–63.

21 In fact, three years earlier they had stolen Deane's brother Simeon's letter to him and published it in *Lloyd's Morning Post*, August 26, 1778. See DP, in *New York Historical Society*, 2:465.

22 King George III, July 19, 1781, DP, in *New York Historical Society*, 4:503.

23 King George III, August 7, 1781, ibid., 4:503.

24 Washington to Joseph Reed, May 28, 1780, Varick transcripts, series 3h, GWPLC.

25 Arthur Lee to Samuel Adams, August 12, 1781, DP, in *New York Historical Society*, 4:447.

26 Ebenezer Huntington to Jabez Huntington, December 21, 1778, in *Letters Written*, 77–78.

27 Ebenezer Huntington to Andrew Huntington, July 7, 1780, ibid., 87–88.

28 Silas Deane to Trumbull, October 1781, 974.6.t 76, TP, CSLA, 15:206.

29 Barnabas Deane to Jacob Sebor, November 11, 1781, DP, in *New York Historical Society*, 4:531–33.

30 Silas Deane to Thomas Mumford, September 24, 1781, ibid., 4:468–74.

31 Benjamin Tallmadge to Barnabas Deane, November 11, 1781, in *Collections of the Connecticut Historical Society* (Hartford: Connecticut Historical Society, 1930), 23:163.

32 Tallmadge to Silas Deane, December 27, 1781, DP, in *New York Historical Society*, 4:494–95. Trumbull wrote a similar reply the following spring, refuting each of Deane's points, and then placed copies of both letters in the state archives, as Deane requested.

33 Deane to Tallmadge, October 20, 1781, ibid., 4:494–95.

34 Deane to Bancroft, November 8, 1781, ibid., 4:528–29.

35 Deane to Bancroft, November 13, 1781, ibid., 4:534.

36 Deane to Bancroft, November 23, 1781, ibid., 4:539.

37 Jay to Deane, February 22, 1783, DP, in *New York Historical Society*, 5:131.

38 Barnabas Deane to Samuel Webb, May 14, 1782, in Webb, *Correspondence and Journals*, 2:395.

39 Cato to Francis Bailey, in *The Freeman's Journal; Or, the North American Intelligencer*, January 2, 1782, DP, in *New York Historical Society*, 5:1.

40 Milton Lomask, "Benedict Arnold: The Aftermath of Treason," *American Heritage Magazine*, October 1967, 86; "Letters from R. M.," *General Advertiser and Morning Intelligencer*, February 9, 22, 1782. The visit to Andre's relatives may be apocryphal, though it is widely reported. For an anecdote about

Arnold visiting Andre's grave in Westminster Abbey, see Henry Van Schaak, *Life of Peter Van Schaak* (New York: Appleton, 1842), 147.

41 *Massachusetts Spy*, October 25, 1781.

42 MSS 106, folder K, L, Papers of Benedict Arnold, 1761–94, Whitney Library, NHM; *Connecticut Journal*, April 18, 1782. Pierpont Edwards bought it on bond.

43 For more on Arnold's cold reception in England, see *Connecticut Courant and Weekly Intelligencer*, December 2, 1783, reprinted from the *Gentleman's and London Magazine* and the *United States Chronicle*, January 22, 1784, et al.

44 Tallmadge, *Memoir*, 50.

45 Mather, *Refugees of 1776*, 342.

46 Tallmadge, *Memoir*, 51–52.

47 "A Circular Letter to States on the Distress of the Army Head-Quarters, Newburgh, New York, June 18, 1783," in Fowler, *American Crisis*, 257–66.

48 Tallmadge, *Memoir*, 60–61.

49 Jonathan Trumbull, "An Address of His Excellency Gov. Trumbull … Declining Any Further Election to Public Office," October 1783 (New London, CT: Green, 1783), CHS, 6, 8.

50 Tallmadge, *Memoir*, 62.

51 *Boston Gazette*, November 10, 1783.

52 David Colden to [?], September 15, 1783, in *American Historical Review* 25, no. 1 (1919): 83.

53 Thomas Jefferson, *Notes on the State of Virginia* (Richmond, VA: Randolph, 1853), 166–67.

54 Ezra Stiles, *The Literary Diary of Ezra Stiles*, vol. 3, 1782–95 (New York: Scribner's Sons, 1901), 70.

55 Fowler, *American Crisis*, 97. They kept the letter secret from the army, so as not to give anyone bad ideas, but kept a record for posterity.

56 George Washington to Robert Livingston, August 14, 1782, Founders Online, National Archives, http://founders.archives.gov.

57 Tallmadge, *Memoir*, 63.

58 Ibid., 64; James Thacher, *Military Journal of the American Revolution* (Hartford, CT: Hurlbut, Williams, 1862), 347–48.

59 George Washington to Thomas Mifflin, December 20, 1783, Founders Online, National Archives, http://founders.archives.gov.

60 Ron Chernow, *Washington: A Life* (New York: Penguin, 2010), 454–56. Chernow and others make it clear that this was one of the most remarkable moments in the history of the world.

61 Tallmadge, *Memoir*, 65.

62 Deane to Robert Morris, October 10, 1783, DP, in *New York Historical Society*, 5:201.

63 Deane to Barnabas Deane, July 25, 1783; and Deane to Benjamin Franklin, October 19, 1783, both ibid., 5:176, 212–15.

64 John Adams to Robert Livingston, August 2, 1783, ibid., 5:184.

65 Benjamin Franklin to John Jay, January 19, 1782, ibid., 5:13.

66 Jay to Deane, February 23, 1784, ibid., 5:280–81. Jay went on to write his share of *The Federalist Papers* and become the first chief justice of the Supreme Court. By then he could probably have helped his friend recover his reputation from the Arthur Lee fiasco at least. But they were no longer friends, and it was too late.

67 Deane to Jay, May 3, 1784, ibid., 5:297–99.

68 John Adams to James Lloyd, March 29, 1815, in John Adams, *The Works of John Adams* (Boston: Little, Brown, 1856), 10:147. By the 1830s Deane was forgiven officially, and his heirs reimbursed some of the vast personal wealth he had donated to the Revolutionary cause. But he has never quite recovered the reputation he deserved for bringing so much French help to the war (including Lafayette himself), and the argument over whether he purposefully gave his letters to the British continues to this day.

69 Deane to Samuel Webb, October 31, 1783, DP, in *New York Historical Society*, 5:218.

70 Deane to Barnabas Deane, November 3, 1783, ibid., 5:220.

71 Deane to Jay, February 28, 1783, ibid., 5:136–40.

72 Arnold to George Johnstone, July 18, 1784; and Johnstone to Arnold July 21, 1784, in *Magazine of American History*, vol. 10 (New York: Historical Publications Company, 1883), 314–17.

73 Ester Clark Wright, *The Loyalists of New Brunswick* (Fredericton, NB: n.p., 1955), 221.

74 *Connecticut Courant and Weekly Intelligencer*, January 23, 1786.

75 *Connecticut Courant*, October 10, 1791. Canadian historian Barry Wilson finds this story questionable and gives a good account of his doubts in *Benedict Arnold: A Traitor in Our Midst* (Montreal: McGill-Queen's University Press, 2001), 207–14.

76 "Benedict Arnold's Rum Bills," *Hartford Courant*, February 16, 1888.

77 Wilson, *Benedict Arnold*, 187; William Kenyon to Josiah Blakely, [1780?], MSS 106, folder C, Papers of Benedict Arnold, 1761–94, Whitney Library, NHM.

78 *New York Journal*, November 16, 1786.

79 *New Jersey Journal*, August 13, 1788.

80 *New Hampshire Gazette*, September 18, 1788.

81 *New York Daily Gazette*, May 27, 1790.

82 Wilson, *Benedict Arnold*, 189–94.

83 Silas Deane to Simon Deane, April 3, 1784, in Webb, *Correspondence and Journals*, 3:33.

84 Silas Deane to George Washington, June 25, 1789, ibid., 135.

85 Silas Deane to Samuel Johnson, June 29, 1789, ibid., 136.

86 James West Davidson and Mark Lytle, *After the Fact: The Art of Historical Detection* (New York: McGraw-Hill, 1992), xxvii–xxxv; James, *Silas Deane*, 119–21. That Bancroft killed Deane is a popular theory, though there is no hard evidence. But it seems clear that only four hours between falling ill and dying means that he was poisoned by *somebody*.

87 "Extract of a Letter from a Gentleman in England to His Friend in This City," *Spooner's Vermont Journal* 7, no. 353 (1790): 3.

EPILOGUE

1 Charles Maurice de Talleyrand-Perigord, *Memoirs of the Prince de Talleyrand*, ed. Duc de Broglie, trans. Angust Hall (London: Griffith, Farrax, Okeden, and Welsh, 1891), 3:174–75.

2 Tower, *Marquis de La Fayette*, 2:166.

3 Peggy Arnold to Edward Shippen, July 6, 1792, MS Am 1446, Benedict Arnold Papers, 1765–1886, Houghton Library, Harvard University.

4 Oversize item 5, MSS 106, Papers of Benedict Arnold, 1761–94, Whitney Library, NHM.

5 Jefferson to James Monroe, July 11, 1790, in Boyd, *Papers of Thomas Jefferson*, 17:25, 77; John Fitzpatrick, ed., *The Diaries of George Lengel* (1925; repr., New York: Kraus Reprint, 1971), 4:136.

6 Washington to Henry Lee, October 31, 1786, series 4, 1741–99, GWPLC.

7 Chernow, *Washington*, 718–26.

8 Ibid., 792.

9 Brian Carso points out the importance of this "we" in Washington's statement after Arnold's treason: "Whom can we trust now?" He writes, "Washington's concern is for the community, the American republic, the same 'we' that would begin the Constitution." Furthermore, Washington's exclamation could have been something retributive like, "I will hang that traitor!" *"Whom Can We Trust Now?,"* 5, 240.

10 Ezra Stiles to Jonathan Trumbull, July 24, 1784, folder 9, box 4, JTP, CHS.

11 Washington to Jonathan Trumbull Jr., October 1, 1785, in Hinman, *Historical Collection*, 323–24. In this wonderful letter Washington talked to Trumbull's son of his "sincere respect" and "friendship" for the governor.

12 Daniel Lathrop Coit, *Memoir of Daniel Lathrop Coit, 1754–1833* (Norwich, CT: Bulletin, 1907), 6–9.

13 Tallmadge, *Memoir*, 69–70.

14 Smith and Vergason, *September 6, 1781*, 46.

15 Harris, *Battle of Groton Heights*, 250.

16 Lafayette Foster, "Address of the Honorable Lafayette S. Foster Delivered before the New London County Historical Society in Old Fort Griswold," September 6, 1880, in *Records and Papers of the New London County Historical Society*, pt. 2 (New London, CT: NLCHS, 1890), 1:20.

17 William Brainard, *An Address in Commemoration of the Sixth of September 1781* (New London, 1825), 26–27.

18 Esmond Wright, "A Patriot for Whom?," *History Today* 36, no. 10 (1986): 29.

19 Sheldon S. Cohen, "Yale's Peripatetic Loyalist: Samuel Andrew Peters," *Journal of the New Haven Colony Historical Society* 25, no. 1 (1977): 3–7.

20 *Connecticut Courant*, June 16, 1800.

21 As historian Carl Van Doren put it, "The wonder is — as Washington understood — not that some of them were false but that most of them were true to the ragged colors of a perilous cause." *Secret History*, 435.

22 John Adams to Baron Van Der Capellen, Amsterdam, January 21, 1781, in *John Adams: Revolutionary Writings* (New York: Library of America, 2011), 447. Adams was wrong about Arnold's wife, of course.

23 Joshua Kendall, *The Forgotten Founding Father* (London: Penguin, 2010), 210.

24 *Connecticut Courant and Weekly Intelligencer*, October 31, 1780, and November 7, 1780.

25 Webster, *Dictionary* (1828), s.v. "society." Webster could have taken this definition wholesale from elsewhere, of course, though it is not in Samuel Johnson's dictionary or any other readily available source. The beginning is adapted from Immanuel Kant, and there seems to be material from Jeremy Bentham and Aristotle.

✷ ✷ ✷
Index

Adams, John, xvii, 24, 79, 80, 83, 178, 179, 199, 202; opinions of Benedict Arnold, xiii, 105, 192

Allen, Ethan, 28–30

Andre, John, 82, 84–86, 90–91, 93–95, 101, 106, 108, 186, 202

Arnold, Benedict, ix–xi, 1, 10, 49, 136, 137, 154, 169, 170, 171, 172, 174, 175, 177, 201; accusations of profiteering, 81–82, 84, 85, 90; battle of Ridgefield, 63–65, 151, 159; Benjamin Franklin opinions of, 72, 98, 100; Benjamin Tallmadge and, xx, 60–61, 89, 91, 92, 95, 97–98, 101; Betsey Deblois and, 62, 71, 82; in Boston, 62, 71; British opinions of 106–8, 119, 165, 166, 186; burning of New London, xv, xvii, xix, xxii, 12, 138, 140–50, 151, 160–61, 164, 166, 167, 172, 173, 184, 200; captain of Governor's Foot Guards, 18, 27, 28; conspiracy to betray West Point, x, xv, xix, 60, 86, 90–92, 97, 103, 108, 160; Continental Congress and, 63, 67, 72, 96, 98, 103, 104, 108, 109, 115, 134, 193; education of, 4, 6–8; Eleazer Oswald and, 63, 67, 72, 96, 98, 103, 104, 108, 109, 115, 134, 193; exile in Canada, 193–95; exile in England, 185–86, 191–93, 197–98; Ezra Stiles opinions of, 97, 105, 164–16; family in Middletown, Conn., 69, 71, 81, 109, 134, 136, 186; first wife (Margaret Mansfield), 19–20, 30; as Freemason, 17–18, 20; in French and Indian War, 10–11; George Washington and, x, xi–xii, xix, xx, 38, 55, 62–63, 67, 68, 72, 84, 85, 86, 90, 92–94, 95, 96, 103, 104, 105, 110–12, 121, 123; Henr Clinton and, xvii, 85, 86, 104, 108, 117, 124; home in Connecticut, xix, xiii, 20, 60, 66, 69, 71–72, 77, 78, 83, 86, 89, 98, 109, 134, 146, 194; injuries of, 64, 69, 72; invasion of Quebec, 37–39, 55, 63, 102; invasion of Virginia, 112–24; John Adams opinions of, xiii, 105, 192; John Lamb and, xx, 38, 39, 62, 67, 91–92, 95–96, 103, 104; Jonathan Trumbull and, xx, 29, 66, 71, 86, 97, 104, 109, 134, 164; loyalist opinions of, xvi, 25, 81, 104; Marquis de Lafayette and, xv, 92–94, 97, 98, 101, 121–23, 126, 197; as merchant, 12, 14, 16, 17, 18–19, 23, 37, 81–82, 193–94; Nathaniel Shaw and, xx, 81–82, 89, 149; in New Haven, Conn., 12, 14, 19, 20, 37, 62, 63, 71, 82, 86, 89, 186, 202; in New York City, 109, 113, 123, 126, 134, 165; in Norwich, Conn., ix, 1–6, 12, 14, 69, 97, 146, 159, 168; in Philadelphia, 63, 67, 72, 79, 81–84, 88, 104, 109, 179, 186, 192, 198; plans to kidnap, 110–12, 120, 134, 199; Richard Varick and, 35, 62, 66, 67, 68, 89–92, 96, 103, 104; reputation of, xii–xvii, 13, 78, 81, 84, 96, 98–102, 105–6, 115, 121, 134, 160–

61, 166–67, 169, 176, 188, 196, 200, 202; at Saratoga, xiii, xv, 67–69, 72, 87, 96, 102, 109, 122; Silas Deane and, xx, 17, 37, 39, 79, 85, 178–79, 185, 191–93, 198; songs and poems about, 100–102, 167–68; temperament of, xii, 18–19, 20, 25, 37, 66, 67, 68, 69, 85–86, 134, 174, 197; at Ticonderoga, 28–30, 62; treason, x–xii, xvii–xxii, 53, 84–85, 86, 96, 97, 103–4, 132, 160–61, 174, 178, 20; uncles and cousins, 5, 134, 168; at West Point, 60, 86–87, 88–90, 92, 102, 109; William Ledyard and, xx, 10, 166

Arnold, Benedict, Sr., 2, 7, 11–12, 97

Arnold, Hannah, 6, 12, 14, 37, 83, 109, 194

Arnold, Hannah King, 2, 6, 10–11

Arnold, Peggy Shippen, 81, 82–83, 84, 86, 89, 91–92, 93, 109, 134, 135, 185, 194, 195

Avery, Ebenezer, house of, 159, 161, 162

Avery, Rufus, 138, 155, 156, 157, 159, 170, 171

Bancroft, Edward, 59–60, 85, 179, 181, 182, 184–85, 195

Beaumarchais, Pierre-Augustin Caron de, 39, 80, 81, 178

Boston, Mass., x, xiii, 16, 17, 25, 26, 27, 28, 40; massacre, 20; Port Act, 23–24; siege of, 29, 31–33, 35, 37, 39, 56

Brooks, Jonathan, 140–41, 143–44, 146–47, 170

Burgoyne, John, 66, 68, 69

Burr, Aaron, xvii, 38

Byrd, Mary Willing, 115, 121

Champe, John, 111–12, 123

Clinton, Henry, 54, 88, 90, 95, 111, 113, 133, 134, 135–36, 137, 166, 172, 173, 174, 193; Benedict Arnold and, xvii, 85, 86, 104, 108, 117, 124

Cogswell, James, 6, 20, 149, 167

Commissary Department of the Army, 34, 70, 72, 130, 192

Connecticut, ix, xii, xvii, 23, 25, 26, 28, 31, 40, 45, 65, 85, 113, 124, 133, 168, 176, 190, 195; attacks on, xix, xx, xvii, xi, 13, 63, 73, 74, 78, 100, 118, 128, 135, 136, 160, 164, 172, 173, 174, 176, 200; as Benedict Arnold's home state, xix, xiii, 20, 60, 72, 83, 86, 89, 98, 109, 134, 194; Committee of Correspondence, 17, 23; economy of, 4, 8, 11, 14, 130–31, 132, 172, 177, 178; government of, 3, 9, 15, 16, 24, 25–26, 34, 35, 86, 97, 109, 130, 181, 188, 199, 200, 201; loyalists in, 51–53, 120, 137, 188; prisoners kept in, 57, 58; refugees in, 54, 55; troops of, 10, 11, 22, 28, 29, 30, 31, 32, 34, 35, 62, 63, 66, 69, 70, 93, 134, 174

Continental Congress, xii, 24, 29, 40, 49, 51, 58, 70, 113, 169, 189, 190; Benedict Arnold and, 63, 67, 72, 96, 98, 103, 104, 108, 109, 115, 134, 193; Connecticut delegates to, 27, 41, 97, 132, 199, 200; orders of, 41, 98, 104, 105, 109, 115, 121; politics of, 114, 130, 132, 182, 193; Silas Deane and, 24, 30, 31, 34, 36, 59, 80, 81, 85, 178, 179, 180, 183, 184, 185, 190, 195

Cornwallis, Charles, x, 124–26, 133–37, 165, 172, 173, 185, 186; surrender of, 174–76, 183

Daggett, Napthali, 20, 21, 22, 75, 76
Danbury, Conn., xvi, 53, 63–64, 66, 73, 118, 134, 168
Deane, Barnabas, 40, 42, 71, 183, 184, 185
Deane, Silas, 17, 22, 27, 28, 52, 82, 124; accusations of profiteering, 59, 79–80, 85, 104, 178; Benedict Arnold and, xx, 17, 37, 39, 79, 85, 178–79, 185, 191–93, 198; Benjamin Franklin and, 58, 80, 178, 179, 192; Continental Congress and, 24, 30, 31, 34, 36, 59, 80, 81, 85, 178, 179, 180, 183, 184, 185, 190, 195; death of, 195; exile of, 184–85, 190–93, 195; in France, 39–40, 58–59, 60, 69, 72, 178–84; intercepted letters of, 180–82, 183–85; reputation of, 80, 85, 124, 132, 178, 184–85, 191–93, 195; temperament of, 17, 30, 37, 80–81, 178, 179, 180, 181, 183, 187; wife of (Elizabeth Saltonstall), 17, 30, 31, 79, 141
Devil's Belt. *See* Long Island Sound
Downer, Avery, 129, 138, 162

Enlightenment, 3, 18, 20
Eyre, Edmund, 151, 154

Fairfield, Conn., 54, 77, 110, 168, 194
Fitch, Thomas, 16, 17
Fort Griswold, 41, 127, 129, 138, 139, 149, 151–55, 161, 164, 165, 166, 169, 170
Fort Ticonderoga, xiii, 28–30, 39, 62, 67, 86
Fort Trumbull, 127, 128, 129, 138, 141, 152, 154
Franklin, Benjamin, 3, 18, 40, 59, 69, 105, 131, 182; opinions on Benedict

Arnold, 72, 98, 100; Silas Deane and, 58, 80, 178, 179, 192
Freemasons, 17–18, 19, 20, 23, 38, 63
French and Indian War, 10–11, 16, 18, 30, 40

Gray, David, 137
Great Awakening, 2–3
Groton, Conn., 2, 10, 17, 36, 37, 138, 139, 171, 177; defense of, 41, 42, 88, 127, 128, 129, 141, 151, 152, 170, 172; destruction of 149, 159, 164
Groton Heights, battle of, xix, 154–57, 160, 168, 169, 174, 200

Hale, Nathan, 21–22, 31–32, 35, 43, 53, 109, 129, 148, 183; as spy, 46, 60, 94–95, 200, 247
Hamilton, Alexander, 47, 82, 90, 92–93, 95, 102, 174, 198
Harris, Joseph, 140, 141, 170
Hartford, Conn., ix, 1, 5, 9, 10, 12, 17, 20, 56, 101, 132, 137, 151; meeting place of Revolutionary War leaders, 24, 41, 43, 86, 90, 92, 126, 133, 159, 164
Hempstead, Stephen, 32, 46, 129, 138, 145, 200; at battle of Groton Heights, 141, 152, 155, 157, 161, 162
Hempsted, John, 140, 141, 143, 144, 148, 162–63, 170
Hinman, Abigail, 146
Homegrown Terror, x, xi, xvii, xx–xxii, 100, 103, 136, 167, 176, 203. *See also* parricide
Hopkins, Ezekiel, 40, 41
Hull, William, 46, 47, 48
Huntington, Ebenezer, 10, 26, 64, 95, 175, 183, 199

Huntington, Jedidiah, 6, 10, 56, 160, 168, 183, 199
Huntington, Samuel, 10, 24, 27, 41, 97, 132, 176, 199

Jay, John, 50, 179, 185, 192
Jefferson, Thomas, xvii, xxi, 113–21, 188, 198, 202

Knox, Henry, 62, 90, 94, 124, 189

Lafayette, Marquis de (Gilbert Du Motier), xvi, 40, 90, 95, 135, 137, 172, 173, 174, 178, 200; Benedict Arnold and, xv, 92–94, 97, 98, 101, 121–23, 126, 197
Lamb, John, 38, 55, 64, 65, 88, 94, 175; Benedict Arnold and, xx, 38, 39, 62, 67, 91–92, 95–96, 103, 104
Latham, William, 138, 151, 156
Lathrop, Daniel, 7, 8, 10, 12, 27, 149, 199
Lathrop, Jerusha, 13–14, 130, 199
Lebanon, Conn., x, 6, 9, 15, 27, 34, 116, 128, 161; as Revolutionary War headquarters, 33, 40, 42, 87, 131
Ledyard, Anne, 37, 127, 135, 162, 171, 200
Ledyard, Ebenezer, 152, 157, 159, 170, 171
Ledyard, Fanny, 55, 161
Ledyard, John, 10, 17, 36
Ledyard, William, 10, 17, 24, 27, 36–37, 41, 42, 57, 134, 135, 136, 140; Benedict Arnold and, xx, 10, 166; in command, 74, 127–29, 137–39, 151–55; death of, 155, 162, 164, 166, 167, 170, 200

Lee, Arthur, 40, 58, 59, 69, 80, 182
Lee, Henry, 110, 111, 123, 198
Lee, Richard Henry, 59, 80
Long Island, ix, 34, 44, 49, 51, 52, 65, 128, 129, 165, 174; Brookhaven, 21, 190; illegal trade with, 54, 104, 186; occupation of, ix, 43, 46, 54, 55, 56, 161, 189; raids on, 51, 54, 57, 74, 78, 110, 133, 169
Long Island Sound, ix, 2, 21, 36, 41, 65, 77, 88, 128, 136, 137, 165, 170, 172; raids across, 42, 45, 46, 49, 54, 66, 74, 110, 134, 169
loyalists, xi, xii, xvi, 55, 60, 81, 84, 117, 171; as spies, 54, 64, 182; contradictory or confused position of, 52, 77, 104, 115, 121; persecution of, 56, 188; serving in the British Army, x, xvi, 73, 77, 111, 112, 148, 151, 168; status after the war, 188, 194. *See also* Tories

Mackenzie, Frederick, 47, 119, 136, 173, 174
Mansfield, Margaret (first wife of Benedict Arnold), 19–20, 30
Martin, Joseph Plumb, xii, 98
McVeigh, Timothy, xvii
Meigs, Return Jonathan, 66
Middletown, Conn., 26, 56, 66, 86, 88, 178, 186; Benedict Arnold's family in, 69, 71, 81, 109, 134, 136, 186
Mix, Jonathan, Jr., 26–27, 41, 57, 75–76, 96
Mix, Jonathan, Sr., 18, 26
Montgomery, Richard, 38, 39
Montgomery, William, 154, 155
Mumford, Thomas, 27, 88, 132, 159, 163, 164, 172, 173, 178, 184

New Haven, Conn., xii, 16, 18, 20, 21, 31, 73, 79, 130, 188, 200, 201; home of Benedict Arnold, 12, 14, 19, 20, 37, 62, 63, 71, 82, 86, 89, 186, 202; invasion of, 53, 74–77, 168; militia and defense activity of, 10, 25, 26, 28, 29, 38, 66, 164, 165

New London, Conn., ix, x, 1, 2, 7, 10, 22, 32, 35, 69, 174, 176, 177, 186, 188, 196, 199; burning of, xv, xvii, xix, xxii, 12, 77, 138, 140–50, 151, 160–61, 164, 166, 167, 173, 200; defense preparations, 31, 42, 62, 73–74, 127–29, 137–39, 164, 170, 172; merchant activities, 9, 18; political activities, 15, 16, 24, 27, 169; privateering, 41, 136, 169; war effort, 36, 40, 56, 57, 88, 113, 134

New York City, 1, 16, 17, 29, 35, 40, 52, 54, 58, 60, 66, 90, 189, 199; American plans for attack on, 125, 133, 134, 135, 136; Benedict Arnold in, 109, 113, 123, 126, 134, 165; British headquarters in, 86, 88, 119, 134, 135, 137, 169, 172, 173, 174, 183; invasion of, 43–45; spies in, 49, 50, 89, 100, 106, 136, 137

Newport, Rhode Island, 26, 40, 41, 97, 128, 165; British occupation of, 45, 62, 73; French in, 87, 88, 97, 121, 130–31, 133, 135

Norwalk, Conn., 11, 46, 51, 57 63, 73, 77–78

Norwich, Conn., xii, 9, 15, 17, 24, 34, 36, 42, 52, 87, 128, 129, 133, 170, 174, 199; during attack on New London, 138, 140, 146, 148, 150, 159, 160, 161; home of Benedict Arnold, ix, 1–6, 12, 14, 69, 97, 146, 159, 168; home of Hunting-ton family, 27, 40, 41, 56, 97, 132, 176

Oswald, Eleazar, 29, 38, 104, 202; Benedict Arnold and, 29, 38, 39, 62, 64, 67, 80, 89, 96

Paine, Thomas, 30, 80
Painter, Thomas, 74
Parsons, Samuel, 28, 71, 104, 188
parricide, xi, xxi, 101, 117, 166, 200
Peters, Samuel, 25, 201
Philadelphia, Pa., x, 16, 26, 36, 69, 89, 92, 96, 98, 133, 134, 135, 137, 145, 169, 172, 175; Benedict Arnold in, 63, 67, 72, 79, 81–84, 88, 104, 109, 179, 186, 192, 198; Continental Congress in, 24, 30, 42, 109, 132; occupied by British, 49, 52, 66, 70, 81–82; Silas Deane in, 24, 30, 79, 179, 192, 198
prisoners, 7, 12, 47, 64, 109, 198; American, 54, 57–58, 62, 109, 114, 116, 123, 132, 157, 159, 166, 169, 170–71, 177; British, 29, 41, 55–57, 58, 66, 78, 94–95, 120, 129, 160, 186; loyalist, 52, 53, 55–57, 169
Putnam, Israel, 16, 24, 26, 32, 35, 44, 47, 50, 53, 73, 74, 88, 130

Quebec, Canada, xiii, xv, 11, 14, 38, 39, 63, 66, 96, 102

Richmond, Va., 113, 115–16, 120, 122, 123
Ridgefield, Conn., xiii, 26, 64, 88, 96, 151, 159
Rochambeau, Comte de, 87, 97, 128, 130, 133, 136, 173, 176, 192; meetings

with George Washington, 90, 124–26, 135, 137

Robinson, Beverley, 53, 84, 117; house of, 88, 91, 92, 94

Rogers, Zabdiel, 146, 148, 160, 163, 167, 169

Saltonstall, Nathaniel, 141, 143, 144

Saratoga, battle of, xiii, xv, 67–69, 72, 87, 96, 102, 109, 122

Schuyler, Philip, 67, 68, 104

Shaw, Nathaniel, Jr., 16, 22, 27, 32, 83, 113, 138, 140, 145; Benedict Arnold and, xx, 81–82, 89, 149; death of, 177; house of, 31, 40, 127, 138, 144, 170, 17; as leader, 17, 24, 36, 41, 42, 56, 66, 88, 128, 129, 137, 162, 163, 169, 170, 172; as merchant, 16, 23, 26, 36, 40, 87–88, 128, 132, 177; wife of (Lucretia), 31, 55, 144, 170, 171, 177

Silliman, Gold Selleck, 27, 54, 64

Smith, Joshua, 90–92, 95

songs and poems, 43, 53, 65–66, 100–102, 167–68,

Sons of Liberty, 15, 18, 19, 23, 25

Stamp Act, 15, 16, 20

Stanton, Amos, 151, 155

Stiles, Ezra, 3, 53, 65, 70–71, 74, 75, 130, 164–65, 199; opinion of Benedict Arnold, 97, 105, 164–65

Stone, Joel, 51–52, 60

Talleyrand-Perigord, Charles Maurice Day, 197

Tallmadge, Benjamin, 21, 27, 43, 54, 58, 132, 181, 183, 184, 187, 188, 190, 200, 202; as spy master, 48–50, 60, 78, 91, 94–95, 109, 111, 133, 186, 189, 200; Benedict Arnold and, xx, 60–61, 89, 91, 92, 95, 97–98, 101; Nathan Hale and, 21–22, 31–32, 43, 60, 94–95; raids on Long Island, 78, 110, 169, 187

Tea Act, 23

Tories, xii, xvi, 26, 37, 42, 50, 58, 79, 82, 83, 171, 176; contradictory or confused position of, 76, 77, 121; persecution of, 24, 27, 51, 52, 56, 132, 188; serving in the British Army, 54, 64, 134; Silas Deane branded as, 181, 185; as spies, 46, 53, 54, 97, 120, 137; status after the war, 188, 189, 201. *See also* loyalists

Trumbull, John, 34, 72, 108–9, 118, 132, 190

Trumbull, Jonathan, 9–10, 22, 40, 42, 43, 71, 80, 116, 132, 136, 159, 167, 169, 175, 186, 199; Benedict Arnold and, xx, 29, 66, 71, 86, 97, 104, 109, 134, 164; daughter of (Faith), 56; George Washington and, 31, 33–34, 62, 66, 69–70, 100, 124, 130, 137, 164, 176, 199; as governor, 17, 26, 27, 29, 31, 33, 35–36, 41, 51, 54, 56, 66, 74, 100, 128, 134–35, 164, 170, 171–72, 176–77; politics, 9, 11, 16, 17, 24, 26, 34, 52, 58, 187–88; as provisions dealer of the army, 10, 34–35, 70, 72, 86, 87, 130–31; wife of (Faith), 34, 132;

Trumbull, Jonathan, Jr., 133, 135, 137, 175, 176, 189, 190

Trumbull, Joseph, 10, 17, 34, 37, 70, 72, 80, 130

Tryon, William, 50, 53, 58, 63–64, 73, 76, 77

Turner, Philip, 6, 30, 129, 162, 177

Upham, Joshua, 144, 148

Valley Forge, xv, xvi, 49, 70, 72
Varick, Richard, xx, 94, 95, 187, 199;
    Benedict Arnold and, 35, 62, 66,
    67, 68, 89–92, 96, 103, 104
von Ewald, Johann, 115, 119–20
von Steuben, Baron Friedrich Wil-
    helm, 116, 117, 122

Wadsworth, Jeremiah, 27, 31, 90, 124,
    130, 131, 192, 199
Washington, George, 18, 32, 35, 54, 73,
    80, 88, 109, 126, 130, 134–36, 182,
    187, 195, 202, 203; Benedict Arnold
    and, x, xi–xii, xix, xx, 38, 55, 62–
    63, 67, 68, 72, 84, 85, 86, 90, 92–
    94, 95, 96, 103, 104, 105, 110–12,
    121, 123; Benjamin Tallmadge and,
    49, 50, 60, 90, 91, 109, 110, 187; as
    general, 30–31, 43–45, 46, 47, 48,
    49, 93–94, 105, 108, 121, 125, 128,
    129, 133, 172–74; Jonathan Trum-
    bull and, 31, 33–34, 62, 66, 69–70,
    100, 124, 130, 137, 164, 176, 199;
    Mount Vernon, 122, 173; Nathaniel
    Shaw and, 36, 40, 41, 42, 88, 128; as

president, 198–99; resignation of,
    189–90
Weathersfield, Conn., 17, 22, 24, 30,
    31, 40, 49, 56, 57, 124
Webb, Samuel, 24, 57, 98, 124, 165,
    185, 192
Webster, Noah, 31, 202–3
West Point, xii, 53, 92, 93, 101, 183;
    Benedict Arnold at, 86–87, 88–90,
    92, 102, 109; conspiracy to betray,
    x, xv, xix, 60, 86, 90–92, 97, 103,
    108, 160
Williams, William, 27, 109, 161
Windham, Conn., 5, 9, 15, 16, 24, 52,
    133
Wooster, David, 18, 25, 27, 38, 39, 63–
    64, 65, 66, 96

Yale College, 20–22, 70–71, 74, 75,
    130, 199, 202; students of, 3, 6, 14,
    17, 20–22, 26, 31, 47, 53, 94, 176,
    183
Yorktown, Virginia, 120, 121, 173, 177,
    183, 184, 185, 186

Garnet Books

Garnet Poems:
    An Anthology of Connecticut Poetry
    Since 1776
    Edited by Dennis Barone
Food for the Dead:
    On the Trail of New England's
    Vampires
    by Michael E. Bell
Early Connecticut Silver, 1700–1840
    by Peter Bohan and Philip
    Hammerslough
    Introduction and Notes
    by Erin Eisenbarth
The Connecticut River:
    A Photographic Journey through the
    Heart of New England
    by Al Braden
Tempest-Tossed:
    The Spirit of Isabella Beecher
    Hooker
    by Susan Campbell
Connecticut's Fife & Drum Tradition
    by James Clark
Sunken Garden Poetry, 1992–2011
    Edited by Brad Davis
The Old Leather Man:
    Historical Accounts of a Connecticut
    and New York Legend
    Edited by Dan W. DeLuca
Post Roads & Iron Horses:
    Transportation in Connecticut from
    Colonial Times to the Age of Steam
    by Richard DeLuca

The Log Books:
    Connecticut's Slave Trade and
    Human Memory
    by Anne Farrow
Dr. Mel's Connecticut Climate Book
    by Dr. Mel Goldstein
Hidden in Plain Sight:
    A Deep Traveler Explores
    Connecticut
    by David K. Leff
Becoming Tom Thumb:
    Charles Stratton, P.T. Barnum, and
    the Dawn of American Celebrity
    by Eric D. Lehman
Homegrown Terror:
    Benedict Arnold and the Burning
    of New London
    by Eric D. Lehman
Westover School:
    Giving Girls a Place of Their Own
    by Laurie Lisle
Crowbar Governor:
    The Life and Times of Morgan
    Gardner Bulkeley
    by Kevin Murphy
Fly Fishing in Connecticut:
    A Guide for Beginners
    by Kevin Murphy
Water for Hartford:
    The Story of the Hartford Water
    Works and the Metropolitan
    District Commission
    by Kevin Murphy

*African American Connecticut
  Explored*
  Edited by Elizabeth J. Normen
*Henry Austin:
  In Every Variety of Architectural
  Style*
  by James F. O'Gorman
*Ella Grasso:
  Connecticut's Pioneering Governor*
  by Jon E. Purmont
*The British Raid on Essex:
  The Forgotten Battle of the War
  of 1812*
  by Jerry Roberts
*Making Freedom:
  The Extraordinary Life of Venture
  Smith*
  by Chandler B. Saint and
  George Krimsky
*Welcome to Wesleyan:
  Campus Buildings*
  by Leslie Starr
Barns of Connecticut
  by Markham Starr

*Gervase Wheeler:
  A British Architect in America,
  1847–1860*
  by Renée Tribert and
  James F. O'Gorman
*Connecticut in the American Civil
  War: Slavery, Sacrifice, and
  Survival*
  by Matthew Warshauer
*Inside Connecticut and the Civil War:
  One State's Struggles*
  Edited by Matthew Warshauer
*Prudence Crandall's Legacy:
  The Fight for Equality in the 1830s,
  Dred Scott, and* Brown v. Board
  of Education
  by Donald E. Williams Jr.
*Stories in Stone:
  How Geology Influenced
  Connecticut History and Culture*
  by Jelle Zeilinga de Boer
*New Haven's Sentinels:
  The Art and Science of East Rock
  and West Rock*
  by Jelle Zeilinga de Boer
  and John Wareham

ABOUT THE AUTHOR

Eric D. Lehman is a professor of creative writing at the University of Bridgeport. His fiction, travel stories, essays, and nonfiction have appeared in dozens of print and online journals and magazines. He is the author of nine books, including *The Insider's Guide to Connecticut* and *Becoming Tom Thumb: Charles Stratton, P. T. Barnum, and the Dawn of American Celebrity.*

ABOUT THE DRIFTLESS CONNECTICUT SERIES

The Driftless Connecticut Series is a publication award program established in 2010 to recognize excellent books with a Connecticut focus or written by a Connecticut author. To be eligible, the book must have a Connecticut topic or setting or an author must have been born in Connecticut or have been a legal resident of Connecticut for at least three years.

The Driftless Connecticut Series is funded by the
BEATRICE FOX AUERBACH FOUNDATION FUND
at the Hartford Foundation for Public Giving.
For more information and a complete list
of books in the Driftless Connecticut Series,
please visit us online at
http://www.wesleyan.edu/wespress/driftless.